AF899829

Clinical Sociology: Research and Practice

Series Editor

Jan Marie Fritz, University of Cincinnati, Cincinnati, Ohio, USA, University of Johannesburg, Johannesburg, South Africa

The series explores key research and practice in this rapidly expanding field. Topics include ethical and legal aspects of intervention; the nature of client relationships; methods of intervention and evaluation; and the role of clinical sociology in specific settings. This open-ended series appeals to practitioners, policymakers, students and professors in sociology, social work, community psychology, public health, health education, social policy and counseling.

Zarine L. Rocha • Kathy L. Davidson
Editors

Applied and Clinical Sociology in Aotearoa New Zealand

Springer

Editors
Zarine L. Rocha
Department of Sociology
University of Auckland
Auckland, New Zealand

Kathy L. Davidson
Registered psychotherapist and independent research-practitioner
Masterton, New Zealand

ISSN 1566-7847
Clinical Sociology: Research and Practice
ISBN 978-3-031-36580-5 ISBN 978-3-031-36581-2 (eBook)
https://doi.org/10.1007/978-3-031-36581-2

© The Editor(s) (if applicable) and The Author(s), under exclusive license to Springer Nature Switzerland AG 2023
This work is subject to copyright. All rights are solely and exclusively licensed by the Publisher, whether the whole or part of the material is concerned, specifically the rights of translation, reprinting, reuse of illustrations, recitation, broadcasting, reproduction on microfilms or in any other physical way, and transmission or information storage and retrieval, electronic adaptation, computer software, or by similar or dissimilar methodology now known or hereafter developed.
The use of general descriptive names, registered names, trademarks, service marks, etc. in this publication does not imply, even in the absence of a specific statement, that such names are exempt from the relevant protective laws and regulations and therefore free for general use.
The publisher, the authors, and the editors are safe to assume that the advice and information in this book are believed to be true and accurate at the date of publication. Neither the publisher nor the authors or the editors give a warranty, expressed or implied, with respect to the material contained herein or for any errors or omissions that may have been made. The publisher remains neutral with regard to jurisdictional claims in published maps and institutional affiliations.

This Springer imprint is published by the registered company Springer Nature Switzerland AG
The registered company address is: Gewerbestrasse 11, 6330 Cham, Switzerland

For G. Reginald Daniel and Peter J. Aspinall:
two scholars who were endlessly generous
with their vast knowledge and kind support,
and who are sorely missed.
ZLR

For all those whose calling takes them beyond
the constrictions of social expectations. And
for those who have inspired me through their
unwavering faith in the human capacity for
integration and growth, including my own:
Trisha, Catherine, Helen, and the
psychosynthesis community.
KLD

Contents

Introduction: Locally Oriented Applications of Sociology in Aotearoa New Zealand

Zarine L. Rocha and Kathy L. Davidson

This volume brings together social scientists from around Aotearoa New Zealand, exploring the applications and practice of sociology in this unique context. Together, drawing on a range of backgrounds and specializations, we look at how sociology is utilized in the country, and what makes sociology clinical in this particular setting. While clinical sociology is a term most often used in North America and France, referring to the application of a sociological perspective to facilitate change (see Wirth, 1931; Glass, 1979, 1991; Freedman, 1982; Swan, 1981; Rebach & Bruhn, 2001), the practice of sociology has a long and varied history in Aotearoa, being applied and practised in many different ways. Responding to Fritz's (2012) call, this book contributes to the study of global sociological practice, in examining the particular role and potential scope for sociology in New Zealand's political, economic and cultural environment.

Our collection of chapters is very much a product of the contemporary pandemic times, seeking answers to questions which now seem much more pressing: What is the point of sociology in Aotearoa? What are we, as sociologists, doing to facilitate change in our country? Sociological practice is as old as sociology itself (Fritz, 2012), and this volume traces its development within the small, rather isolated context of Aotearoa New Zealand, illuminating how these local applications and contextual considerations connect to social issues around the world. As Thorns (2003) suggests, the edges are a good place to view global–local interconnections, and these chapters draw out the importance of these interlinkages. Our contributors highlight the value of sociological work, and the undeniable significance of history

Z. L. Rocha (✉)
University of Auckland, Auckland, New Zealand
e-mail: zarine.rocha@auckland.ac.nz

K. L. Davidson
Independent Practitioner, Masterton, New Zealand

© The Author(s), under exclusive license to Springer Nature Switzerland AG 2023

Z. L. Rocha, K. L. Davidson (eds.), *Applied and Clinical Sociology in Aotearoa New Zealand*, Clinical Sociology: Research and Practice,
https://doi.org/10.1007/978-3-031-36581-2_1

and context. Rather than seeking to understand the application of sociology as something that occurs in the same way across different communities, these chapters illustrate how sociology can be decolonized and reclaimed across societies and populations, to shape locally oriented (and all the more powerful) sociological practices.

Locating Aotearoa New Zealand

Aotearoa New Zealand is a valuable case study in exploring applied and clinical sociology around the world. As a country of just over five million people located in the Southern Pacific, New Zealand has a diverse multicultural population within a bicultural national framework: with 70.2% of the country identifying as NZ European/Pākehā, 16.5% as Māori, 15.1% as Asian and 8.1% as Pacific Peoples[1] (Statistics NZ, 2018). This volume illuminates key features of the development and institutionalization of the discipline of Sociology in this context, as a small, semi-peripheral, settler society: an interesting point of comparison with similar contexts such as Ireland, Canada, Australia and Denmark (Crothers, 2016; Spoonley, 2015). We position Aotearoa within the wider global context in which practitioners are 'doing sociology' (see Thorns, 2003), and explore the ways in which sociological practice has developed and changed in the face of key challenges and constraints.

The name we use for the country itself highlights a unique and complex history, with echoes of colonialism that have powerful impacts to this day. In this introduction, and throughout the volume, we have deliberately chosen to name the country in both official languages, in te reo Māori[2] and New Zealand English. When using both, we say Aotearoa New Zealand, without a hyphen or an either/or: both languages, together, representing the bicultural reality of the state and seeking to decolonize our ways of knowing and doing.

Tangata whenua ('we who stand here' or 'people of the land'), the Indigenous people of the country, were well established in Aotearoa New Zealand at the time of British settlement, with markedly different understandings around land ownership and control. As Larner and Spoonley (1995, p. 41) describe: "Although the country was not densely populated, it was actively occupied with established territorial demarcations between *iwi* (tribes) and *hapu* (sub-tribes), and well-known corridors of exchange. Land was not only an economic base, it was also of spiritual, cultural and symbolic importance. Tribal connections and individual identity were both integrally linked to the physical landscape". Initial social relations were

[1]We would like to clarify that these populations are themselves extremely diverse, and we are not assuming an overarching sameness within each population group. We use the terms "Māori" and "Pākehā" throughout the volume with this understanding in mind, as eloquently stressed by Barnes (2013).

[2]Please refer to the glossary for translations as necessary.

characterized by the power imbalances between the colonized and the colonizer, Māori and Pākehā, epitomized in the 1840 signing of the Treaty of Waitangi, and the colonial annexation of the territory (Orange, 1997; Larner & Spoonley, 1995; Spoonley, 1993).

As the British consolidated their hold on power in the country, New Zealand was constructed as a colonial project, creating a better 'Britain of the South Seas', and largely limiting migration to white origin countries through deliberately racially exclusive immigration policies from the late 1800s to the mid-1960s (Spoonley, 2015; Leckie, 1985). Over time, Māori political activism grew further in strength, and by the 1960–70s, it was increasingly recognized that the colonial state had sought to maintain racial hegemony at the expense of Māori. The Indigenous population was given a new constitutional status, effectively acknowledging the bicultural reality of the country, with recognition for Māori "... as signatories to a settlement agreement (Treaty of Waitangi 1840); as having been disadvantaged in various ways by colonization and therefore as deserving of reparation; as requiring state support for the maintenance of the Māori language and culture; and as a particular client group of the state" (Spoonley, 2015, p. 655).

With shifting and ever-more diverse migration flows, contemporary Aotearoa New Zealand is distinctly multicultural within this bicultural national framework, setting the country apart from many others (Spoonley, 2015; Grbic, 2010). Over the past years, since the onset of the COVID-19 pandemic in 2020, New Zealand has been increasingly distinct on the global stage, with a strong public health response and one of the lowest mortality rates in the world. However, as Barber and Naepi (2020) stress, while the positive outcomes of the pandemic response are tangible, the response itself lacked sensitivity to the cultural and socio-economic realities of Māori and Pasifika Peoples in the country. These recent years have highlighted the ongoing impacts of colonization for Māori: "Moments of crisis, whether financial, viral or both, register their effects across every domain of the social. What were seemingly more fractured experiences of inequality—in whatever area we choose to look—become discernible as parts of a more totalising structure: colonial domination and accumulation that operates through racial inequality" (Barber & Naepi, 2020, p. 694).

The practice of sociology in Aotearoa New Zealand then must take these diverse experiences and ongoing inequalities into account: applying sociology in ways which are aware of global processes, but equally how these processes are filtered through local realities and structures (Thorns, 2003). Orienting sociological practice to Aotearoa is crucial. As described by Crothers: "If New Zealand sociologists do not produce a New Zealand sociology no one else will" (2008, p. 4).

Applied, Clinical and Public Sociology

Looking elsewhere, applications of sociology around the world have historically been practical and multidisciplinary, employed from micro to macro levels; from individuals and families, social groups and communities, to national and international structures. The practical, public face of sociology is highlighted by Burawoy (2021), emphasizing that sociology is more than just theory: it *matters*, as an engaged discipline that actively intervenes in the world. Fritz (2021) further outlines clinical sociology as a creative, humanistic, rights-based and interdisciplinary specialization that aims to improve life situations for individuals and groups across contexts, combining research, analysis and intervention. However, the idea that sociology can be clinical and directly applied is still somewhat peripheral, even in settings where the therapeutic potential of sociological interventions is more widely recognized.

Despite growing recognition and promising beginnings in the United States in the 1930s and 1940s, and a resurgence of interest in the 1970s/80s that brought about the formation of a number of organizations including the Society for Applied Sociology and the Sociological Practice Association (which merged to become the Association for Applied and Clinical Sociology in 2005), the idea of clinical sociology as established practice is not well known. Yet, regardless of labels, the practical impact of sociology and sociological practitioners can be far reaching. As described by Rebach and Bruhn, referring to the United States in particular (2001, p. 8): "Clinical sociology *is* sociology. Clinical sociologists do the same things that other sociologists do—they theorize, conceptualize, observe, test, evaluate, teach, do research, and become involved in professional and community service. What clinical sociologists do that other sociologists do not we call *intervention,* active involvement in various social systems with the goal of positive social change."

A key characteristic of clinical sociology is its applicability across and between societal levels. As Mills (1959) highlighted the interconnections between personal troubles and public issues, clinical sociology works to make meaningful links between individual struggles and social problems, and the practical ways these interconnections can effect change for the better (Hall, 1990). Social context is always key in assessing and approaching any socio-clinical work: levels of practice and analysis are interdependent and ultimately inseparable in everyday life. Sociological intervention can thus take place at any level, from personal, individual interactions (sociotherapy, counselling, social work) to group/societal level work (family counselling, community consultation, support groups) to the state level (policy development and governance): each level has significant interactions and implications for the others (Bruhn & Rebach, 2007). Dunham (1982) suggests that clinical sociology starts out micro, but through practice contributes to macro sociology, with Payne and Cross (1993) highlighting this as a particular strength of the discipline—its capacity to bring both macrosocial and microsocial factors and processes into play.

Clinical sociologists thus shift away from researcher/respondent relationships, towards clinical practitioner/client interactions, across social levels. As a clinical, applied branch of sociology, it complements the diversity of approaches which make up sociology itself, and illustrates the wide spectrum within the discipline, ranging from purely theoretical to practical and applied (Wan & Wan, 2020). While social research is often driven by both a quest for knowledge and a drive to improve social life, linking research and practical intervention or policy has frequently been controversial, with a separation maintained between the creation of social scientific knowledge and its use (Thorns, 2003). However, as Payne and Cross (1993) highlight, the distinction between "pure" and "applied" is not necessarily helpful, and misses the inevitable interactions within this spectrum, and the ways in which much sociology and sociological research is already applied in everyday life (see also Bulmer, 1993).

Going back to Burawoy (2008, 2021), sociology can be seen as more than just a discipline, but rather as a vocation. Sociological theory and practice are inextricably intertwined, and translating theory to practical change remains a key challenge. Burawoy outlines four options for sociological work: policy, professional, critical and public (see Spoonley, 2023 for more detail): and he queries, "How can sociologists make common cause with publics and still retain their integrity?" (Burawoy, 2008, p. 355).

Thorns (2003) suggests that applying sociological research with the aim of practical change is a delicate balance, drawing on political, social and inevitably ethical judgements about what individual and collective well-being signifies in context. While many sociologists go into research and practice to make a positive difference, it is not always clear what this means in reality. Gary C. David, former president of the Association for Applied and Clinical Sociology finds that link within applied sociology itself: finding connection with people's lives in ways that have impact and meaning (David, 2022). Linking research and practice, sociologists can work towards becoming socially relevant social scientists, "scholars who can take their research out of the academy and bring it to the public sphere in meaningful ways" (Iloh & Connor, 2022, p. 319).

Applied, Clinical, Public: Different Names, but the Same Search for Meaning

The chapters in this volume explore how this social relevance has emerged in Aotearoa New Zealand, looking at many different aspects of sociology, and their applications. Although clinical sociology is not established as a discrete discipline in Aotearoa New Zealand, there are examples of use and practical development both here and around the world, most notably in the US, Quebec and France, as well as in Greece, China, Brazil, Mexico, Japan, Italy, the Netherlands, Malaysia, Spain, Colombia and South Africa (Fritz, 2012, 2021). In the Pacific region, Spencer

(2009) describes the expanding role of clinical sociology interventions in Australia, particularly looking at clinical applications and analysis within the Victorian Workcover Authority, using a "bio-psycho-social" model of health. Payne and Cross suggest that clinical sociology remains in its infancy in the UK (1993), while Wan and Wan (2020) discuss how the practice of sociology in many developing countries is frequently by necessity practical or clinical, as practitioners work to address key social issues through research and intervention.

Sociology as a practice is thus clearly labelled as such in some contexts, while in others, such as Aotearoa, this practical perspective exists, but not always under the clinical banner. At the international level, the International Sociological Association maintains research committees on clinical sociology (RC46) and sociotechnics/ sociological practice (RC26), while other national sociological associations may also have practical/clinical sections (such as l'Association française de sociologie) (Fritz, 2021). Sociologists across the world then work in research, analysis and often application, with issues of importance and sociological understandings differing from country to country, and region to region.

Interestingly, in exploring the practice of sociology in Aotearoa New Zealand, our contributors have chosen different terms in their writing, illuminating this practical side of sociology as applied, clinical and public. There is significant overlap between these terms, and we provide a broad outline here:

- Sociology (or theoretical sociology, or foundational sociology), generally refers to the development and use of key theories, concepts and methods in research, within and for a primarily academic context (David, 2022). Sociological practice is frequently not included within this general definition, and various qualifiers are then added to clarify what this type of practice or invention might entail (Fritz, 2012).
- Applied Sociology takes these theories, concepts and methods within sociology to audiences outside of academia, working to further understanding for community organizations, policy makers and business groups: translating sociological findings for social use (David, 2022).
- Clinical Sociology takes the same sociological theories, concepts and methods in order to implement practical change, and in some contexts, creating interventions to effect change outside of academic work (David, 2022). Clinical is not intended to indicate pathology, but rather practice: moving away from medicalized perceptions of abnormality, clinical sociology seeks to address problematic issues and behaviours as responses to the larger social context (Wirth, 1931; Wan & Wan, 2020).
- Public Sociology, as a more recent term, focuses on bringing sociology into conversation with publics, often with a focus on civic groups—turning outwards to engage with people in everyday life and using sociology and sociological practice in a meaningful, understandable way (Burawoy, 2008; Fritz, 2012).

Thus, the practice of sociology has various names and nuances in its many forms in Aotearoa and elsewhere, drawing on the drive of many sociologists to make the world a better place (Turner, 1998). It is based on the hope that it is possible to make both individual lives and society better through intervention and implementation of research-based best practices, often combining sociology with other disciplines (Vissing, 2021; Fritz, 2012). Applications of sociology are underpinned by the idea that all individuals are social (although that can mean different things), and everyone is located in and influenced by their social contexts as well as their choices: we are all best understood through our relationships with wider societal forces, our interrelationships, institutions, gendered socializations, cultures, communities, and histories (Fein, 1997; Straus, 1979; Cavanagh, 2021). Clinical, applied and public sociologists aim to go beyond providing research and analysis, and could work to promote and implement constructive social change (Swan, 1981; Jaeckel, 1991). To do this effectively, sociological practice needs to be visible and impactful outside of the discipline and, as this volume shows, it must be applied in ways that are contextually appropriate (see Bulmer, 1993). This could develop from a form of open, contextualized dialogue between grounded theory, comprehensive research and careful application (Blane, 1993): as a locally oriented, decolonized sociological practice (Spoonley, 2023).

A Sociology of and for Aotearoa New Zealand

Sociology in Aotearoa New Zealand has its foundations in the development of the social sciences that took place in late nineteenth century Europe and England, though social analysis was occurring in this country long before the formal existence of university-based sociology departments (Brickell, 2007). In terms of organizational history, however, the late 1950s through to the late 1960s is considered a founding decade for sociology in Aotearoa and the basis for the subsequent development of the discipline (Crothers, 2014). In 2013 the Sociological Association of Aotearoa New Zealand (SAANZ)[3] celebrated its 50th anniversary. Through employment in the country's university system and affiliation with the national body of SAANZ, sociologists have maintained a strong sense of disciplinary identity, however this sense of identity has been more difficult for those sociologists working outside academia, 'in the margins' as it were (Crothers, 2016). Of relevance to this volume is the lack of a coordinated professional body for sociologists working outside academia, particularly those who work in applied settings.

In recent times scholars based in this country, several of whom are contributing to this volume, have begun to reflect more explicitly on what a sociology of and for Aotearoa New Zealand might look like (see, for example, Barber & Naepi, 2020; Crothers, 2014, 2016; Spoonley et al., 2016). The discipline itself is relatively young

[3] In 1963 the Sociological Association of Australia and New Zealand was formed and was referred to as SAANZ. This changed in 1988 when New Zealand members formed an independent body separate from the previous association with Australian sociologists, and from that time onwards, the acronym refers to the Sociological Association of Aotearoa New Zealand.

here and its contextualized historical development not well understood even by some sociologists and post-graduate students (Crothers, 2014). A feature of (post-)colonial New Zealand, like other colonialist projects, has been a neglect of its own socio-cultural characteristics, assumptions and silences. Historians and sociologists alike have developed many a cogent critique of this lack of awareness and have brought to light a variety of consequences that were a result of this absence (Bell et al., 2017; Brickell, 2008; Phillips, 1987; Salmond, 1998). Presumptions of the superiority of Western 'scientific' approaches to research, and their presumed neutrality, illustrate the continued influence of colonization and remain discriminatory in relationship with indigenous peoples around the world, including in Aotearoa (Tuhiwai Smith, 1999). Authors and researchers cognizant of these limitations thus continue to work at shedding light on what has too often gone unnoticed: this country's sociologists can continue to bring awareness to the way ethnocentrism can shape both public and sociological debate (see Barber & Naepi, 2020).

The scant access to research funds from the likes of private philanthropic trusts in Aotearoa has meant a heavy reliance on the state for tertiary education and research funds (Thorns, 2003). This has an impact on what kind of research gets done, whether by independent researchers or those with institutional homes within the university system. One result of this heavy reliance on state funding is that the research agenda in Aotearoa New Zealand can experience a high level of vulnerability to the 'push and pull' of political agendas (Spoonley et al., 2016; Thorns, 2003). Many of those who might be identified as sociologists through their educational foundations find employment in other important social settings. Yet their identification as sociologists becomes less visible once located outside academia and subsequently the contribution their disciplinary perspective may make to public issues is lost from view.[4]

Any reflection on a sociology of and for Aotearoa New Zealand would be incomplete without mention of the influence the neoliberal turn has had on how sociology is taught and practised here. The precarious nature of employment in our academic institutions needs noting, including the gendered and racialized nature of this precarity (Simpson et al., 2022; Stringer et al., 2018). More specifically to sociology, the pervasive influence of neoliberal policies in our institutions of higher learning has created tensions in how social theory is taught and resulted in questions about the ongoing viability of independent sociology programmes (McManus, 2006; Crothers, 2008, 2016). Within such an environment, questions that have been raised about the viability and applicability of the sociological gaze become ever more relevant.

These are the parameters that have shaped and continue to influence the development of sociology—whether academic, clinical, applied or public—in Aotearoa

[4]Prominent examples include, but are by no means are limited to, former Labour government minister and current chair of Pharmac, Accident Compensation Corporation and Education New Zealand Steve Maharey, and CEO of the National Collective of Independent Women's Refuges, Dr. Ang Jury (ONZM).

New Zealand. They are not unique to this place but rather part of a global picture which privileges some forms of knowledge and research over others, and that sees merit in a move towards closer linkages between research and policy (Thorns, 2003). The drive for policy to be "evidence-based" (defining "evidence" very narrowly), co-exists alongside the work of scholars such as Tuhiwai Smith (1999) and Barber and Naepi (2020) who highlight the fragile nature of much of what has been understood as 'factual'.

Uncertainty with regard to the future of sociology has been voiced at various times over the past decades (see Crothers, 1999; McManus, 2006) and the capacity of sociology to help 'right' what is 'wrong' with its own discipline has been raised in the international literature (Woolcock & Kim, 2000). This disconnect in New Zealand has been linked to the changes being felt as neoliberal policies have radically reshaped the scene of higher education over the past decades (Olssen & Peters, 2005). Fiscal imperatives, such as those at the heart of neoliberal frameworks, have had and are continuing to have a significant impact on tertiary education in Aotearoa, as Rowe-Williams (2018) points out regarding the application of a "financialised mindset" to the management of New Zealand universities.

While this has caused some to question whether the discipline will be able to maintain itself (as in Crothers, 1999), others point to the continued employment of sociologists and the emergence of new sociology programmes as evidence that although the discipline may be changing in new and unfamiliar ways, there remains cause for optimism in the new millennium (Spoonley, 2015; McManus, 2006). Within this context, we might cautiously suggest that the contributors to this volume look hopefully at sociology's capacity to ask the important questions that need addressing. These chapters offer the prospect of an on-going, vibrant sociological discussion in Aotearoa that spans disciplinary divides and keeps the value of a sociological perspective apparent.

Locally Oriented Sociology in Aotearoa New Zealand

Sociology in Aotearoa thus has a long history as an academic discipline, and applications of sociology have been varied and diverse. However, many contemporary sociologists remain frustrated that sociology often lacks a public voice, and as policy priorities shift, the importance of social research and practice can be lost (Spoonley et al., 2016). While sociological research often focuses on the ongoing impacts of colonization, and the deeply entrenched ethnic inequalities within society, sociology itself remains limited in its practice and application. The majority of professional sociologists (particularly within universities) are Pākehā (Tuhiwai Smith, cited in Barber & Naepi, 2020), and much sociological theory is heavily based on other contexts. However, local sociologists are increasingly exploring what a critically re-oriented and decolonized sociological practice would look like—how sociological research can become "a unique expression of this place" (Barber &

Naepi, 2020, p. 701), with a better sense of the distinctiveness and value of Aotearoa's intellectual and practical contribution (Spoonley et al., 2016).

As Barber and Naepi describe, a locally oriented sociological practice in Aotearoa will look different from sociology elsewhere: "For sociology to remain a vital voice in the years to come it must be transformed by its encounter with other ways of thinking, learning and knowing. If the sociological imagination is to be opened by a perspective on itself other than its own, then the primary relationship it must develop, in Aotearoa, is with the long memory and thinking of this place that Māori give voice to" (Barber & Naepi, 2020, p. 701).

Thus, Aotearoa New Zealand faces unique challenges and opportunities in the social sciences and in the global community. As a small country, we have a vibrant social scientific community, a diversity of scholars and practitioners, and innovative and often unusual approaches to addressing social problems: our privileged national standpoint during the COVID-19 pandemic has highlighted this positioning. Our bicultural national framework based on Te Tiriti o Waitangi, together with our multicultural population sets us apart as a national context, and while much research in the country emphasizes the importance of Māori approaches to the theory and practice of sociology, the realities of colonial inequalities linger. Significant social challenges face Aotearoa, and as Spoonley describes in this volume: rising to the challenges of these times is "...an exciting, challenging, terrifying, place to be—but isn't it exactly where sociology ought to be?" (p. 34).

The case studies in this book then bring much that is new to the clinical sociology literature, including Indigenous-centered sociological applications and practice. Our volume builds on recent international work, providing new perspectives on the challenges and potential of applying sociology in everyday life in Aotearoa—from the level of the state, through social policy and different communities within the country, to the micro level of sociological therapy and understandings of mental health. While clinical and applied sociology are not terms often heard in the Aotearoa New Zealand context, these chapters describe an active sociological community, and many examples of sociology informing and transforming social life, interweaving public and private issues. By reorienting the field of study to look specifically at Aotearoa New Zealand, we illustrate the history and future potential of applying sociology in this country, and the possibilities for change and intervention through locally oriented sociological practice, across micro, meso and macro applications.

Volume Overview

While this volume focuses on sociological practice, it is also interdisciplinary, crossing boundaries and bringing together work across fields. We do not aim to delimit clinical and applied sociology as separate fields of study and practice—it is precisely the interconnections and overlaps, the whanaungatanga within the social sciences, that make the practice of sociology so valuable in addressing the complexities of everyday life. This book then includes chapters from sociologists and social scientists from around Aotearoa New Zealand, looking at how a sociological perspective is important, and how sociology can make a difference. Chapters draw on research across disciplines, to explore both the past and the present through contributions that see theory and practice as two sides of the same coin (see Glass, 2001).

We are delighted to include a diversity of contributors, reflecting the diversity of the country—but it is important to note that many others wished to contribute to the volume, but were prevented from writing by a variety of very real public and private issues. Unpaid writing work in pandemic times is more difficult than ever before, and this burden is heavier on the shoulders of our Indigenous and marginalized colleagues. We want to recognize how hard the authors of these chapters have worked, drafting and revising chapters in this unsettled time. Bringing together a collection of chapters is not the same process as it was before 2020, and every single author who contributed, or who sought to contribute but was unable to, has worked to overcome all sorts of challenges—in terms of health, family, work, and just the general difficulties of life as we know it. It is with great sadness that we acknowledge the passing of one of our authors, Charles Crothers, an influential sociologist who put much time and effort into this volume, and wasn't able to see it completed. We remain very grateful to everyone for persisting, and the following eight chapters represent an important contribution to the field.

As co-Editors, we found our own positionings both a challenge and an advantage: as insiders (sociologists) and outsiders (psychotherapists and self-employed contract workers), we fall somewhere in between academic and practical work. We are both women with multiple national and ethnic ties, who have created somewhat unique career paths to allow for a balance between family and professional commitments. The authors of these chapters play equally complex roles—they include some of New Zealand's most established and well-known sociologists, and others who are earlier in their careers and who bring new, exciting approaches and energy to the discipline. Rather than seeing ourselves as experts in curating these chapters, we have taken an approach of curiosity and inquiry, and we have learned a lot from all participants who saw the potential in this volume.

These eight chapters then explore the history of applying sociology in Aotearoa New Zealand, and future possibilities for change and intervention through sociological practice, across micro, meso and macro levels.

Paul Spoonley's chapter on Making a Difference opens the volume, as he outlines the idea of a public sociology in Aotearoa: what it means and why it matters, and how sociological practice can lead to transformation. Speaking from personal experience, as one of Aotearoa's most publicly recognized sociologists, Paul positions public sociology within this unique context. He highlights how much previous work in the field was shaped by North American and European concerns and theorization, and how decolonial work has significant implications for both conceptual understanding and sociological practice. He describes the importance of a locally oriented sociological practice, drawing out the potential of public sociology to make a difference in everyday life.

Awanui Te Huia's chapter follows, illustrating the importance of a sociological lens in understanding Māori identities, Māori in English-medium education, and te reo Māori revitalisation in a colonial context. Her piece emphasizes the history and importance of Māori culture in Aotearoa, and the ongoing impacts of colonial harm for indigenous ancestral language learners in a colonial settler society. Awanui describes how te reo Māori is being revitalized, with increasing numbers of Māori language learners, and how sociological and psychological perspectives illuminate how these individuals are located and influenced by history and social context. This chapter deftly outlines the ways in which public issues and private anxieties intersect, as structural racism and the historical devaluation of te reo Māori contribute to personal feelings of inadequacy or whakamā for Māori seeking to learn their ancestral language.

The next chapter, by Zarine L. Rocha, keeps the focus on this individual-social interplay, in exploring the idea of sociologically-informed psychotherapy, or sociotherapy, in the context of Aotearoa New Zealand. She highlights how psychotherapeutic and sociological frameworks intersect, and how each is inextricably linked to the context in which these frameworks were developed. The chapter emphasizes the holistic approaches to therapy grounded in Kaupapa Māori, and the important ways in which seeing clinical sociology and (socio)therapy through this lens of Indigenous knowledge shifts the focus of therapy to these interconnections and complex positionings: *working with* people within culturally appropriate and locally sourced social frameworks, rather than *working on* individual troubles as divorced from public issues.

Chapter five, by Charles Crothers, traces a detailed overview and analysis of the various modes of social knowledge production in Aotearoa New Zealand and how applied sociology and applied sociologists are embedded in these. Drawing on his own significant work in the development of sociology in the country, as well as a comprehensive review of the work of others, this chapter outlines the role of applied sociology within the main academic, governmental and other public and private institutions of the country. He highlights key individuals and projects which have been particularly influential, before outlining two important types of practical contributions that have developed in New Zealand: Social Impact Assessment and Programme Evaluation.

Robert Didham then provides a detailed case study of the clinical sociology of the intersections between identity, categories, labelling and policy. In exploring the frames within which clinical sociology and clinical sociologists operate in Aotearoa New Zealand, Robert's wealth of practical experience in the field informs his nuanced discussion of categorizing ethnic identities: highlighting how research on Pacific populations tends not to adequately take account of the cultural and social diversity within the population, and can also ignore the ways in which other populations of interest intersect. He stresses that labelling of populations carries with it embedded prejudices and implicit 'othering', and these issues present challenges when it comes to effective public policy development. Careful applications of sociology can thus assist in effective policy formulation and a deeper, more nuanced, understanding.

Chapter seven outlines how sociology is applied within healthcare research and practice in Aotearoa New Zealand, written by a leading sociologist and practitioner in the field, Kevin Dew. He clearly outlines how the subdiscipline of the sociology of health has had a very strong presence in New Zealand, tracing the long history of research and policy work on medical or health sociological concerns. The chapter highlights the importance of sociological work in illuminating the systemic racism and inequalities faced by the Māori population, and how such research can have key practical outcomes. Kevin's piece stresses the significant work undertaken by New Zealand sociologists, and those in allied disciplines, including sociolinguistics and Māori health researchers, in facilitating different ways of thinking about and acting on healthcare delivery.

Chapter eight remains in the field of healthcare, with Aimee B. Simpson providing a detailed dramaturgical analysis of health, lifestyle, and body size in healthcare settings. In applying a sociological lens to issues of healthcare, particularly the meanings of 'fat' and 'healthy', she explores how these beliefs contribute to a stigmatising healthcare environment, in which fat people must navigate assumptions about their health status and lifestyle habits in the process of accessing care. Drawing on Goffman's framework, she carefully outlines how fat people 'perform' health in order to overcome the barriers they face in healthcare, and how a convincing health 'performance' can be a fundamental part of accessing treatment, tests, or advocacy. Using this theoretical framework for practical ends, Aimee demonstrates how this novel application of sociological analysis in clinical settings can illuminate the impact of stigma on healthcare delivery and receipt, and thus contribute to changes that lead to more equitable health outcomes.

Kathy L. Davidson's piece closes the volume, exploring the productive space at the confluence of sociology and psychotherapy and bringing together key threads of sociological practice across levels of analysis. Her chapter traces her personal story of applying sociology to her psychotherapeutic work, linking the wider sociology of healthcare to individual experiences of mental health(care). This thoughtful and reflective piece on her experiences bringing together sociology and psychotherapy—both theoretically and practically—highlights the importance of interdisciplinary work in the reality of sociological practice. She questions limitations around what is and is not sociological, what is and is not psychological: entertaining the possibility of incorporating both in order to support the emergence of something new.

As this collection shows, the practical uses and future potential for clinical and applied sociology in Aotearoa are vast. Clinical, applied and public sociology illustrate how human life and social concepts are not limited to a single method of explanation or analysis, and crucially, clinical sociology does not seek to work in contradiction to other approaches, disciplines or methods (Fritz, 2021; Straus, 1979). In this context, and elsewhere, we firmly believe that in addressing practical change in everyday life, it is impossible to delineate clear boundaries—and this is a strength, not a weakness. As eloquently described in the whakataukī by the late Māori language and tikanga expert, Kūkupa Tirikatene:

E kore e taea te whenu kotahi ki te raranga i te whāriki kia mōhio tātou ki ā tātou. Mā te mahi tahi ā ngā whenu, mā te mahi tahi ō ngā kairaranga, ka oti tēnei whāriki. I te otinga me titiro tātou ki ngā mea pai ka puta mai. Ā tana wā, me titiro hoki ki ngā raranga i makere nā te mea, he kōrero anō kei reira.

[The tapestry of understanding cannot be woven by one strand alone. Only by the working together of strands and the working together of weavers will such a tapestry be completed. With its completion let us look at the good that comes from it and, in time we should also look at those stitches which have been dropped, because they also have a message.]

References

Barber, S., & Naepi, S. (2020). Sociology in a crisis: Covid-19 and the colonial politics of knowledge production in Aotearoa New Zealand. *Journal of Sociology, 56*(4), 693–703.

Barnes, A. (2013). *What can Pākehā learn from engaging in kaupapa Māori educational research?*, Working Paper 1, New Zealand Council for Educational Research.

Bell, A., Elizabeth, V., McIntosh, T., & Wynyard, M. (Eds.). (2017). *A land of milk and honey: Making sense of Aotearoa/New Zealand.* Auckland University Press.

Brickell, C. (2007). Those "other sociologists": Social analysis before sociology. *New Zealand Sociology, 22*(1), 4–27.

Brickell, C. (2008). *Mates and lovers: A history of gay New Zealand.* Random House.

Bruhn, J. G., & Rebach, H. M. (2007). *Sociological practice: Intervention and social change* (2nd ed.). Springer.

Blane, D. (1993). Clinical sociology: What it might be. In M. Cross & G. Payne (Eds.), *Sociology in action: Applications and opportunities for the 1990s.* Palgrave Macmillan.

Bulmer, M. (1993). Successful applications of sociology: Can Britain learn from America? In M. Cross & G. Payne (Eds.), *Sociology in action: Applications and opportunities for the 1990s.* Palgrave Macmillan.

Burawoy, M. (2021). *Public sociology.* Polity Books.

Burawoy, M. (2008). What is to be done? Theses on the degradation of social existence in a globalizing world. *Current Sociology, 56*(3), 351–359.

Cavanagh, S. L. (2021). Sociotherapy in the time of COVID-19: A critical position paper on the importance of sociology. *Journal of Applied Social Science., 15*, 211–225. https://doi.org/10.1177/1936724421998275

Crothers, C. (2016). *Sociologies of New Zealand.* Palgrave Macmillan.

Crothers, C. (2014). History of New Zealand sociology: An introductory editorial. *New Zealand Sociology, 29*(4), 3–26.

Crothers, C. (2008). The state of New Zealand sociology: An updated profile. *New Zealand Sociology, 23*(1), 3–29.

Crothers, C. (1999). New Zealand sociology in the new millennium. *New. Zealand Sociology, 14*(2), 203–219.

David, G. C. (2022). What's phase 2? Crafting the value proposition for applied and clinical sociology. *Journal of Applied Social Science, 16*(2), 371–381.

Dunham, H. W. (1982). Clinical sociology: Its nature and function. *Clinical Sociology Review, 1*, 1, 5.

Fein, M. L. (1997). Clinical sociology and the individual client. *Clinical Sociology Review, 15*,1, 6.

Freedman, J. A. (1982). Clinical sociology: What it is and what it isn't – a perspective. *Clinical Sociology Review, 1*,1, 6.

Fritz, J. M. (2021). Introduction. In J. M. Fritz (Ed.), *International clinical sociology* (2nd ed.). Springer.

Fritz, J. M. (2012). Including sociological practice: A global perspective and the US case. In D. Kalekin-Fishman & A. Denis (Eds.), *The shape of sociology for the twenty-first century: Tradition and renewal*. Sage.

Glass, J. (2001). Foreword. In H. M. Rebach & J. G. Bruhn (Eds.), *Handbook of clinical sociology* (2nd ed.). Springer.

Glass, J. (1991). Foreword. In J. G. Bruhn & H. M. Rebach (Eds.), *Handbook of clinical sociology*. Springer.

Glass, J. (1979). Reviewing an old profession: Clinical sociology. *American Behavioral Scientist, 22*(4), 513–529.

Grbic, D. (2010). Social and cultural meanings of tolerance: Immigration, incorporation and identity in Aotearoa, New Zealand. *Journal of Ethnic and Migration Studies., 36*(1), 125–148.

Hall, C. M. (1990). Identity empowerment through clinical sociology. *Clinical Sociology Review, 8*, 1, 7.

Iloh, C., & Connor, C. (2022). Making the case for the socially relevant social scientist. *Journal of Applied Social Science, 16*(1), 318–327.

Jaeckel, M. (1991). Clinical sociology. *Teaching Sociology, 19*(1), 96–102.

Larner, W., & Spoonley, P. (1995). Post-colonial politics in Aotearoa/New Zealand. In D. K. Stasiulis & N. Yuval-Davis (Eds.), *Unsettling settler societies: Articulations of gender, race, ethnicity and class*. Sage.

Leckie, J. (1985). In defence of race and empire: The white New Zealand league at Pukekohe. *New Zealand Journal of History., 19*(2), 103–129.

McManus, R. (2006). Shifting practices in New Zealand sociology. *New Zealand Sociology, 21*(2), 270–288.

Mills, C. W. (1959). *The sociological imagination* (Vol. 46, p. 355). Oxford University Press.

Olssen, M., & Peters, M. A. (2005). Neoliberalism, higher education and the knowledge economy: From the free market to knowledge capitalism. *Journal of Education Policy, 20*(3), 313–345.

Orange, C. (1997). *The treaty of Waitangi*. Bridget Williams Books Ltd.

Payne, G., & Cross, M. (1993). An active sociology? In M. Cross & G. Payne (Eds.), *Sociology in action: Applications and opportunities for the 1990s*. Palgrave Macmillan.

Phillips, J. (1987). *A man's country? The image of the Pakeha male, a history*. Penguin Books.

Rebach, H. M., & Bruhn, J. G. (2001). Theory, practice, and sociology. In H. M. Rebach & J. G. Bruhn (Eds.), *Handbook of clinical sociology* (2nd ed.). Springer.

Rowe-Williams, J. (2018). The financialisation of tertiary education in Aotearoa/New Zealand. *New Zealand Sociology, 33*(2), 41–68.

Salmond, A. (1998). *Between worlds: Early exchanges between Maori and Europeans, 1773–1815*. Allen Lane.

Simpson, A, Jolliffe Simpson, A. D., Soar, M., Oldfield, L., Roy, R. P., & Salter, L. A. (2022). *Elephant in the room: Precarious work in New Zealand universities*. The University of Auckland. Report. https://doi.org/10.17608/k6.auckland.19243626.v2.

Spencer, L. (2009). The expanding role of clinical sociology in Australia. *Journal of Applied Social Science, 3*(2), 56–62.

Spoonley, P. (1993). *Racism and ethnicity* (2nd ed.). Oxford University Press.

Spoonley, P. (2015). New diversity, old anxieties in New Zealand: The complex identity politics and engagement of a settler society. *Ethnic and Racial Studies, 38*(4), 650–661.

Spoonley, P. (2023). Making a difference: practicing public sociology in Aotearoa. In Z. L. Rocha & K. Davidson (Eds.), *Applied and clinical sociology in Aotearoa New Zealand*. Springer.

Spoonley, P., Fraser, G., & Maharey, S. (2016). A New Zealand sociological imagination: The Massey story. *New Zealand Sociology, 31*(3), 60–63.

Statistics NZ. (2018). *Ethnic group summaries reveal New Zealand's multicultural make-up*. Accessed February 27, 2023, from https://www.stats.govt.nz/news/ethnic-group-summaries-reveal-new-zealands-multicultural-make-up/

Straus, R. A. (1979). Introduction: The reemergence of clinical sociology. *American Behavioral Scientist, 22*(4), 477–485.

Stringer, R., Smith, D., Spronken-Smith, R., & Wilson, C. (2018). "My entire career has been fixed term": Gender and precarious academic employment at a New Zealand university. *New Zealand Sociology, 33*(2), 169–201.
Swan, L. A. (1981). Clinical sociology: Problems and prospects. *Mid-American Review of Sociology, 6*(2), 111–127.
Thorns, D. C. (2003). The challenge of doing sociology in a global world: The case of Aotearoa/New Zealand. *Current Sociology, 51*(6), 689–708.
Tuhiwai Smith, L. (1999). *Decolonizing methodologies: Research and indigenous peoples*. Zed Books.
Turner, J. H. (1998). Must sociological theory and sociological practice be so far apart?: A polemical answer. *Sociological Perspectives, 41*(2), 243–258.
Vissing, Y. (2021). Children's human rights as a buffer to extremism: A clinical sociology framework. In J. M. Fritz (Ed.), *International clinical sociology* (2nd ed.). Springer.
Wan, P. M., & Wan, A. H. (2020). *Clinical sociology: Moving from theory to practice*. Springer.
Wirth, L. (1931). Clinical Sociology. *American Journal of Sociology, 37*(1), 49–66.
Woolcock, M., & Kim, J. (2000). Can what is right with sociology solve what is wrong with sociology: A view from the 'come-back' generation. *The American Sociologist, 31*(1), 15–31.

Zarine L. Rocha is a sociologist and researcher, the Editor-in-Chief of *Sociology Compass* and Managing Editor of *Current Sociology*. She is an Honorary Research Fellow at the University of Auckland, and an Affiliated Researcher with the Department of Sociology, National University of Singapore. Zarine specializes in issues of mixed race/mixed ethnic identity, narratives of belonging, multiculturalism and diversity, and clinical/applied sociology in Asia and the Pacific, and has worked as a researcher in academic institutions and international organizations, including at the United Nations Research Institute for Social Development, the United Nations Environment Programme and the World Economic Forum. She has published widely on issues of identity and belonging, race and ethnicity, and applications of sociology.

Kathy L. Davidson is a sociologist and registered psychotherapist currently working in private practice in Wellington and the Wairarapa. She has a PhD from Massey University, an honours degree in sociology, and a BA with a double major in psychology and sociology also from Massey University. She holds diplomas in Psychosynthesis Counselling and Psychotherapy from the Institute of Psychosynthesis NZ. Kathy's diverse research interests include emotional labour and occupational identity, disaster management, and mental health. She has coordinated a bicultural participatory action research project into the mental health and well-being of youth/rangatahi.

Making a Difference: Practicing Public Sociology in Aotearoa

Paul Spoonley

Introduction

There is a useful debate about the similarities and differences between and amongst clinical, applied and public sociology which is usefully summarized by Fritz (2012) and Burawoy (2005, 2021). Fritz (2012: 3) notes that what she refers to as "engaged public sociology" can be encapsulated under the label of clinical sociology as a form of sociological practice. The normally used terms—clinical, applied and public sociology—do have a number of similarities and for some commentators, such as Fritz, it is possible to stress the similarities of "sociological practice" under the rubric of clinical sociology. However, I am persuaded by Burawoy's (2007: 28) definition of public sociology as bringing sociology "into a conversation with publics" as sociologists are "read beyond the academy". I would go further and stress this public engagement as defining an important tradition and form of practice within sociology. As will become apparent in this chapter, I think this outward facing and engaged sociology holds considerable promise. It sits as one variant of clinical sociology but my inclination is to stress the public ambitions and practice, and I therefore prefer the label of "public sociology" as a way of reflecting this particular emphasis.

If public sociology is, at its core, an engagement by sociologists with non-sociological[1] communities, then the discipline—from its origins—can lay claim to be 'public' in various ways. But the recent international debate concerning

[1] The phrasing seems clumsy—and it is. In this context, "non-sociological" includes every community that is not directly involved in the teaching and research of the discipline as a member. There are communities that are—and should be—the focus of partnership in the project that is public sociology. More of this as the chapter proceeds.

P. Spoonley (✉)
Massey University, Auckland, New Zealand
e-mail: P.Spoonley@massey.ac.nz

© The Author(s), under exclusive license to Springer Nature Switzerland AG 2023
Z. L. Rocha, K. L. Davidson (eds.), *Applied and Clinical Sociology in Aotearoa New Zealand*, Clinical Sociology: Research and Practice,
https://doi.org/10.1007/978-3-031-36581-2_2

public sociology, beginning in the 1980s and then intensifying in the early 2000s, argued for a much-enhanced degree of engagement from the discipline and its practitioners and to deliberately seek to influence policy and political debates. This might be done in a variety of ways, from working intimately with communities, being a contributor to public debates via the media, or helping shape policy and service delivery as part of policy development. This interest in public sociology was sparked, in part, by the discipline's perceived irrelevance during the 1980s and 1990s (especially as neo-liberal economics grew in influence) and the decline in the numbers of students and faculty at universities, especially in the USA. Public—and clinical—sociology was part of a reaction that sought to make sociology more relevant and visible.

It is an interesting debate, not simply because of how confusing it is (what exactly is public—or clinical, or applied—sociology? And what defines these sociological approaches and practices in terms of activities?) but because there has been a considerable and negative reaction, including from within the ranks of the discipline itself. These debates about public sociology have tended to be a reflection of the situation and concerns faced by American sociology. It is a useful debate to have but the issues and possibilities are situationally determined and driven. Therefore, most of the discussion will concern public sociology in a New Zealand context. The discipline has northern hemisphere roots and has been transplanted to a colonial and settler society to be part of the knowledge-making and policy-development of a contemporary liberal-democracy (Crothers, 2005). However, there are powerful alternatives to these northern sociological ontologies and traditions which are so deeply embedded in European expansionism and colonialism. For example, Raewyn Connell (2007, 2020), in *Southern Theory,* provides a critique of classical sociological theory as too based in global-north points of view and establishes the case for sociologists to take more notice of key thinkers and approaches from the global south and indigenous perspectives. More of this soon.

The argument here is that sociology ought to be public in various ways but that there are historical and contemporary pressures that limit sociology's contribution or impact. These need to be addressed. And the discipline needs to be public in relation to the exigencies and considerations of a particular location. There are a range of considerations, if sociology is to be truly public in its connections and impact, that need to be considered. Most are not easy, either in their conception or in the way in which sociologists negotiate the issues. What does a truly decolonised and public sociology look like? What does it mean to partner with communities as part of sociological practice? Is advocacy and political engagement something that all sociologists should do—or are capable of doing? Should sociologists engage with the media—and which media and in what way?

Given the variety of sociological approaches, the very different circumstances that sociologists find themselves in and the relevance of being public for some topics and issues—and not for others—it is perhaps inevitable that there is no one approach or type of public sociology but rather a spectrum that depends on circumstances and skill. This chapter aims to offer some guidance on the possibilities but I accept that we need to recognise that there are many sociologies, with often little in common in terms of framing or practice. That said, the excitement, rewards and transformative potential of public sociology, whatever the circumstances and the approach adopted, deserves attention and, I would argue, should be a defining characteristic of the discipline in the twenty-first century in Aotearoa.

Public Sociology: A Brief History

The contemporary literature tends to date the interest in public sociology from Herbert Gans' Presidential address to the American Sociological Association in 1988 (Gans, 1989). He followed it up with a note in the ASA *Footnotes* (Gans, 2002) titled "More of us should become public sociologists". Gans appeared most concerned about what he called 'public intellectuals' and the number of sociologists in the media or contributing to public and policy debates and, specifically, the lack of such public profile and contribution. It was another Presidential address, this time by Michael Burawoy in 2004 along with a subsequent article and then a book (Burawoy, 2005, 2021), that sparked a new wave of interest and debate. As Burawoy noted:

> …the challenge of public sociology is to engage multiple publics in multiple ways… [involving] taking knowledge back to those from whom it came, making issues of private troubles, and thus regenerating sociology's moral fiber (Burawoy, 2005: 4–5).

He goes on to argue that there are four types of sociology: *professional* (concerned with developing a corpus of theory, concepts and empirical data), *critical* (the role here is to examine and critique the foundations of sociology or, as Burawoy puts it, "critical sociology is the conscience of professional sociology"; Burawoy, 2005: 10), *policy* (sociology which provides useful and practical knowledge that has implications for policy) and *public*.[2] Although he often talks as though public sociology represents a single and singular approach, he also concedes at other points that there is a "multiplicity of public sociologies" which reflects "not only different publics but different value commitments on the part of sociologists" (Burawoy, 2005: 8).[3]

Burawoy's writing on public sociology provided an influential and compelling argument for a sociology which was engaged with different areas of civil society and with a range of publics, or rather communities. It came at a moment when sociology had experienced a troubling decade as neo-liberalism and conservative economists and economic views were paramount while sociology, in terms of both influence and

---

[2]While I am attracted to the Burawoy notion of public sociology, I am also aware that the distinctions he makes between the four types—professional, critical, policy and public—are at times conflated in sociological practice. Further, in the context of this book, it might be more appropriate to consider more umbrella terms such as applied or clinical—and, of course, public—sociology.

[3]There were a lot more contributions to what was entailed in public sociology than the thoughts of two American Sociological Association Presidents; see Hossfeld et al. (2021).

numbers, had stagnated in many countries. In the growing managerialism of the universities, and the often narrowly applied focus of funding agencies, sociology needed to reassert its relevance. The interest in public sociology was timely and it ignited some lively debates, although not all sociologists were convinced. There was a considerable sociological constituency who were critical of any conception of public sociology.

Jonathan Turner (2005), for one, was certainly not convinced and argued that the public sociology espoused by Burawoy exposed the ideological biases of sociology. He went on to assert:

> ...the morality of sociologists is several standard deviations away from that of the publics we might influence. They are not likely to listen to left-wing ideology of sociologists; and indeed, if the public finds out that the discipline is so left and so mired in political correctness, we could permanently hurt our chances of influencing anyone... (Turner, 2005: 28).

Even while he confesses to sharing a left-leaning view with Burawoy, Turner was concerned that this ideological orientation represented a major issue for engaging with communities. Subsequent headings in his article expand on this theme ("The dangers of critical theory", "Tower of babble") before he ends with a plea to avoid the advocacy inherent in the sort of public sociology advocated by Burawoy.

Turner is not alone.

Fatsis (2017) provides a somewhat different assessment of public sociology and the debates rehearsed above. He favours public sociology but asks whether the advocacy for this approach to sociology has "amounted to little more than a rhetorical gesture or a self-righteous posture, rather than as a defining feature of our daily scholarly lives". He is concerned that there is too little public sociology because of the pressures of managerialism and the tendency to prioritise what counts over what should matter (Fatsis, 2017). He ends with some useful questions:

- What do we mean by public sociology?
- Whether we do it all
- How to best practice it and
- Whether we [I assume here that he is referring to all sociologists wherever they are located and whatever their focus of sociological work] are "truly willing to commit to in ways that go beyond a mere symbolic attachment to a utopian flight of fancy" (Fatsis, 2017).

These seem exactly the questions that should be central to the debates about public sociology. My only addition would be to invite any discussion or debate to be contextualised so that we are not continuing the tradition of some earlier contributors in assuming a similarity or common set of drivers and expectations in very different settings. Of particular significance here are national contexts but also the relevance of locational factors within a particular society.

Public Sociology: A Definition

As Fatsis (2017) points out, 'public sociology' is routinely evoked as a shorthand to describe a bewildering variety of related ideas and propositions whose very breadth makes public sociology extremely resistant to a clear definition. He might be right but that does not mean that a definition should not be offered.

A good starting point is to acknowledge that the founding 'fathers' of the discipline were all public sociologists in some form—Emile Durkheim, Max Weber and Karl Marx—primarily because they were intimately involved with the major social and economic issues of the day and provided compelling conceptual and theoretical insights into matters such as religious influences on suicide, religious values and economic systems and the nature of capitalism and class conflict. Each participated in different forms of social engagement and activism (cf. Nichols, 2017: 316–317). As Marx had inscribed on his grave: "Philosophers have only interpreted the world, in different ways. The point is to change it".

I would argue that the origins of the discipline and those who were most influential in establishing it provide some guidance in terms of some of the core elements that could—and should—embody a public sociology, notably a critical engagement with major social, economic and political issues of a particular time and place and then, following Marx's exhortation, making a difference in real world lives and settings. Burawoy (2021) notes that Weber was clear that sociology was more than a discipline; it was a vocation to be practiced everywhere and by everyone. As Crothers (2005) notes, these classical thinkers and their conception of how sociology should be practiced were influential in the New Zealand context, especially in the early phase of the establishment of the discipline (1960s–1980s), particularly as much of the local sociology was highly derivative and was practiced by sociologists who were originally European or North American—or were New Zealanders who had trained in the northern hemisphere. What also should be acknowledged was that this influence often precluded sociological thinkers and practitioners who were people of colour or women, as Connell (2007, 2020) observes.

The discipline grew to maturity influenced by its European, North American and Western science origins, frameworks and practices. Sociology reflected a mixture of influences: the Enlightenment, modernity and liberal and democratic values. But it also took place in a wide range of national and societal settings through a range of historical periods. One question that arises from this disciplinary trajectory is whether these scientific origins and influences have inhibited the discipline. Located in a settler society that is grappling with a colonial past and the ongoing impacts of this past, do the assumptions and traditions of a sociology that reflects its European and North American roots need to be recognised, challenged and altered? The answer here is contextualisation is important if a public sociology is to be relevant and effective.

In the debates about decoloniality (see Ndhlovu, 2016; Mignolo, 2011; Smith, 1999; Meghji, 2021), the concern is that sociology, along with other disciplines, remains too committed to elements of modernity and universalism, and does not recognise or respond adequately to ongoing power relations and material differences, especially where these reflect racialised and colonial notions and assumptions. The same concerns are relevant to gender and transgender issues or socio-economic dynamics and outcomes. The recent challenges offered by movements such as Black Lives Matter or #MeToo highlight the ongoing repressive and discriminatory nature of systems, including knowledge systems. Can sociology and sociologists demonstrate that they can not only address such concerns but that there is the potential for transformative change that benefits the colonised and dispossessed? Can sociology demonstrate both an ability and willingness to be 'public' in its connections to communities as well as 'public' in its impact on policy and community well-being? These issues become especially relevant in settler societies.

The public sociology discussed below relates to the issues and challenges of a settler society, Aotearoa New Zealand, and what then becomes appropriate in terms of community and public engagement in a specific nationalised territory.[4] More of this soon. But first I want to return to the definition of public sociology deployed here.

As a starting point, it is important to acknowledge that sociology, including public sociology, is defined by its past as a discipline of the north and as a product of European expansionism, by its traditions and core theoretical and methodology approaches and its institutional settings, past and present. For those wanting to develop a public sociology, it is critically important to recognise these traditions and influences and to develop a reflexive sociology that acknowledges conceptual and praxis limitations. A decolonial sociology is one option.

The next question is which publics, or which agencies or communities, are appropriate partners in the practice of a public sociology? This typically involves whakawhanaungatanga, or the development of meaningful relationships, rather than transactional or distant encounters. What sort of relationships best serve the community in knowledge generation and understanding? How do sociologists negotiate and develop these relationships? Beyond the development of a relationship (or relationships), the next question is what will the benefits be from the research or relationship involved, what outcomes will there be and will the safety and well-being of those involved be assured or, hopefully, improved? Public sociology is about active community engagement and the establishment of relationships with clear agreements about the sharing of power and knowledge, and the identification of outcomes that will be beneficial to that community.

To respond to the question put by Fatsis (2017), public sociology is not public sociology if it simply refers to the aggregation of activities that sociologists might undertake in public; it should involve a genuine and meaningful attempt to embody

[4]There is an interesting admission in the Burawoy (2005: 21, 22) article where he states: "…it [American sociology] strides like a giant over world sociology. Many of the leading sociologists teaching in other parts of the world were trained in the United States". He then goes to talk how American sociology has become "world hegemonic" and there is a need to "provincialise" sociology. Then "provincialise" sociology we will, and seek to decolonize it as well.

civic engagement in sociological practice and the possibility of transformative and positive outcomes for the communities ('publics') of those involved.

Sociology is not the only discipline to discuss these issues. There has been a parallel discussion in relation to public criminology.

Public Criminology

There has been an enthusiastic debate about the nature and desirability of a 'public' criminology that began not long after a similar debate in sociology, again, notably in the USA (see Loader & Sparks, 2010; Mears, 2010; Uggen & Inderbitzen, 2010; Clear, 2010). Like those advocating for a public sociology, public criminology was characterised as a "field of engaged social enquiry" that could intervene in "societal conversations and social action around their subject matter" (Loader & Sparks, 2010: 771).

This public criminology is only part of the spectrum that constitutes criminology in what Loader and Sparks (2010: 773) describe as "a disputatious plurality of theoretical assumptions and perspectives, by affiliations to different surrounding disciplines, by a wide range of objects of interest and enquiry, by competing methodologies and ways of knowing, and by a range of different styles of criminological engagement". This is equally true of sociology but does not invalidate the attempt to develop a form of engaged and impactful disciplinary practice.

The following understanding goes some way to suggesting the nature of a public criminology at the core of these debates:

> [public criminology makes] . . .explicit the connections that inescapably exist between crime and its control and the repertoire of ideas (order, justice, authority, legitimacy, freedom, rights, etc.) and traditions (liberalism, but also conservatism, social democracy, feminism, republicanism, environmentalism, etc.) that comprise modern political thought (Loader & Sparks, 2010: 777).

Others saw this public criminology as an attempt to "reframe[e] cultural images of the criminal. . .reconsidering rule-making. . .evaluating social interventions. . .and assembling social facts" (Uggen & Inderbitzen, 2010: 726–727).[5]

These understandings of the core aspects of public criminology stress the importance of influencing public understanding and political decisions by contributing to the task of provoking and unsettling "political imperatives" and "pos[ing] questions about our responses to crime" (Loader & Sparks, 2010: 778). Clear (2010: 722) discusses the prime audience for public criminology as being:

> . . .the crime/justice consumer publics (both those who make crime policy and those who are affected by it) . . .This entails talking *to,* talking *with,* and talking *about* those publics in the production of criminological scholarship.

---

[5]There are those that are critical of a public criminology (see Rock, 2010, 754, who suggests that the matters of concern are a product of political contingency).

This emphasis in public criminology on communicating findings to public audiences and directly participating in public and political debates certainly constitutes one of the key elements in what is defined here as public sociology. But there are still the same concerns that have emerged in debates about public sociology: the need to be politically engaged in ways that expose the ideological assumptions of the discipline or its advocates. Moreover, there is a repeat of the concern that public criminology relies on "news-making criminology" and that it empties "criminology of any meaningful content so that all that matters is getting one's favoured discourse heard" (E. Turner quoted in Wilson, 2013: 543).

Do these debates about public criminology add anything to guide the development of a public sociology? The applied and highly contested nature of crime, and what works by way of societal measures and responses, provides a public criminology with a rich array of possibilities to enter and influence public and policy understanding and options. But there is little by way of a discussion of community engagement or the need, as I have framed it here, to develop relations with communities as partners in the research as a precursor to any contribution to public understanding and policy interventions. Moreover, and given the earlier discussion about the need to decolonise sociology in a settler society, Aotearoa New Zealand, I would argue that the discussion of a public criminology offers a partial and ultimately inadequate framing of a 'public' disciplinary approach or practice.

Public Sociology: Issues and Possibilities in Aotearoa

It would be misleading to suggest that there has been no interest in public sociology in the history of the discipline in New Zealand. A quick survey of the interests and activities of sociologists (see Baldock, 2005 as one example) indicates that there are multiple examples of sociologists seeking to develop a locally grounded sociology that is built on partnerships as well as looking to influence policy and political debates. There are even examples of sociologists using the term 'public sociology' to describe their ambitions for an engaged and activist sociology, in one case, in relation to a certain period of sociology at Massey University (see Spoonley et al., 2016). But the nature of this public engagement and the possibilities of a more deliberate public sociology of the sort envisaged by Gans and others has stuttered and started—or stopped—as advocates have come and gone, or the vicissitudes of a modern managerial university have placed new demands and limitations on staff, or sociology has been downsized and underfunded in a particular period. Nevertheless, there are some developments which have rightly placed sociology back at the centre of engagement and influence—and shaped what that should look like.

Debates about decoloniality and the decolonisation of sociology, along with contributions on how best to position the discipline and those practicing it in the context of Te Tiriti and tino rangatiratanga, have all provided new strategies for engagement and have made it clear that it is possible to articulate and practice a sociology that is public in what it does and how it seeks to do it. Moreover, the core components of this approach, which rely on a degree of reflexivity and exhibiting decolonising principles, and which embody Māori values (see below for a further discussion of what these might entail), provide a basis for considering and partnering with marginalised groups. These developments invite a different mindset, a different sociology and a different set of activist options which, in turn, provide the elements of a locally oriented public sociology. It is to these that I now turn.

(i) **Te Whakapakari Te Mana Tangata**[6]

If public sociology is to achieve its potential in Aotearoa, then it needs to centre Te Tiriti obligations and to decolonise its practice and assumptions, as well as to act as an agent of decolonisation (including within institutional contexts such as the university), to establish effective and appropriate partnership arrangements and to be transformative in practice and outcomes. Can a discipline that has its roots in Europe and North America decolonise to the point where it is recognised as having relevance in Aotearoa in the twenty-first century? Can practitioners, notably Pākehā, contribute to a decolonial disciplinary future?

In the New Zealand context, one of the challenges is to understand the subjectivity and power inherent in being a member of the dominant Pākehā group (see Bell, 2022). What does this membership mean in terms of addressing both the ethnic hegemony of those wanting to deliver on the ambitions of a public sociology and the appropriate relations with those who have been oppressed and marginalised by colonialism, notably (but not only) Māori?[7] There is an interesting and helpful literature on this aspect of addressing the asymmetrical relationships and power differentials (see Showden et al., 2022; Hoskins & Bell, 2021; Bell et al., 2021) and the need to develop decolonising projects. Central to this is an understanding, along with actions, that embody decoloniality amongst those who are settler subjects. This includes "highlighting and critiquing settler logics and in identifying changes that it is within the power of settler peoples themselves to make as a contribution towards Indigenous-led decolonisation" (Bell et al., 2021). They follow this invitation with the observation that key to this are settlers (in the case discussed in this chapter, Pākehā sociologists) "learning to be 'in relation' with Indigenous worlds and people outside the deeply habituated logics and practices of domination" (Bell et al., 2021). Hoskins and Bell (2021) argue that rather than a turning away from the state as part

[6]The title for this section comes from Ngahiwi Tomoana and was part of a project, *Mahi Awatea*, in which Taiwhenua o Heretaunga were granted funding along with Massey University to undertake a survey of the marae that constituted the Taiwhenua and to identify their social, cultural and economic resources as the basis for creating a development plan. One of the initial tasks was to establish how iwi Māori would work with a sociologist (me) and what benefits would accrue to the partnership. The results of this discussion and agreement are to be found in Teariki et al. (1992).

[7]See Margaret (2019) for an interesting autobiographical exploration of what being Pākehā means, especially in relation to Te Tiriti o Waitangi and colonisation. Ani Mikaere is quoted: "There is nowhere else in the world that one can be Pākehā. Whether the term remains forever linked to the shameful role of the oppressor or whether it can become a positive source of identity and pride is up to Pākehā themselves".

of "an alternative politics of (indigenous) resurgence and refusal", for Māori, "'turning up' is the ethical and correct practice of politics, a practice stemming from the relational ontology of the Māori world" so that the "embodied, face-to-face encounter" becomes central to these politics. This is an interesting argument that has implications for those wanting to practice a public sociology, both in relation to the respectful relational connections with Māori as well as providing a guide to sociological practice.

This is further expanded by research on the nature of 'decolonising activism' by Showden et al. (2022). They acknowledge that contributing to decolonisation "is a difficult and imperfect process" and they provide a helpful outline of the literature on what this might entail in various settler societies (see Showden et al., 2022: 666). The question becomes how best to reflect decolonising processes and options and to develop alliances. Showden et al. (2022: 667) note:

> Engagement in the big work of being a settler ally presents the challenge of how to speak about colonizing processes and their impacts on Indigenous peoples from the perspective of a beneficiary of those processes. This has to be done only in spaces where it is appropriate and in a way that does not recentre white stories or take the focus off those who are oppressed. . .Allies understand that they should not speak *for* Māori; rather, they should speak to the problems of colonization and shifts they can make in their own practices.
>
> Activists need to learn to navigate conflicts and contradictions in allyship. . .and to be reflexive about whiteness, power, privilege and one's motives in speaking with and for others.

They talk later about the importance of "reflexivity and relationality" as central to settler colonial responsibilities. At the same time, it is important—as Higgins (2018) reminds us—to acknowledge and theorise "settler colonial landscapes and their multiple subjectivities beyond a white/non-white binary". It is the positioning in these landscapes of white hegemony and the importance of decolonising strategies that restore mana and voice to those colonised, as part of reflexive practice that enables the relationality identified as critical by Showden et al. (2022). Following on from this is the task of how to co-construct knowledge and to amplify the voices of those participating from oppressed groups (Flavell & Cunningham, 2022).

There are also the challenges of overcoming the disincentives that exist because of the key dynamics of the discipline and its institutional base. Currie (2007: 186) refers to what he characterises as the "modern research university, and the professional disciplines which increasingly drive the university's conception of itself" that include certain "publication imperatives", "narrow research findings" and the dismissal or even the penalising of work that seeks to have impact. This is an issue in the New Zealand context, both in relation to the potentialities of a public sociology as well as for Indigenous researchers "who mobilise public/tribal scholarship alongside native publics and counter-publics" in the context of a neoliberal university context, especially in "settler-colonial institutions" (Kidman, 2019). It has been compounded in recent years by a debate about the scientific status of mātauranga Māori (see Henry, 2022; Trafford, 2022; Barber & Naepi, 2022; Parke & Hikuroa,

2021) and the dismissive and disrespectful assertions being made about the merits of mātauranga Māori relative to western science traditions.

Barber and Naepi (2022: 2) question whether "we practice social science not as social scientists who happen to Māori and/or Pacific but as Māori and/or Pacific social scientists". They go on to argue:

> Our ways to give full expression to our [Māori/Pasifika] ways of knowing, thinking and doing takes place in adversarial conditions, whether these conditions are the tinnitus of structure or the vocal antagonism of colleagues and canon. ...our research only finds adequate expression when it breaches, works on or against or escapes in some way the constraints imposed upon it by the relations of knowledge production in the University. (Barber & Naepi, 2022: 2).

As Macfarlane and Macfarlane (2019: 48) observe, "culturally relevant and inclusive approaches to research need to be the policy of choice and must be the policy of necessity". They go on to argue for power-sharing based on culturally grounded frameworks that combine Indigenous and Western knowledge systems and approaches. The institutional location of sociologists and the imperatives of the modern managerial university, combined with the origins and traditions of the discipline, present a major challenge to those wanting to develop a decolonised public sociology.

These matters and tensions raise a series of issues which are challenging for any claims for public sociology in Aotearoa:

- The ontological and epistemic roots of sociology;
- The clash between such Western knowledge systems and, in the New Zealand case, those of Māori and Pasifika;
- The institutional base of knowledge production and the way in which this inhibits forms of knowledge production or acknowledges the authenticity or value of Māori and Pasifika knowledge systems;
- The asymmetrical relationship and power between sociologists and marginalised and impoverished communities of Māori and Pasifika;
- The commitment to meaningful change as part of a broad sociological project that has positive outcomes for communities.

Mignolo (2007) has argued that it is important to:

> ...introduce a fracture with both the Eurocentred project of post-modernity and the project of post-coloniality... [in order] to foreground other epistemologies, other principles of knowledge and understanding and, consequently, other economy, other politics, other ethics.

The decolonisation of knowledge allows for the "re-construction and the restitution of silenced histories, repressed subjectivities, subalternized knowledges and languages" (Mignolo, 2007). On this basis, it becomes possible to develop a decolonised sociology along with meaningful relations and relationships with those who are partner communities, although the territory is fraught and seldom easy as the above literature makes clear.

(ii) Advocacy

This is an interesting and challenging dimension of public sociology. As Turner (2005) and others have suggested, advocacy undermines sociology's credibility because it 'exposes' the ideological inclinations of the discipline and its practitioners. But in the same way that it would be unusual to encounter those today who would believe in value-free science, the same is true in terms of most being open about their interest as sociologists in making a difference and to do this by declaring or contributing to an agenda of social change. This has been part of the tradition of sociology which has become even more significant given the way in which diverse bodies, groups and communities have been recognised as politically and sociologically important over recent decades. How do sociologists engage with these communities in ways that respect these differences but which also address questions of marginalisation, discrimination and exploitation? Neutrality is not an option and the challenge is a political one: what are you/we, as sociologists, doing to mitigate or address these forms of oppression and "othering"?

At this point, the question becomes one of seeking change and to do that, advocacy becomes an inevitable part of sociological practice. McGregor (2021) is clear on this point:

> **Sociologists should be advocates for inclusion** [emphasis in original]. As sociologists, we need to be the voice for those who may not have a voice. This could be the voice of marginalised communities, but also experiences of others who can shed light into emerging problems not yet understood or examined sociologically. Social justice is at the heart of sociological practice.

Advocacy becomes an inevitable part of a public sociology and the question is really what sort of advocacy is most effective and/or most appropriate. Who speaks? And to whom? With regard to a decolonised public sociology, it is hard to think of any circumstances which do not require advocacy and, as a result, political engagement.

(iii) Being a public intellectual

One final area of public activity and contribution is, in my view, problematic and yet a very important activity in relation to an effective public sociology. For some, contributing to public debate and understanding by having a major online presence via social media, or being a public speaker, or a regular contributor in the media is part of public sociology as a 'public intellectual' (cf. Nichols, 2017). For others, the distance between author/commentator as sociologist and audiences means that it is something of a faux public engagement (see Fatsis, 2017). Further, by participating in this way, there is always the challenge of sociological insights being trivialised by media gatekeepers, by the tendency of some in the media, or even by those sociologists who contribute in this way, to dramatise what is being said or argued. And communicating via the media, in whatever form, seldom allows the time and space to provide a nuanced explanation of complex social issues.

There are two questions here. One is the question of whether a public sociology inevitably requires the sociologist to be a public intellectual. This implies a role as a 'critic and conscience' and 'speaking truth to power' as part of being a contributor to public and policy debates. This requires a certain skill set—confidence, ability to communicate to a range of audiences, availability—that is not necessarily part of sociological training. Nor does it suit all personalities and is often a highly stressful aspect of public sociology that exposes those involved to criticism and attack. There is always the challenge, as Fatsis (2017) rather grandly notes: "...brandishing public sociology is one thing but bringing it down from its lofty and exclusive station to transform it into something tangibly public is quite another". Perhaps, the expectation that public sociology inevitably involves communicating (and advocating) in a range of public media spaces needs to be qualified—it is important but contingent on, firstly, those involved having the required skills and that secondly, that this engagement is seen as relevant to the outcomes.

The second question is *where* this advocacy and communication should take place. To some extent, this rather depends on the nature of the relationship with partner communities and the aim of the research process. Who is the audience? How do they normally engage with knowledge and policy issues? There are challenges in using certain media, say social media, to communicate with others, especially with the possibility that the political economy of the media and institutional practices can easily subvert the message or the authenticity and authority of the sociologist involved. Being a public intellectual in the cause of public sociology is, at best, fraught and, at worst, counterproductive.

These issues—of decolonising sociology and establishing relations with partner communities, of advocacy, and of operating in public domains, especially in relation to the media—provide some of the components of a public sociology in Aotearoa. It might be helpful to provide some examples of what this might look like in practice. Here are two that provide some guidance of a locally grounded public sociology.

Public Sociology in Aotearoa

Ranginui Walker: A Role Model for Public Sociology?

In many ways, the late Ranginui Walker (Whakatōhea, 1932–2016) embodied the values and activities that might be expected of a public sociologist. As part of the post-war migration of Māori from a rural rohe (in his case, Ōpōtiki) to Auckland, he gained access to educational qualifications that led him into a teaching and research career, ultimately as Pro Vice-Chancellor (Māori) at the University of Auckland. It was his large variety of roles, and the way in which spoke with and for marginalised communities, in both Māori and non-Māori worlds, that qualifies him as something of an exemplar as a public sociologist.[8]

[8] Walker's disciplinary background and identity was varied, and he was influenced by a range of sociological, anthropological, decolonial and Māori knowledge sources and systems. Depending on context, he might self-describe as an anthropologist or sociologist but more often than not, he would stress his reliance on Māori epistemologies in later life.

As he completed his PhD and began work firstly at the Auckland Teachers College and then in Extension Education at the University of Auckland, he began an intellectual journey which combined the arguments of liberation theorists, emancipatory education with decolonisation writers. Key works by Frantz Fanon, Aimė Cėsaire, Antonio Gramsci and Paulo Freire were influential (Spoonley, 2009). Education was to provide understanding and emancipation. But alongside this growing intellectual journey, Walker was also being called upon to help Māori organisations and iwi including Ngati Whātua and Māori wardens. And then, as he organised an educational conference in 1970, he encountered a group of young Māori activists who went onto become Ngā Tamatoa. As he acknowledged, he was radicalised by them and took a much more critical intellectual approach accompanied by involvement in both communities and agencies of the state.

Throughout his career, Walker saw education as a means both of control and of liberation, and he become a major player in supporting (and often critiquing) Māori organisations and politics but he reserved his most trenchant criticisms for the state and its failure to deliver on its Treaty of Waitangi obligations. But this criticism was almost always accompanied by constructive options and extensive relations/activities with both the activist world and those in power. He was directly involved in qualification reviews (six major ones, mostly of Māori tertiary institutions or those with large numbers of Māori students, staff or client Māori communities), he was a member of the Waitangi Tribunal and a long-standing member of the Māori Council and of its most radical branch, the Auckland District Māori Council. He combined his activism with membership of a range of state agencies and Māori communities and organisations.

This participation in public life was further highlighted by his publications, notably a column in the *New Zealand Listener* as well as some powerful books which revised public understanding of New Zealand history and the way in which that history denied and marginalised Māori. His book, *Ka Whawhai Tonu Matou: Struggle Without End*, is ranked as one of the most widely read and influential in late twentieth century New Zealand. He often wrote with a Pākehā audience in mind, he appeared regularly in the media as an expert commentator and he spoke on many occasions and to many audiences. He was a compelling and authoritative communicator who played a major role in the debates in the 1970s, 1980s and 1990s as New Zealand and New Zealanders struggled with Māori tino rangatiratanga ambitions and the state sought to develop new ways of interacting with Māori. He was as much interested in ensuring that Aotearoa New Zealand was and remained nuclear free, or in poverty reduction, as he was with the performance and equity that resulted from educational processes, or the renegotiation of the place of Māori and their well-being in a contemporary Aotearoa.

He sought to use his intellectual knowledge, positions and skills to empower communities. He played a direct role in many spheres of New Zealand life and politics, from his own iwi, Whakatōhea, through to local and often quite small communities, to the state. There are two things to be said about the example he provided: his public sociology was especially relevant to the time and place that New Zealand found itself in and he was able to provide a powerful and highly relevant sociology to those times and that place; and he had the required skills that meant he could participate in a variety of ways. Not all of it was easy: there were major disagreements, including with his own iwi, and his public profile often meant abusive and dismissive reactions, including from at least one Prime Minister. He straddled two very different social and cultural landscapes, as he noted in *Ka Whawhai Tonu Matou: Struggle Without End.*

Researching Policing in Aotearoa New Zealand

Internationally, relations between police and marginalised communities have been the subject of political debate and protest over recent decades, especially in relation to Black Lives Matter and the ongoing issues concerning the way in which the Metropolitan Police in London had addressed the racism involved as they responded (and continue to respond) to the killing of Stephen Lawrence (see Macpherson, 1999; Home Affairs Select Committee, 2021). As the Home Affairs Select Committee (2021) noted, although many of the issues of concern had been identified in 1999, 22 years on, they had still to be addressed. More than that, there was a denial in some quarters (police, certain politicians, and some media) that racism was an issue at all in the police response. This was vehemently disputed by community activists and those communities most impacted by police racism. The New Zealand Police Commissioner sought to sponsor a research project that would provide evidence of local relationships and behaviour, as well as identifying options in terms of policies and procedures that would help address any issues that would be identified.

In 2020, the then Commissioner of the New Zealand Police/Ngā Pirihimana o Aotearoa, Andrew Coster, invited a group of community representatives and academics to provide advice to him and his senior leadership team in order to help frame a research project that would provide evidence of whether systemic racism and bias existed in relations between police and communities.[9] This was known as the "Understanding Policing Delivery" (UPD) project and concerned three particular areas of police-community contact: who police stop and speak to, as well as how police engage with those stopped; decision-making around the use of force; and decisions about the laying of charges. The advisory group are known in this project as the Independent Panel.

The Independent Panel was tasked with framing this research. It represented a challenging and unique opportunity to develop an approach that would embody many of the elements that reflected a public criminology/sociology: how to undertake research on a major government agency, the New Zealand Police, that would

[9]The Independent Panel consisted of the following: Tā Kim Workman (Chair), Phylesha Brown-Acton, Katie Bruce, Fa'anānā Efeso Collins, Penny Hagen, Helen Leahy, Lady Tureiti Moxon, Jo McLean, Grant O'Fee, Rahui Papa, Khylee Quince, Paul Spoonley, Anne Waapu and Glenn Wilcox, with 50% of the Panel being Māori.

identify matters of critical importance for key communities, specifically whether they experienced systemic racism and bias when the police interacted with them in various ways; whether the research and researchers could maintain a degree of independence and authority in a way that would reassure communities that this was a genuine exercise in community engagement; the need to embody Māori values and a recognition of Te Tiriti o Waitangi; whether various communities, including the police themselves, could be convinced that this research would help improve police-community interactions; and whether it would transform and improve policing in Aotearoa New Zealand. It needed to be 'public' in establishing and developing relationships and impact.

The Independent Panel were the key agents in developing the research expectations and in commissioning the research. The police were involved in the process; there were regular reports to a 'Leads Group' on progress and emerging issues. There was also a group of frontline staff from the police, labelled the Operational Advisory Group, who could provide advice and react to the project as it developed. And there was a Research Steering Group who were made up of a range of police from different sections who also provided advice and guidance although this was later disbanded.

The research was couched as addressing matters of fairness and equity in policing. This was informed by two literature reviews, one carried out by Te Puna Haumaru/New Zealand Institute for Security and Crime Science at the University of Waikato (completed in October 2021) and the other by Te Atawhai o Te Ao (November 2021). Following on from this, the Independent Panel developed an approach that identified Māori as a key partner in this research and required those who would undertake the research to have a clear statement of Kaupapa Māori, or Māori-centred research, or Vision Mātauranga. (All terms were used on the assumption that the researchers would address the expectations of one—or perhaps several—of these approaches to research practice and would embody Māori values and mana). Each of these components were carefully outlined as part of the invitation for researchers to submit proposals. To reinforce these requirements, a number of values or mātāpono were identified as central to the research, along with statement that the Independent Panel expected to see these embedded within the research approach and practice. These included:

- Kaitiakitanga
- Whakamana
- Manaakitanga
- Whanaungatanga

It was made clear the research should recognise and contribute to the rangatiratanga of partner Māori communities. The notion of partnership was key to both the research practices to be adopted along with an agreement about the ownership of outputs and the delivery of outcomes. The Mana Ōriti agreement, (see https://www.inaiatonunei.nz/mana-orite-agreement) that emerged in 2021 as part of a Hui Māori (Inaia Tonu Nei) initiative to seek reform in the justice sector, was also identified as providing guidance in terms of the partnership values that should be central to the research. The researchers were required to consider the colonial context of policing, the possibility of re-traumatisation, how stories could be collected and told, and data sovereignty.

The research guidelines for those applying to be the research providers also specified that the research outputs had to be in a form that would impact meaningfully on police-community relations. The Independent Panel, along with an Ethics Committee which was specifically formed to help consider various ethical matters, would guide the research as it took place but would also help manage the transfer of data to those responsible inside the police.

In late 2022, research providers were contracted to undertake the research. There remained a number of challenges and risks in the research as outlined especially given the exigencies of a complex research project and the fact that it involved a powerful government agency, the New Zealand Police. The framing that was produced by the Independent Panel, and which was agreed to by police leadership, provides one example of how to operationalise public sociology. The research is designed to deliver transformative change to police policies and procedures in a practical way. The early discussion of a decolonial sociology has not been a major aspect of the framing of the research but the nature and impacts of colonialism are certainly an element that required recognition and acknowledgement in this project.

Conclusion

In 2004, Michael Burawoy argued for a sociology that needed to "...embark on a systematic back-translation, taking knowledge back to those from whom it came, making issues out of private troubles, and regenerating sociology's moral fiber" (Burawoy, 2005: 6). The notion that sociology ought to share its insights and strategies for social change with communities is a good but insufficient starting point. As this chapter has argued, the aim is to work in partnership with communities, not as is suggested by Burawoy, by patronisingly returning knowledge that was the community's knowledge in the first place. And while taking 'private troubles' and making them public might be appropriate in some circumstances, again, this requires some humility and the skills necessary to communicate such issues in an appropriate form of public engagement. How private troubles might be made public, and in what sort of way, is something that requires understanding and agreement from those for whom it is private in the first place.

In elaborating on this starting point, I have argued that in a settler society that has been shaped by colonialism, then a form of decoloniality needs to take place to ensure that the sociology is grounded in local realities and expectations. This is designed to address both the impacts of a settler colonialism in Aotearoa New Zealand, including the hegemony of Pākehā, and the disciplinary origins and assumptions of sociology. Alongside the importance of a decolonised sociology, the 'public' in public sociology requires establishing relations with partner communities in order to co-define research problems, methodologies and outputs/outcomes. Moreover, there are other considerations which are often fraught: advocacy and the challenges of operating as a public intellectual. To illustrate the possibilities and some of the characteristics of a public sociology, two examples were provided, one of an academic activist, Ranginui Walker, and the other of a research project which seeks to explore whether systemic racism and bias occur in police-community relations.

None of this is easy. There are issues of negotiating agreement, participation and partnership with communities, of producing knowledge outputs that help transform the circumstances of those communities, and of being exposed with all that this entails by being so public. Nichols (2017: 319) has argued that "public sociology puts sociologists in the middle of the complicated 'unscripted problems' facing organizations, communities and societies in a globalized context". That is an exciting, challenging, terrifying, place to be—but isn't it exactly where sociology ought to be?

It is helpful to end by noting that while public sociology implies some sort of singularity of purpose, method and practice, the actuality of public sociology is in fact a product of many and often diverse sociologies, of very different social and political contexts and employs a range of strategies to make sociology truly public in some sense. This plurality is inevitable and both a strength and weakness. Diverse forms of engagement, of relationships and of sociological practice are needed for complex and diverse social issues. Sociologists have different skill sets, different conceptual and methodological approaches and different values. They occupy different material and political spaces and are the product of different socio-economic backgrounds. Inevitably, a public sociology is a function of different publics and different sociologies. It would be unfortunate if that diversity becomes a reason not to participate in a sociology which aims to be public in its practice and impact.

Acknowledgement I would like to acknowledge Tā Kim Workman's agreement to include material on the New Zealand Police research that we have been involved with—and to point to a very interesting literature on public criminology.

References

Baldock, C. V. (2005). Sociology in Australia and New Zealand. In J. Germov & T. R. McGee (Eds.), *Histories of Australia sociology*. Melbourne University Press.

Barber, S., & Naepi, S. (2022). Introduction. *New Zealand Sociology, 37*(1), 1–19.

Bell, A. (2022). Building stamina, fighting fragility: The account of a white settler 'recovering racist'. *Ethnicities, 22*(5), 685–704. https://doi.org/10.1177/14687968211062671

Bell, A., Yukich, R., Lythberg, B. J., & Woods, C. (2021). Enacting settler responsibilities towards decolonisation. *Ethnicities, 22*(5), 605–618. https://doi.org/10.1177/14687968211062675

Burawoy, M. (2005). For public sociology. *American Sociological Review., 70*, 4–28. https://doi.org/10.1177/000312240507000102

Burawoy, M. (2007). For public sociology. In D. Clawson, R. Zussman, J. Misra, N. Gerstel, R. Stokes, D. Anderton, & M. Burawoy (Eds.), *Public sociology: Fifteen eminent sociologists debate politics and the profession in the twenty-first century* (pp. 23–65). University of California Press.

Burawoy, M. (2021). *Public sociology: Between utopia and anti-utopia*. Polity Press.

Clear, T. R. (2010). Editorial introduction to "public criminologies". *Criminology and Public Policy, 9*(4), 721–724.

Connell, R. (2007, 2020). *Southern theory. Social science and the global dynamics of knowledge* (2nd ed.). Allen and Unwin (2007)/Abingdon, Routledge (2020).

Crothers, C. (2005). History of sociology in New Zealand. In J. Germov & T. R. McGee (Eds.), *Histories of Australian sociology* (pp. 67–80). Melbourne University Press.

Currie, E. (2007). Against marginality. Arguments for a public criminology. *Theoretical Criminology, 11*(2), 175–190.

Fatsis, L. (2017). The practice of public sociology: Common practice or wishful thinking? [online]. *The Sociological Review Magazine* (27 March). https://thesociologicalreview.org/collections/public-sociology/the-practice-of-public-sociology-common-practice-or-wishful-thinking/

Flavell, M., & Cunningham, E. (2022). Engaging in research with Pacific communities as a non-Pacific researcher: Reflecting on lessons learnt. *Kōtuitui; New Zealand Journal of Social Science Online*. https://doi.org/10.1080/1177083X.2022.2108465

Fritz, J. M. (2012). Including sociological practice: A global perspective and the U.S. case. In D. Kalekin-Fishman & A. Denis (Eds.), *The shape of sociology in the twenty-first century*. Sage.

Gans, H. J. (1989). Sociology in America: The discipline and the public. American Sociological Association, 1988 Presidential Address. *American Sociological Review., 54*(1), 1–16. https://doi.org/10.2307/2095658.JSTOR2095658

Gans, H. (2002). More of us should become public sociologists. *ASA Footnotes*, July/August. https://www.asanet.org/sites/default/files/savvy/footnotes/julyaugust02/fn10.html

Henry, E. (2022). Busting myths about mātauranga Māori. *The Spinoff*, 14 November. https://thespinoff.co.nz/atea/14-11-2022/busting-the-myths-about-matauranga-maori

Higgins, K. (2018). Tense and other: Temporality and urban multiculture in Auckland Aotearoa New Zealand. *Transactions, 44*(1). https://doi.org/10.1111/tran.12257

Home Affairs Select Committee, House of Commons. (2021). *How has the Macpherson report impacted racism in policing in the UK*. House of Commons. https://houseofcommons.shorthandstories.com/home-affairs-committee-macphersonreport/index.html

Hoskins, T. K., & Bell, A. (2021). Being present: Embodying political relations in indigenous encounters with the crown. *Contemporary Political Theory, 20*, 502–523. https://doi.org/10.1057/s41296-020-00439-9

Hossfeld, L., Kelly, E. B., & Hossfeld, C. (Eds.). (2021). *The Routledge international handbook of public sociology*. Routledge.

Kidman, J. (2019). Whither decolonisation? Indigenous scholars and the problem of inclusion in the neoliberal university. *Journal of Sociology, 56*(2), 247–262. https://doi.org/10.1177/1440783319835958

Loader, I., & Sparks, R. (2010). What is to be done with public criminology? *American Journal of Criminology, 9*(4), 771–781.

Macfarlane, A., & Macfarlane, S. (2019). Listen to culture: Māori scholars' plea to researchers. *Journal of the Royal Society of New Zealand, 49*(1), 48–57. https://doi.org/10.1080/03036758.2019.166.1855

Macpherson, W. (1999). *The Stephen Lawrence inquiry*. Home department, Secretary of State. https://assets.publishing.service.gov.uk/government/uploads/system/uploads/attachment_data/file/277111/4262.pdf

Margaret, J. (2019). Becoming 'really Pākehā. E-Tangata 8 December. https://e-tangata.co.nz/reflections/becoming-really-pakeha/

McGregor, C. (2021). How to work with other researchers? A guide for sociologists. *Sociological Association of Aotearoa New Zealand Newsletter* (blog), 28 May. https://www.saanz.net/2021/05/28/how-to-work-with-other-researchers-a-guide-for-sociologists-by-casimir-macgregor/

Mears, D. P. (2010). The role of research and researchers in crime and justice policy. *Criminology and Public Policy, 9*(4), 799–805.

Meghji, A. (2021). *Decolonizing sociology: An introduction*. Polity.

Mignolo, W. D. (2007). Delinking. The rhetoric of modernity, the logic of coloniality and the grammar of decoloniality. *Cultural Studies, 21*, 449–514. https://doi.org/10.1080/09502380601162647

Mignolo, W. D. (2011). Border thinking, decolonial cosmopolitanism and dialogues among civilisations. In M. Roviso & M. Nowicka (Eds.), *The Ashgate research companion to cosmopolitanism* (pp. 329–348). Ashgate.

Ndhlovu, F. (2016). A decolonial critique of diaspora identity theories and the notion of superdiversity. *Diaspora Studies, 9*(1), 28–40. https://doi.org/10.1080/09739572.2015.1088612

Nichols, L. (2017). Public sociology. In K. O. Morgan (Ed.), *The Cambridge handbook of sociology*, Vol. 2, Speciality and interdisciplinary studies. Cambridge University Press.

Parke, E., & Hikuroa, D. (2021). Let's choose our words more carefully when discussing mātauranga Māori and science. *The Conversation*, 4 August. https://theconversation.com/lets-choose-our-words-more-carefully-when-discussing-mataurnaga-maori-and-science-165465

Rock, P. (2010). Comment on "public criminologies". *Criminology and Public Policy, 9*(4), 751–767.

Showden, C. R., Nairn, K., & Matthews, K. R. (2022). So people wake up, what are we gonna do?: From paralysis to action in decolonizing activism. *Ethnicities, 22*(5), 663–684.

Smith, L. T. (1999). *Decolonising methodologies. Research and indigenous peoples*. Zed Books.

Spoonley, P. (2009). *Mata Toa. The life and times of Ranginui Walker*. Penguin Books.

Spoonley, P., Fraser, G., & Maharey, S. (2016). A New Zealand sociological imagination: The Massey story. *New Zealand Sociology, 31*(3), 40–63.

Teariki, C., Spoonley, P., & Tomoana, N. (1992). *Te Whakapakari Te Mana Tangata: The politics and process of research for Māori*. Department of Sociology, Massey University.

Trafford, W. (2022). Despite 'not being real science' jibe, mātauranga conference at Auckland Uni. *Te Ao Māori News*, 24 November. https://www.teaomaori.news/despite-not-real-science-jibe-matauranga-conference-auckland-uni

Turner, J. (2005). Is public sociology such a good idea? *The American Sociologist, 36*(3/4), 27–45.

Uggen, C., & Inderbitzen, M. (2010). Public criminologies. *Criminology and Public Policy, 9*(4), 2725–2749.

Wilson, D. (2013). Counterblast: The public criminologist and the democratic under-labourer. *The Howard Journal, 52*(5), 543–545.

Paul Spoonley was, until 2019, the Pro Vice-Chancellor of the College of Humanities and Social Sciences, at Massey University. He retired from Massey University in April 2021. He is the author or editor of 29 books, the most recent being *The "New" New Zealand. Facing Demographic Disruption* (2021) and *The History of Hate* (2023). He was made a Fellow of the Royal Society of New Zealand in 2011. He is currently a member of the Marsden Fund Council, and Co-Director of He Whenua Taurikura (Centre for Countering Violent Extremism). He has been a longtime participant in the Metropolis network and recently became the Co-Chair.

The Interlocking of History, Identity, and te reo Māori: Language Revitalisation in a Colonial Context

Awanui Te Huia

Introduction

Individuals are shaped by our societies that we occupy. As Māori, our lived experiences are diverse. Our ability to engage with our culture and language is connected to both our collective histories, and our current realities. This chapter illustrates how sociological and psychological perspectives can be integrated to illustrate how individuals are located and influenced by history and social context. It explores two prominent factors that impact on the language learning experiences of tangata whenua from a range of diverse backgrounds. These two factors include the devaluation of te reo Māori and experiences of Māori within a predominantly mainstream education system, and some of the reasons for experiencing language based whakamā, which is tied to the colonial experience

Te reo Māori is still in the process of revitalisation. The Maihi Māori 2017–2040, the most recent Māori language strategy put forward by Te Mātāwai[1] in collaboration with iwi representatives, and Māori language community stakeholders, is focused on te reo Māori use within homes and communities (Te Mātāwai, 2017). The focus of this strategy is to create conditions that support te reo Māori usage outside of the home. Part of this strategy includes looking at factors that influence people's perception of their identities and "domains where reo and tikanga are normalised and have relevance" (Te Mātāwai, 2017, p. 3).

[1] Te Mātāwai is an independent entity set up under Te Ture mō Te Reo Māori (the Māori Language Act), which aims to promote the use of te reo in homes and the community.

A. Te Huia (✉)
Te Kawa a Māui (the School of Māori Studies), Te Herenga Waka, Victoria University of Wellington, Wellington, New Zealand
e-mail: awanui.tehuia@vuw.ac.nz

© The Author(s), under exclusive license to Springer Nature Switzerland AG 2023

Z. L. Rocha, K. L. Davidson (eds.), *Applied and Clinical Sociology in Aotearoa New Zealand*, Clinical Sociology: Research and Practice,
https://doi.org/10.1007/978-3-031-36581-2_3

Looking at some of the challenges that speakers of te reo Māori face, we can see that Pākehā dominant society has a role to play in the ability of language speakers to turn around the ever-looming threat associated with language endangerment. The late Te Wharehuia Milroy (in Te Rōpū Tohutohu Reo Māori, 2015) writes "In instances where people have changed to another language and have given up their own entirely, it is usually as a result of political suppression, social discrimination and economic deprivation" (p. 6). As one of our cherished reo Māori revitalisation leaders, these words carry significant weight, and help us to understand some of the conditions that have created language loss within our Māori communities.

Within the context of education, authors have commented on the role of mainstream education in the devaluation of te reo, indicating that "One aspect of this 'civilising agenda' has been the devaluing of the language and cultural practices of Māori" (McKenzie & Toia, 2014, p. 240). Kuia Merimeri Penfold (Ngāti Kurī) was part of the generation who were abused at school, and she recalls: "The rule in the schools was, 'Do not speak the Māori language'; therefore, this is what we followed because we would be beaten by the teachers. We were the children who were caught speaking Māori. We did not do anything wrong." (2014, p. 27). This kuia was 94 years old at the time of writing these words. The violence that was enacted throughout schools in this country towards Māori speaking children for speaking their mother tongue has very real current day implications. Although these violent acts are memories held by our elderly, the moral injury that descendants of our tūpuna experience should not be minimised. Moral injury is described as occurring "when there has been (a) a betrayal of "what's right"; (b) either by a person in legitimate authority (author's definition), or by oneself" (ibid., p. 182). The pain that individuals feel in thinking about their tūpuna being punished as children is chilling and extremely painful. The fact that these acts were carried out by individuals with authority granted by the government may exacerbate feelings associated with moral injury.

The context of where we are currently with te reo Māori is not strictly linked to the treatment of Māori children in mainstream education. Māori academic Bruce Biggs noted "In the early years of this century virtually all Maoris [sic] spoke Maori and as late as 1950 between one half and three-quarters of the Maori children attending Maori schools spoke or understood it. Since that time there has been a massive migration of Maoris [sic] from rural communities where they were often in a Maori-speaking community." Post World War 2, there was a significant shift of Māori working within the primary industries into manufacturing related industries (Pool & Kukutai, 2023). These shifts in employment options saw an exponential growth in the number of Māori who relocated to urban centers from rural townships. Derby (2023) notes that "In the 50 years between 1936 and 1986, the Māori population changed from 83% rural to 83% urban, one of the fastest rates of urbanisation in the world." The communities into which Māori families migrated were predominantly English speaking. The availability of individuals who could communicate in te reo outside of the home, as well as pressures for Māori to assimilate contributed to a reduction in Māori language use in the home.

Returning to the present, we have a need for systems that reinforce positive cultural identities, highlighting the intertwining between the sociological and the psychological: the inseparability of the person from the culture. When we are embedded within communities that reinforce our Māori identities as something worth celebrating, these spaces can have a positive impact on our health and wellbeing. In comparison, Durie (2003) notes that "poor mental health often stems from an insecure identity, and second, unsatisfactory relationships with others—individuals and institutions—contribute similar to personal problems and lack of wellbeing." He continues by indicating that "insecure identity is most often a reflection of impaired access to the institutions within which culture is nurtured, and from which individuals draw strength and confidence." (p. 49). What these observations demonstrate is that we require institutions that know how to enhance our ability to express ourselves in culturally enriching ways.

Some of the challenges that we see in Māori language learning contexts are experiences of whakamā. The conditions of whakamā can occur in response to a person feeling that they have transgressed a particular moral or norm agreed to by the wider group. In her study of whakamā, Metge (1986) indicates that "Not only individuals but whole groups can be whakamaa and individuals can be whakamaa on behalf of others and as group members. To understand whakamaa it is necessary to be aware of the part tupuna and group membership play in the formation of Maori personal identity and the pressures exerted on the individual to conform to group expectations and to place group interests above individual ones." (p. 148). The expectations that we as Māori have of ourselves to claim ingroup membership can contribute to feelings of whakamā when these conditions are not met. Failing to meet expectations that allow us ingroup belongingness are directly related to experiences of anxiety in language learning settings (Rātima & May, 2013; Pohe 2012; Te Huia, 2013).

The ways in which Māori identities have been defined and redefined since the process of colonisation began in this country have contributed to how Māori interpret our identity boundaries. Existentialist beliefs, such as who is more or less Māori based on a set of entry criteria have colonial derivations. These are discussed in detail by the late Moana Jackson who notes that "I have often talked about this defining of the Māori self because it was captured and controlled by the colonisers very early in the dispossession of our people. Sadly, because this is what colonisation does, many of our people have been taught and have had to learn their definitions rather than our own" (2011, p. 74). Our feelings of whakamā within a Māori language learning context can be traced to the self-definitions that have been assigned to us, not always from within Māori communities.

What is happening in Māori language classrooms includes a complex array of social negotiations and interactions between both teachers and learners, and within the learner communities themselves. As Māori, we are in the process of reclaiming our ancestral language. This means that we are also constructing what it might mean to become a member of a Māori language speakers' community, which includes the role of imagination. Norton (2013) notes that "the target language community may be, to some extent, a reconstruction of past communities and historically constituted relationships, but also a community of the imagination, a desired community that offers possibilities for an enhanced range of identity options in the future." (p. 3). Indigenous experiences of colonisation mean that individuals might not have been exposed to having their mother tongue transmitted intergenerationally for many generations. Therefore, some learners may be using their imaginations to create relationships with significant others, which can be healing.

Te reo Māori in the Education System

As of July 2021, most students (71.9%), including both Māori and non-Māori were "not involved in Māori language education" (Education Counts, 2023). While some of the rationale behind not having any Māori taught in schools was due to institutions not meeting funding criteria (such as alternative education, or international fee-paying students), a considerable proportion of schools who were eligible for Māori language programme funding did not provide Māori language learning at any level for a sizeable proportion of students (totalling 242,099 or 29.2%). This means that almost a third of schools in Aotearoa have access to funding, but are not offering *any* reo Māori to their students.

These findings indicate that although government can make funding available, if te reo Māori is not a priority for schools then it is unlikely that Māori students will gain an education that meaningfully integrates their ancestral language. An additional issue could include the limited number of Māori teachers available to teach te reo Māori. As te reo Māori becomes more profitable as part of professional employment, the appeal of becoming a Māori language teacher may not be as enticing as other opportunities available to Māori who hold tertiary qualifications, and are proficient users of te reo.

Method and Methodology

Methodology

The process of engaging with Māori research is part of a wider set of goals for the reclamation of mātauranga Māori. This research was undertaken with the goals and principles of kaupapa Māori in mind. Given our histories of colonial experiences, it is important that as researchers, we are encouraged to think critically about the process of how knowledge is created, assumed and shared. Leonie Pihama writes "the impact of colonisation on our knowledge, on our beliefs, our reo, our world views, epistemologies, everything has been disrupted. What kaupapa Māori theory does generally, philosophically, is seek to return to old ways of thinking in order to interrupt some of those processes. It brings our ways of thinking forward into a contemporary context where we can draw upon the deep knowledge that our people have had for many generations" (2011, p. 50). This research project aims to contribute to the goal of cultural reclamation.

We engaged in this research with respect and manaakitanga for those who shared their personal and profound experiences with us as researchers. Professor Linda Smith (2012) notes that "From indigenous perspectives ethical codes of conduct serve partly the same purpose as the protocols which govern our relationships with each other and with the environment. The term 'respect' is consistently used by indigenous peoples to underscore the significance of our relationships and humanity." (p. 125). It is our hope that the respect that we have for our participants' stories come through in this research.

Participants

The qualitative parts of our study (which are included in this chapter) include 38 wāhine, and 19 tāne. Ages ranged from 18–74 years with an average age of 39.7 and a median age of 38.5 (see Fig. 1). The length of interviews ranged from 22 min, to 1 h and 37 min. On average, interviews were 47 min and 21 s long.

Participants from Te Ataarangi, Whare Wānanga/Universities (Victoria University of Wellington, and Massey University Palmerston North), whānau, hapū, and workplaces were invited to participate.

A total 57 individuals who self-identified as Māori (who were affiliated with 54 iwi) were interviewed across nine regions included, Te Taitokerau, Tāmakimakarau, Kirikiriroa, Waipā, Whakatāne, Rotorua, Tauranga, Manawatū, Te Whanganui a Tara, Hokitika. Three participants were interviewed in locations

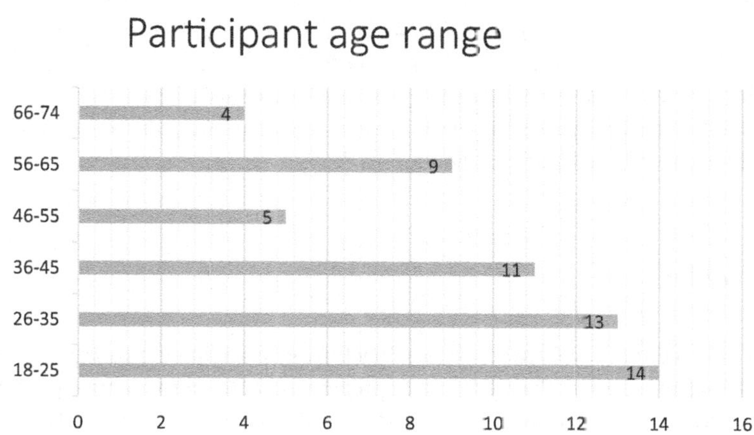

	18-25	26-35	36-45	46-55	56-65	66-74
Participant age range	14	13	11	5	9	4

Fig. 1 Participant age range

outside of their residential region: the residential region of participants recorded outside of their hometowns included Ōtautahi, Otepoti, and Manawatū. After each quotation provided in the results below, the age of the participant is given alongside their residential region, as opposed to the place that they were interviewed or their iwi affiliation. This decision was partly made to protect participants' privacy, particularly those who wished to have their identities remain confidential.

Research Tools and Process

We designed a semi-structured interview schedule that was used by all three interviewers (including Tai Ahu, Dr. Maureen Muller and the author). While most respondents (39) used te reo Māori and English intermittently during interviews, 13 used solely English, and 5 interviewed solely in te reo Māori. Most participants were known to researchers, and in instances where there were no prior relationships, we sought out a connection through mutual friends or colleagues. Given the highly personal nature of the research, it was important that the research team had existing relationships with participants. Sharing experiences related to Māori language learning, and language trauma can be triggering for research participants, which requires researchers to be mindful of the research context, including the development and nurturing of relationships. Having prior relationships with participants helps to maintain an ongoing connection between the researchers and the interviewees subsequent to the interviews taking place and is consistent with principles of Kaupapa Māori methodologies (Smith, 2012). Furthermore, concepts of manaakitanga, and aroha ki te tangata are readily upheld within such relationships.

Participants chose between using their given name or a pseudonym. A koha of $40 (in voucher form) was gifted to each participant. We chose to hold interviews in workplaces, kura, home, at marae, or in cafes. The location of the interview was chosen based on convenience and comfort for participants. All the interviews were recorded and later transcribed by research assistants who all signed a confidentiality agreement. Transcribed interviews were sent to participants for their feedback, with the option to make amendments.

Analysis

Once we had received transcripts back from participants, I undertook a process of thematic analysis. This research approach allowed me to identify patterns or themes in the research data (Braun & Clarke, 2006; Clarke & Braun, 2013). As there were multiple interviewers and transcribers involved in this study, all interviews were analysed by the author for purposes of cohesion and consistency. All interviews were analysed in written form. Common themes were grouped together with quotes from participants to highlight these themes. Given the extensive amount of data that is available from the 57 interviews, the results in this chapter focus on key specific themes that came through. Other themes have been written about elsewhere (Te Huia et al., 2019; Te Huia, 2022).

Results

The results of this study are divided into two themes, highlighting the way in which individual experiences are shaped by social context: the first relates to the experiences of Māori students in mainstream education systems. This theme discusses some of the conditions that encourage or inhibit Māori students from choosing to see te reo Māori as valuable or relevant in their lives. The second theme is the expectations of Māori in a colonial context.

Theme 1: Te reo Māori and Māori Student Experiences in Mainstream Education

Young participants in this study reflected on the time when they were in formal education in mainstream schools. These experiences illustrate how challenging it is to see te reo Māori as valid, and normal when Māori students are operating in Pākehā dominant spaces, such as in mainstream education.

One issue that was raised in this study is that although te reo Māori may be offered as a subject at school, the rest of their education is conducted in English, and the norms that govern student and staff behaviours are more aligned to Pākehā cultural behaviours than aligned to tikanga Māori, or Māori ways of being. An example of this experience is raised by Te Reimana in the excerpt below.

Te Reimana Once you know you leave that Māori class you just got, I just went back into my mainstream like you know Pākehā classes. (Kihikihi, 18–25)

One thing that participants in this study highlighted was that although some participants attended mainstream schools, in instances where Māori offerings, such as te reo, and kapa haka were made available for students, having these spaces where Māori could celebrate being Māori was highly important for their development. Ariana speaks to these experiences in the excerpts below:

Ariana I went through mainstream school and Primary School we did, we were one of the 'good schools', um quotation marks, that learnt waiata, did haka um not hardcore, very Pākehā, but we, we did that. And I felt very proud about that in that space. Umm at Intermediate, it came up again by that point I was starting to be hit by quite a bit of racism, so I was feeling a bit more um, had a bit more anxiety around things, but also very staunchly because of those initial messages from my whānau that, well, 'hei aha the anxiety' [. . .] out of all these classes, Spanish, Japanese, blah, I'm gonna pick te reo', (Te Whanganui a Tara, 26–35)

The point that Ariana draws out towards the end of this quote is that when she reached intermediate school, and racism become a more prominent experience, this was also the time that her anxiety relating to being Māori and learning te reo Māori became more salient. Having one's Māori identity highlighted in hostile environments can be immensely challenging for Māori students who are attempting to navigate a mainstream, Pākehā dominant education system that is not affirming of being Māori. The quote from Ariana above also indicates that the affirmation she received from her whānau that supported her to claim and own her identity as a member of her whānau, was influential when it came time to explicitly choose which topics that she engaged in and why. When Māori students need to intentionally select to learn te reo Māori as a subject over other subject options, how they feel about being Māori is a sizeable consideration for students to make.

A total of 40.7% of school students learn "simple words, greetings or songs in Māori" (Education Counts, 2023). The results from our study indicated that although the inclusion of te reo or waiata might seem basic or tokenistic, they are better than having no Māori at school. These minor exposures to te reo sometimes had positive impacts on students who then pursued te reo Māori for themselves later on as adults.

Participants in this study who had attended both Māori medium education (such as kura kaupapa Māori, kura ā-iwi, or wharekura), and mainstream education were more cognisant of the differences in treatment that Māori students received across both systems. Māori medium education provided students with a space where being Māori was normalised, and all the elements that contribute to being Māori were actively supported in Māori medium education. Some of these points are raised by Phillip in the excerpt below:

Philip I think it was more as the care for students [in my previous kura Kaupapa Māori]? Whereas um Māori students that were attending that [mainstream] school were being neglected from a lot of things. So, there were school trips that we were missing out on just because of our behaviour towards others. So, yea. (Palmerston North, 18–25)

In the extended interview, Phillip spoke about how student behaviours were often misinterpreted by teachers, or behavioural related challenges were not well managed in the mainstream school. When teachers in mainstream schools are unaware of their own prejudices and the racism that they may feel toward Māori has not been critically analysed, these views and values can have a negative impact on our Māori students. Teachers are the power holders in educational institutions, therefore, their ability to negate or reinforce racism is heightened when they are acting in their occupational roles.

The devaluation of te reo Māori can impact the choices that are available to Māori students at school. Devaluation tended to occur as a result of racism towards Māori people, which extended to te reo Māori. Ways in which values and resourcing can impact on whether Māori students willingly take up te reo Māori at schools include:

- whether a school provides te reo as an option;
- the timeslots in which te reo Māori is offered (such as offering te reo at a time where there are few clashes with other subjects popular with Māori students, such as physical education or other subjects);
- support for teachers to develop resources, making financial resourcing available to Māori language teachers to attend professional training to support best practice teaching methods;
- how non-Māori language teachers are integrating te reo into their classes. If te reo is seen as a stand alone subject that has little relevance to other subjects, this makes it harder for students to see the relevance of te reo outside of their specific Māori language class;
- how te reo is marketed to students within the school: for instance, whether it's seen as a subject that holds credibility amongst peers and teachers; and
- how parents view te reo Māori and whether it's seen as a viable subject that contributes to the goals and aspirations that the whānau have for their child.

Māori language learners do not live in a silo. They are part of a wider system of relationships, each of which has the ability to impact on our decisions to make te reo Māori a meaningful part of our daily lives. For some Māori speakers in our study, the decision to be a speaker began at school. The points above demonstrate some of the conditions that are helpful for encouraging Māori students to take up te reo Māori while in mainstream schools. Each of the factors raised above have an influence on Māori language learners, however, the impact of how each of these factors these play out in reality can vary. One key point comes from Corban, a now highly proficient user of te reo Māori. He recalls some of the challenges that he traversed when choosing to learn te reo Māori at high school.

Corban I te tīmatanga kāre ōku mātua i te whakaae ki te tuku i au ki te ako i te reo Māori. He pōhēhē nō rāua tē taea, kāore he hua tō te ako i te reo Māori. Nā reira,[2] yeah, started off learning Chinese and um decided I didn't really like Chinese and all my friends were doing Māori and I wanted to be with my friends. So um, think I may have forged Dad's signature on a paper or two, given it to the principal and yeah, found myself learning Te Reo. (Te Waipounamu, 26–35)

What we see in the excerpt above is that as a student, Corban's parents may have had the power in the relationship to decide on his topics of study. In Aotearoa, at a societal level, there have been strong narratives that have acted to devalue the role of Māori economies. The idea above demonstrates that perhaps his parents perceived that by taking a Chinese language, as opposed to Māori language, they would be

[2] *At first my parents didn't agree to let me learn te reo Māori. They didn't think it could be done, and mistakenly thought that learning te reo Māori was pointless. So...*

supporting their children to achieve their economic aspirations. Wanting economic security is a valid concern for Māori parents who have seen our economic prosperity taken away through systemic level violence and oppression, through colonial actions. The removal of our lands, and our political structures has meant that as a people, we have needed to redevelop our economic prosperity within a colonial structure. While Māori economies are prospering considerably, these achievements are not always well recognised by those who are not directly impacted by such growth.

Corban I don't think they saw any value in learning Te Reo. It wasn't gonna take me overseas or, it wasn't something that was gonna get me a job. Didn't take them long to realise that wasn't the case but um, yeah I think just they didn't see the value, or the need. And it probably goes back to the fact that, you know, kāore tōku pāpā i tipu mai i te reo Māori. I te mōhio ia he Māori, engari, yeah just kāore ōna mātua i te whāngai atu i te reo ki a ia.[3] But yeah, I think it was this whole idea of, you know, te reo wasn't gonna give me a career, or take me overseas. Engari, mā te ako i te reo Hainamana, reo Wīwī, Paniora rānei, koirā ngā reo o te ao, me kī. Engari,[4] yeah I just don't think they saw any value in, whatsoever. (Te Waipounamu, 26–35)

The second point that Corban makes in the first of his excerpts is that despite his parents' decision to enrol him in a non-Māori language subject, the fact that his peers saw value in te reo Māori was an over-riding factor for him. The power of social peer relationships during these years of development are crucial for supporting what it means to be Māori, and the role that te reo Māori plays in this identity development phase.

Theme 2: Expectations of Māori in a Colonial Context

This theme discusses some of the ways in which Māori who were learners of te reo experienced being learners of their ancestral language. Some of the challenges raised in by participants spoke to the expectations that they felt that as Māori within language learning settings, as well as expectations from work settings.

Within the context of employment, participants spoke about the challenges that came with being competent speakers of te reo Māori during a time when there are low numbers of speakers to fulfill cultural roles that require a person to have knowledge of te reo. For younger speakers of te reo Māori, having knowledge of

[3] *My father did not grow up speaking Māori. He knew he was Māori, but, yeah, his parents didn't pass down the language.*

[4] *But, learning Chinese, Mandarin, or Spanish, those are the languages of the world, so to speak. But…*

te reo Māori meant that they were asked to take on roles of kaikōrero or kaikaranga during occasions that felt inappropriate to them due to their limited contextual knowledge about a given event. For instance, some individuals felt that they were being called in to perform such roles without being fully briefed about the context, or having a wider set of relationship connections to those who they were formally engaging with in their roles as kaikōrero or kaikaranga.

Furthermore, within the context of education settings, following on from the previous theme, the expectations that were placed on kaiako Māori tended to be extensive and unrealistic for some. Louise provides an example of how Māori within education contexts are treated in mainstream employment.

Louise The expectation is so huge that I pull out of stuff now, I pull out. So with school I do the kaikaranga which is fine, I feel confident in doing that now, we did one yesterday, we did a pōwhiri yesterday for some new teachers and a significant kuia passed away over in [names the place] and our cluster of schools wanted to go, the principal's and the deputy principal's, 'Oh Whaea Louise will do the karanga.' I've never actually done a karanga for a tangi and I don't ... I'd only met this kuia once and I didn't feel comfortable so I said I couldn't do it. They didn't ask why I didn't have to say why but in my heart they expected me to. But personally, I wasn't at that level yet, so I pulled out. So expectation is huge when you're a Māori, when you have this certain role, when people view you as **that** (emphasis) person and sometimes you're not. You've got to know within yourself ... I can give you what I know and that's it. (Tauranga, 26–35)

There are many points that Louise raises in the excerpt above. Firstly, she is the one kaiako who is called upon to regularly perform a cultural role for her school. Secondly, the management (principal and deputy) both expected her to perform a karanga on behalf of their school without understanding the wider context of karanga. The fact that management are willing to put Louise into a culturally vulnerable situation without an appreciation for some of the risks that she might encounter demonstrates a lack of appreciation for the role. What this excerpt also demonstrates is that Māori who are working in mainstream organisations must have clear boundaries around when and how they participate in culturally specific roles, such as kaikaranga. If the individual is being pressured into performing a particular cultural role without adequate training or support, it is often the individual who wears the risk, rather than the institution that they're representing.

Another challenge that Māori face when learning te reo Māori is whakamā. Whakamā generally arose in discussions with participants when they spoke about being a member of a cultural group who is still in the process of reclaiming the ability to communicate in their ancestral mother tongue.

Despite the varied and complex ways in which colonial violence led to the current state of Māori language revitalisation, Māori who are learning our ancestral language can still be made to feel that their inability to know te reo is down to a set of personal choices that they have made, rather than seeing their reduced levels of proficiency as part of a wider systemic design on the part of colonial forces. Some of these points are reiterated in the excerpt below by Anahera:

Anahera And it's really distressing and frightening, and you feel so whakamā because you feel like it's somehow your fault that you haven't got your language, which I totally don't believe. You know, for me that's **not** (emphasis) the case. It is **not** (emphasis) your fault and so the point at which I decided to come back and learn the reo even though I'm much older was the point at which I realised that it's **not** (emphasis) my fault. I did not do this to myself, you know. Oh, it makes me so upset! (Te Whanganui a Tara, 46–55)

The point that Anahera makes is that when Māori as indigenous peoples can recognise the wider set of circumstances that led to Māori language decline, they're more able to see that the blame for not being able to speak our language does not lie at an individual level. Rather, when a person is given the wider context for language decline, the use of colonial violence to silence te reo Māori, Māori language learners can place the blame for language loss outside of themselves. Being able to accurately redirect blame for language loss in the direction of colonial systems provides Māori language learners with the knowledge that they are not at fault for not being born into families where te reo was transferred from mother to child. While this wider contextual knowledge is still deeply painful for the language learner, it does allow individuals to see their personal experiences as part of a wider set of narratives, which can be empowering.

Whakamā, which has roots in colonial violence that prevented intergenerational transmission, has the ability to impede language learning processes, from language input, through to the production of language. For older participants in this study, it was especially challenging for some of them who were attempting to learn our ancestral language given the additional difficulties associated with language learning as an older person. This point is emphasised in the discussion with Wikitōria:

Wikitōria I mean sometimes I've just got say something really simple you know like "kei whea tō pēpi" or whatever. And then in my head I know the answer, but that question is running through my head. I know the answer, but because the question is running through my head, it blocks the answer? (Palmerston North, 56–65)

One of the challenges that Māori language learners face is the fact that there are high expectations of Māori people to be proficient speakers irrespective of our colonial experiences. A number of participants spoke about the fear that they experienced about making mistakes in te reo Māori. It is important to take into consideration the wider colonial context that on the one hand, has systematically removed the ability of most Māori to be competent users of te reo, while on the other hand raised wider social expectations that Māori who identify as Māori have cultural and linguistic competence.

Given that te reo Māori is highly valued amongst Māori people, it is not surprising that learners of te reo Māori want to demonstrate competence in this skill when using te reo Māori with others who share similar values. These points are reiterated in the discourses below:

Hoana It's always been the same. I would love to learn and speak fluently. I haven't been able to grasp it umm and I think I've shied away from, because I'm frightened to be wrong. (Kirikiriroa, 66–74)

The fear of being incorrect is a challenge for many Māori ancestral language learners. This fear partly comes down to the connection that people make between being competent speakers of te reo Māori, and claiming a Māori identity.

The issues posed in these statements have to do with wider issues that are attached to notions of language purity. Fishman (2006) states "There is a widespread popular assumption that proper languages are "clean" or "pure"." He continues "Actually, 'purity' may be more honoured in theory than in practice, probably because it is usually far more attainable in theory than in practice." (p. 25). While these quotes are not specifically about language innovation, the underlying principles of having a language that is "correct" or pure is part of the colonial context in which we are striving to keep our language as closely tied to the language that our ancestors spoke as possible. A further example is provided by Sahrn:

Sahrn It just comes down to me I guess. But then I guess that's that fear of getting it wrong again so that's another barrier for me as well as being judged, 'oh he should know that he's a Māori'. It shouldn't be what people think, shouldn't even take that into account but I don't know, I guess that's just how some people react. (Tauranga, 26–35)

Fears surrounding being correct in our language use can impede the process of language learning, as they shift a person's focus from the action of processing language to focusing on self-presentation. If we are to improve our chances of achieving language revitalisation, the over-emphasis that is placed on learners being correct while they are still attempting to learn needs to be examined.

An additional challenge that has been created in the colonial context of language revitalisation is that we now have Māori with a range of proficiency levels who are all navigating the same space. Younger Māori people are attempting to regain te reo Māori, while also needing to be very careful about the needs and life experiences of older Māori who have experienced pressures of forced assimilation. For generations, Māori people were discouraged from learning and using te reo Māori. We are now at a point where young people and older people are faced with our current reo Māori realities, which can play out in uncomfortable ways. In an excerpt that captures some of these tensions, Georgia explains:

Georgia What if I'm making them feel bad? All those sorts of things we really need to break through them and just kōrero. But I think what we really need is people being funded to do this sort of thing, to get these things up and running because at the moment we're just doing it because we love it. (Kirikiriroa, 26–35)

The point that Georgia makes above indicates that by speaking Māori, it could make others feel badly. Māori language learners are making a number of social judgements to ensure that the wellbeing of those who they engage with is kept intact. What she subsequently indicates is that while Māori people are creating reo Māori changes in our communities, these initiatives are largely under-funded. The access for individuals and groups who have Māori language aspirations needs to improve if we are to see positive language changes occurring at a large scale, rather than in more haphazard ways. Furthermore, Māori people contribute significantly to our unpaid economies. It is not surprising that tangata whenua who are engaging in Māori language revitalisation efforts would see their contributions in voluntary ways, rather than the fact that they are contributing to correcting a wider set of Treaty breaches which should be remunerated by the government.

Given the history of colonisation in Aotearoa, it is not surprising that Māori would feel a range of emotions when it comes to large numbers of Pākehā learning te reo Māori. The conditions created by colonisation mean that tangata whenua are not only reclaiming our language, we are also reclaiming our mātauranga or knowledge sets, we are attempting to assert our tino rangatiratanga in local spaces to prevent further degradations of our lands, and waterways, all of which cost us time and energy. Furthermore, the challenges that come with Māori language learning can be emotionally evocative, particularly given the historical trauma that exist within our collective experiences as indigenous peoples.

An additional challenge came from having non-Māori teaching te reo Māori for a few students. As there weren't many participants who had been taught by Pākehā, this wasn't a common theme that was raised, however, the points that Anahera discusses below are relevant to others who may have shared similar experiences.

Anahera [I went to] [location] at [University name] with famous, [Pākehā lecturer]. And I hated it. So I sat there and I felt like so this is that whole kōrero about why is it hard, what was hard? So a Pākehā woman was teaching me and I felt angry. How dare you tell me. And the way she taught me didn't make sense to what I grew up understanding, even though I hadn't really picked it up at home I felt [that] clearly I had understood something and I felt really, 'this isn't right. What are you doing?'. [...] It felt really [pauses]. But I had issues. I had issues. You know I felt all angry and issued and, 'how dare this white woman be telling me how to do this thing' and that was mine. I bought that with me [into the language classroom] but I couldn't get rid of it, so I quit. I quit for a number of reasons. I quit in my first year for many, many reasons that, most of them to do with the fact that I felt really isolated being Māori in this extreme Pākehā world. Totally even worse than school. (Te Whanganui a Tara, 46–55)

What Anahera's quote above demonstrates is that when Māori students are exploring some of the challenges associated with being an ancestral learner of te reo Māori, given that so few Māori can speak te reo Māori due to colonial oppression, having a Pākehā teacher of te reo Māori was conflicting. When it seems that

Pākehā are in positions of authority within Māori language spaces, this can cause discomfort for Māori learners who are in the process of reclaiming their language. The power discrepancy between learner and teacher, combined with the historical power related challenges that contributed to language loss are important to consider when exploring Māori language learner experiences. The isolation that many Māori experience in tertiary education (see Naepi et al., 2021) is also an issue that is compounded when Māori are attempting to reclaim their ancestral language within an institution that is predominantly governed by Pākehā ways of engaging with students. The act of language reclamation is one that is tied to our histories, which are complicated, and laden with memories or trauma that students might be unpacking in the process of trying to also to learn their ancestral language.

A final aspect that is discussed by participants in this study was the financial costs of enrolling in a language course. While the costs of individual language courses can vary, the financial cost associated with taking time off work, or arranging childcare is a cost that can be challenging for many Māori who have intentions of improving their reo Māori, but who do not have high levels of expendable income. An example of this point is affirmed by Whaea Judy in the quote below.

Whaea Judy I guess one of the biggest barriers that I find here is that students having to give up their financial stability. Um, that's a big thing for whānau and not being able to do without that financial stability—to give up their job. (Rotorua, 46–55)

These points were reiterated by our quantitative findings outlined in Te Huia (2022), where participants who had not engaged in learning through to those who were competent users of te reo Māori indicated that the cost of studying te reo was the central barrier to learning te reo. As more and more Māori have begun learning te reo as a second language through formal methods, such as through educational institutions, the costs of studying need to be examined by language planners moving forward, if the goal of one million Māori language speakers by 2040 (as specified by Te Mātāwai, 2017) is to be an achievable goal.

Discussion

Drawing on applications of sociology and psychology, this chapter focuses on three main areas: firstly, the subtle ways in which te reo Māori is devalued within the context of mainstream education; secondly, the ways in which whakamā is connected to learning te reo Māori as an ancestral language learner in a colonial context and finally, some of the identity related challenges that are tied to demonstrating one's ability to correctly use their ancestral language. The results of this study highlight the importance of a sociological lens, and provide room to consider the wider societal context that directly impacts on Māori language learners and their ability to reclaim their ancestral language.

What we know is that students enrolled in Māori medium education make up merely 2.8% of the student population (Education Counts, 2023). Māori communities have fought hard to reach these levels of participation in Māori medium settings (which have steadily increased from 2016). We know that in Māori medium education settings, Māori student identities and language are able to be taken as normative and valued. However, the numbers presented here indicate that these experiences of having our language and culture validated within mainstream education in Aotearoa are a luxury for most Māori parents and their children.

The changes that are required to make mainstream settings viable institutions where Māori identities can thrive (or at least survive) require a system wide approach. The change that we require means assessing how education systems actively challenge themselves to engage in ways that do not perpetuate racism. The rationale behind having such limited access to te reo in mainstream schools can be traced back to the unspoken policies that saw Māori students violently abused physically and emotionally for speaking their ancestral language in schools (see WAI 11 for examples, Waitangi Tribunal, 1986). These histories are not tied to a particular timeframe, and these events have had lasting impacts on te reo Māori, and tangata whenua use of te reo Māori. Biggs (1981) notes "A few years ago, in response to Maori opinion, the Education Department changed its longstanding policy of neglect or active opposition to the language, and introduced it in a number of schools…". (p. ix).

We are at a point where te reo Māori as a language being transmitted from parent to child is in dire need of support. Māori learning te reo Māori in formal settings is much more of a reality now than it has been in previous times, as predicted by Māori, such as Biggs. He notes that "One may confidently predict that as the natural learning of Maori declines its formal study will increase" (1981, p. ix). Formal education environments, where Māori language learning takes place, have assumed a task of great responsibility in reversing language shift.

There have been positive examples of how te reo Māori has been meaningfully integrated into schools, including Te Kotahitanga, and the Whakapiki professional development programme. For instance, findings from the Whakapiki study indicated that teachers appreciated discussions about te reo and teaching te reo which was enhanced by their "whole-school and in-school approach" (McKenzie & Toia, 2014, p. 249). Providing teachers with adequate resources partly supported their learning and allowed teachers to monitor their progress. Taking on a whole-school approach acted to support more of a community of learners. The study confirmed the need to "focus on second language acquisition development along with teaching pedagogy specific to language development" (p. 252). Therefore, steps can be taken to improve current systems.

Language learning is a highly emotional process, particularly for Māori who are learning our ancestral language as a second language. Māori ancestral language learners in this study often attributed their language related struggles to personal characteristics rather than deep seated historically based issues. For instance, learners attributed language learning struggles with not being "good language learners". Due to the high motivation of many Māori to be proficient language speakers, the pressures associated with language learning are high, which put Māori language learners in positions of vulnerability as they progress through their language journeys (Te Huia, 2022). Our results indicate that when whānau have contextual information surrounding colonial processes that impact on intergenerational language disruption, ancestral language learners can see their own learning journeys as part of wider set of circumstances: as both public and private. Māori learners of te reo can feel empowered when they understand that their personal language learning related challenges are related to wider colonial processes that specifically aimed to prevent indigenous language maintenance, as opposed to attributing their ancestral language related struggles to personal deficits.

Language theorists acknowledge that "language becomes associated with the emotional and behavioural texture of what it means to be a member of a cultural group. This may be why we affectionately refer to our first language as our "mother" language and why we are generally willing to fight to preserve it" (Padilla & Borsato, 2010, p. 12). This year marks the 50th anniversary since the Māori language petition was carried to parliament with over 30,000 hand written signatures agreeing that te reo Māori should be recognised as an official language of this country and taught in all schools. Fifty years on, we are grateful for the hard work of our predecessors who fought to keep our language alive for future generations.

Te reo Māori revitalisation is firmly political. As Moana Jackson proposes, the questions that Māori researchers need to raise are those concerning "both the little everyday colonisations that manifest themselves wherever we turn in this country and the broader-based colonisation of our ongoing political, legal, and constitutional disempowerment." Both the small acts and the larger shifts to prevent the ongoing impacts of colonisation are necessary. Previous generations of Māori, and non-Māori allies who have opposed racism to ensure that te reo Māori is a language of functional communication have done so at a personal cost. Helen Potter explains that as part of the process of decolonisation, "There is a need for more conscientisation. We need to be irritated and be the bearers of discomfort" (2011, p. 69). People who are willing to shoulder discomfort are part of a collective of individuals who will make positive change for te reo Māori.

Making language errors while we are trying to revitalise te reo has become a real challenge. Partly because it means that the language is changing, and in some ways the intended meanings being transmitted differ from those that are produced by new speakers of te reo. Being correct in our Māori language delivery is part of a wider set of challenges—having integrity in te reo matters (Kelly, 2014), as our intentions need to be conveyed through a set of systems that are created by language. However, in order to achieve the goal of revitalisation, Māori ancestral language learners need to feel safe enough to practice using te reo Māori without the stresses associated with an over emphasis that is placed on correctness, particularly at the beginning phases of their language journeys. As they progress to higher levels, it is possible for these language errors to be ironed out. What we need to shy away from is the association between making Māori language errors and what it means to claim ingroup membership as tangata whenua. These associations can create marginalisation within our communities, particularly for tangata whenua who are in the process of reclaiming their identity as Māori.

On a final note, language learning requires us to look at the conditions that either enhance or suppress its growth. Part of those conditions include adequate resourcing by government agencies to rectify the harmful role that the government has played in the language's decline. The late Te Wharehuia Milroy (in Te Rōpū Tohutohu Reo Māori, 2015) further notes that "Keeping the language alive is knowing how to engage with modern life, and not think that te reo Māori is only limited to the past. Like the seasons, it needs to change and adapt with the changes in society. Whānau, hapū and iwi play a critical role in ensuring that young ones are exposed and engaged regularly with the language so that it is relevant and a living language. But this cannot be done in isolation. We also need to have some material and moral support from the Crown in order for some of these things to take place." (p. 6). Language revitalisation requires a multipronged, interdisciplinary approach. The benefits of achieving language revitalisation are well worth fighting for.

References

Biggs, B. (1981). *The complete english-Maori dictionary. In.* Auckland University Press/Oxford University Press.

Braun, V., & Clarke, V. (2006). Using thematic analysis in psychology. *Qualitative Research in Psychology, 3*(2), 77–101.

Clarke, V., & Braun, V. (2013). Teaching thematic analysis: Overcoming challenges and developing strategies for effective learning. *The Psychologist, 26*(2), 120–123.

Derby, M. (2023). Māori–Pākehā relations - Māori urban migration. Te Ara - the Encyclopedia of New Zealand. http://www.TeAra.govt.nz/en/maori-pakeha-relations/page-5. Accessed 16 Aug 2023.

Durie, M. (2003). *Ngā kāhui pou: launching Māori futures*. Huia Publishers.

Education Counts. (2023). *Māori language in schooling*. Retrieved March 15, 2023, from https://www.educationcounts.govt.nz/statistics/6040

Fishman, J. A. (2006). *Do not leave your language alone: The hidden status agendas within corpus planning in language policy*. Routledge.

Jackson, M. (2011). Hui reflections: Research and the consolations of bravery. *Kei Tua o Te Pae hui proceedings: The challenges of kaupapa Māori research in the 21st century*, 71-78. Retrieved March 15, 2023, from https://www.nzcer.org.nz/system/files/Hui_Procedings__v3_Web_1.pdf

Kelly, K. (2014). Iti te kupu, nui te kōrero: The study of the little details that make the Māori language Māori. In R. Higgins, P. Rewi, & V. Olsen-Reeder (Eds.), *The value of the Māori language: Te hua o te reo Māori* (pp. 255–268). Huia.

McKenzie, T., & Toia, R. (2014). The road to language proficiency is always under construction. In R. Higgins, P. Rewi, & V. Olsen-Reeder (Eds.), *The value of the Māori language: Te hua o te reo Māori* (pp. 239–254). Huia.

Metge, J. (1986). *In and out of touch: Whakamaa in cross cultural context*. Victoria University Press.

Naepi, S., Wilson, E., Lagos, S., Manuela, S., McAllister, T. G., Kidman, J., & Kokaua, J. (2021). Where are we now? Patterns of Māori and Pasifika enrolment in the natural and physical science and society and culture fields in Aotearoa New Zealand. *Higher Education Research & Development, 40*(1), 90–103.

Norton, B. (2013). Identity and language learning. In *Identity and language learning (pp.?)*. Multilingual Matters.

Padilla, A., & Borsato, F. (2010). Psychology. In J. Fishman & O. Garcia (Eds.), *Handbook of language and ethnic identity*. Oxford University Press.

Penfold, M. (2014). Ko te rere o te reo/The decline of the language. In M. Kawharu (Ed.), *Maranga mai! Te reo and marae in crisis?* (pp. 11–34). Auckland University Press

Pihama, L. (2011, 5–6 May). *Keynote: A conversation about Kaupapa Māori theory and research.* Paper presented at the Kei tua o te pae hui proceedings - the challenges of kaupapa Māori research in the 21st century, Pipitea marae, Wellington.

Pohe, E. J. (2012). *Whakawhanautanga a-reo: An indigenous grounded theory for the revitalisation of Maori language speech communities*. Victoria University Wellington.

Pool, I., & Kukutai, T. (2023). Taupori Māori – Māori population change - Post-war changes, 1945–1970, Te Ara - the Encyclopedia of New Zealand. http://www.TeAra.govt.nz/en/photograph/31325/state-housing. Accessed 16 Aug 2023.

Rātima, M. T. (2013). *Kia matatau ki te reo: Factors influencing the development of proficiency in te reo Māori with adult learners. (Doctor of Philosophy)*. University of Waikato.

Smith, L. T. (2012). *Decolonizing methodologies: Research and indigenous peoples* (2nd ed.). Otago University Press.

Te Huia, A. (2013). *Whāia te iti kahurangi, ki te tuohu koe me he maunga teitei: Establishing psychological foundations for higher levels of Māori language proficiency*. (PhD). Victoria University of Wellington. Retrieved on March 15, from http://researcharchive.vuw.ac.nz/xmlui/bitstream/handle/10063/3459/thesis.pdf?sequence=2

Te Huia, A. (2022). *He Reo Tuku Iho: Tangata Whenua and Te Reo Māori*. Te Herenga Waka University Press.

Te Huia, A., Ahu, T., Muller, M., & Fox, R. (2019). *Manawa ū*. Retrieved March 15, 2023, from https://www.tematawai.maori.nz/assets/Research-Reports/Manawa-u-ki-te-reo-Maori-A-study-of-language-motivations-to-enhance-the-use-and-acquisition-of-te-reo-Maori.pdf

Te Mātāwai. (2017). *Maihi Māori 2017–2040.* NZ Government. Retrieved March 15, 2023, from https://www.tpk.govt.nz/docs/Maori%20Language%20Advisory%20Group%20Final%20Report%20English%20Version.pdf

Te Rōpū Tohutohu Reo Māori. (2015). *Pūrongo ki te Minita Whanaketanga Māori: Te whare o te reo mauriora*. NZ Government. Retrieved March 15, 2023, from https://www.tpk.govt.nz/docs/Maori%20Language%20Advisory%20Group%20Final%20Report%20English%20Version.pdf

Waitangi Tribunal. (1986). *Report of the Waitangi Tribunal on the Te reo Māori claim (WAI 11)*. The New Zealand Government.

Awanui Te Huia is a senior lecturer at Te Herenga Waka, Victoria University of Wellington. While she is interested in areas relevant to tangata whenua (Māori), and iwi taketake (Indigenous peoples) more broadly, her research predominantly focuses on learners of te reo Māori, and the dynamics that are at play in bicultural settings. She applies her research background in psychology to help create further understanding about some of the psychological enablers and barriers that impact on Māori language learners, as well as understanding how colonisation impacts on our lived realities as Māori.

Locating Sociology Within Psychotherapy: Possibilities for Sociotherapy in Aotearoa New Zealand

Zarine L. Rocha

Introduction

Sociology and psychotherapy each encompass a diversity of practices and theoretical frameworks. As disciplines which explore and seek to understand the vast multiplicities of human experience, from individual troubles to social structures, they are nevertheless quite distinct in terms of approach and aims, having developed along differing institutional paths (Brossard & Sallée, 2020). In exploring the practical applications of sociological and psychotherapeutic theory, it is notable how each often seems to evade the other—with psychotherapy formulated as if sociological theorization had little to no relevance, and sociology being quick to dismiss the validity of psychotherapy as a framework for understanding (Chodorow, 2014).

This chapter explores the intersections of these disciplines through the possibility of a sociologically informed psychotherapy, or sociotherapy, in the context of Aotearoa New Zealand. Using a clinical sociology lens, it looks at opportunities for cross-disciplinary collaboration and interconnections between theory and practice in both sociology and psychotherapy, while seeking to acknowledge the very real roles of race and power in everyday social structures and individual experiences. Beginning with an overview of the histories and theoretical bases of the disciplines, this piece looks at how each has been inextricably shaped by its (largely Western, European) developmental context, and the invisible nature of such "methodological whiteness" (Bhambra, 2017). The concept of sociotherapy as a practice is then outlined, highlighting key case studies from Europe, Latin America, Africa and Australia. I look at how this approach practically aims to connect sociological theory

Z. L. Rocha (✉)
University of Auckland, Auckland, New Zealand
e-mail: zarine.rocha@auckland.ac.nz

© The Author(s), under exclusive license to Springer Nature Switzerland AG 2023

Z. L. Rocha, K. L. Davidson (eds.), *Applied and Clinical Sociology in Aotearoa New Zealand*, Clinical Sociology: Research and Practice,
https://doi.org/10.1007/978-3-031-36581-2_4

to social change at the micro level: *working with* people within culturally appropriate and locally sourced social frameworks, rather than *working on* individual troubles as divorced from public issues (see Fritz, 2021a). This is then linked to the unique context of Aotearoa New Zealand, emphasizing the holistic approaches to therapy grounded in Kaupapa Māori, and the ways in which seeing (socio)therapy through this lens of indigenous knowledge shifts the focus of therapy in important ways. Repositioning the fundamental therapeutic stance by drawing on Kaupapa Māori seeks to break with the often-unnoticed biases inherent within psychotherapeutic (and sociological) theorization (Wilson et al., 2022), decolonizing knowledge and opening up alternative pathways.

As a critical sociologist and tentative psychotherapist myself, as a non-Māori scholar and Tangata Tiriti, I have written this chapter as an exploration, a way to find a home for my new psychotherapeutic training within my sociological understanding of the world and my place in it. I am a scholar with both Pākehā and non-Pākehā ancestry, I live in Aotearoa as a descendent of immigrants and settlers, and my belonging as Tangata Tiriti is defined by my relationship with Tangata Whenua (Delahunty, 2021). As Dam describes, identifying as Tangata Tiriti is not a passive identity, but rather a relationship with ethical and political responsibilities: to understand and engage with critical histories of Aotearoa, to recognize the inherent inequalities of colonization, and to support Māori struggles for equity and justice (Dam, 2022). In this chapter, my discussion of Kaupapa Māori comes from a place of learning and respect: as Kaupapa Māori is research and knowledge undertaken by Māori, for Māori, and of direct benefit to Māori (Tuhiwai Smith, 2012; Barnes, 2013).

For a non-Māori sociologist and psychotherapist, this creates complexity and sometimes confusion, working to locate myself as Pākehā within methodologies and bodies of knowledge which are not mine, but which have significant value for Aotearoa (Barnes, 2013). From this position, influenced as I am by my background, my chapter then looks towards collaboration and discussion: drawing out what sociotherapy could mean in Aotearoa if it were developed in collaboration with Māori and non-Māori practitioners, acknowledging the fundamental value of Kaupapa Māori approaches to psychotherapy as already understood by Māori practitioners, and exploring how all forms of therapeutic work might be enriched through this wider engagement.

Developing Sociology and Psychotherapy outside of Aotearoa

Broadly, the disciplines of sociology and psychotherapy were shaped and solidified at around the same period in history—drawing on late nineteenth and early twentieth century intellectual work primarily in Western Europe and North America, with each fundamentally changing previous intellectual approaches through new methods and theoretical understandings around what it means to be human (Calhoun, 2014). As Calhoun (2014) further notes, there were key differences in initial sociological and psychotherapeutic approaches, with sociology drawing on its roots in social movements and progressive thought and reform, eventually moving into universities. By contrast, psychotherapy grounded itself in more medicalized academic settings, maintaining separate intellectual and training institutes even as medical education was formalized within the university setting.

The conflicts and disjunctures, whether actual or perceived, between sociological and psychotherapeutic approaches remain stark in both theory and practice. Psychotherapy seeks to explore the complexities of individual thought, personality and character, while sociology is conceived of at the level of the social, locating each individual within their social world. Although each is concerned with understanding what it means to be human, the perspective is different: sociology moving from the external to the internal, from collective action to individual explanation, and psychotherapy beginning with the individual, moving outwards from there (Alexander, 2014; Chancer, 2014). The individual person is the fundamental unit of analysis for psychotherapy, while for sociology, a person is shaped not only by intra-psychic forces, but through balancing human agency with external conditions, influences and constraints (Smelser, 2014).

Interestingly, there are also significant overlaps between and within each approach. Brossard and Sallée (2020) suggest that these linkages and borrowings, rather than being exceptional, are ubiquitous yet often unacknowledged parts of the sociological and psychotherapeutic disciplinary canons. Within sociology, microsociological approaches inherently focus on the individual level of analysis, and qualitative work highlights the value of rich detail and depth of understanding. There have been several prominent examples of theorists who worked to bring together the psychological and the social, the individual and the collective, and interdisciplinary spaces have emerged, such as social psychology, which entwine the two (Calhoun, 2014). Cooley, at the turn of the twentieth century, highlighted the impossibility of analysing one without the other, refusing the arbitrary institutional distinctions between the disciplines (Brossard & Sallée, 2020). Durkheim, while being highly critical of uncritical acceptance of psychological explanations, saw value in the relationship between sociology and how the individual psyche was understood, seeking to potentially sociologize psychology in order to locate the personal within the sociological (Alpert, 1939; Brossard & Sallée, 2020).

In the North American context, some sociological theorization in the 1940s and 1950s took on a particularly psychoanalytical bent (Cavalletto & Silver, 2014). C. Wright Mills focused his work on the interactions between personal troubles and public issues, believing that the personal was inherently sociological (Mills, 1959; Chancer, 2014). Talcott Parsons, famously trained as both a sociologist and psychoanalyst, drew on Freud's vast theoretical work in seeking to integrate psychology and sociology: he sought to develop an overarching framework, a productive fusion of sociology with parts of psychoanalysis, psychology and anthropology, grounded in the work of Durkheim, Weber and Freud[1] (Cavalletto & Silver, 2014).

A number of psychotherapeutic approaches also emphasize social relations as the shaping influences of individual psychological frameworks, although perhaps in a less critical way, with questions of socioeconomic status, ethnic group and gendered social structures often less explored than emotions and individual memory. The discipline of psychotherapy itself is not simple to define, with many types of therapy being included under the wider understanding of a psychologically grounded "talking cure" (Owen, 1993). Therapies can be wide ranging, based on individual or group interactions, some highly interventionist, and others based on supportive companionship. [2] Certain therapeutic strands place a stronger emphasis on the social dimension in therapy relationships, from radical and liberation therapy to feminist therapy and psychodynamic social relations (Tudor, 2012a).

Interestingly, reviews of psychotherapeutic work find that overall, therapy frequently effects positive change for the client, but this is not about the type of therapy or the psychotherapeutic techniques used (Asay & Lambert, 1999). Key studies suggest that client improvement is related more to an empathic, respectful relationship between therapist and client (Owen, 1993), and that up to 40% of positive change seems to be as a result of external client variables and extra-therapeutic influences—not the therapy itself (Asay & Lambert, 1999). This highlights the importance of the socio- in the psycho-, and the intertwining of the sociological within psychotherapeutic practice (Tudor, 2012a). However, Calhoun suggests that perhaps for psychotherapists, "...the social world is rather simpler than for sociologists" (2014, p. 14). The emphasis on the individual which underpins the mechanisms of psychotherapy highlights a very particular ideology of meaning, drawing on psychological theorization which has become prevalent in the West: "...it has made up the kind of society that we inhabit, and the kinds of people we have become." (Brossard & Sallée, 2020, p. 5).

Exploring psychotherapy with a sociological lens draws out the complexity of the intersections between psychotherapeutic theories and the reality of practice, seeking to unpick the different strands and processes that make up "therapy", as placed in social context (Owen, 1993). Focusing on the sociological emphasizes that no psychotherapeutic theory or technique is context and agenda free: no social interaction is free from interpersonal meaning, and psychotherapy in particular has developed implicit understandings of right and wrong ways of living (Asay & Lambert,

[1]Parsons noted in 1958: "Had Freud lived long enough to enter more deeply into the technical analysis of the object-systems to which the individual becomes related, he would inevitably have had to become in part, a sociologist, for the structure of these object-systems is—not merely influenced by—the structure of society itself." (1958, p. 338).

[2]While there are hundreds of different psychotherapeutic models available, Huft (2022) suggests that these can be broadly grouped into psychoanalytic/psychodynamic, existential, person-centered, experiential, behavioral, cognitive/cognitive-behavioral, feminist, narrative, and solution-focused approaches.

1999; Owen, 1993). In the Western world, the discourses of power and knowledge are heavily influenced by neoliberal structures around the value of capital, social responsibility and correct ways for an individual to function: people understand themselves through contextual knowledge of what is "real", which is (invisibly) shaped by the dominant ethical and moral codes and discourses around behaviour in each culture (McDonald & O'Callaghan, 2008).

Thus, shaped by these discourses around expert knowledge and rationality within the human sciences, individuals and societies learn to recognize and label what is normal and what is not—what is instead deemed pathological (McDonald & O'Callaghan, 2008; Pickersgill, 2014). In the field of mental health in the Western world, such discourses are powerful, and closely tied to the interrelationships between psychiatry, psychology and psychotherapy, as reflected in the power of diagnoses and the leading role of the American Psychiatric Association's (APA) Diagnostic and Statistical Manual of Mental Disorders (DSM) in legitimizing the labels used in this process. Jutel's analyses of the role of and authority behind medical diagnoses highlight this frequently taken-for-granted power (Jutel, 2021): diagnosis is key to the governance of social and clinical life (Pickersgill, 2014) and the DSM is held up as defining (and perhaps inventing) a "standard of sanity", around which psychological work revolves across the world (McDonald & O'Callaghan, 2008), including here in Aotearoa New Zealand.[3] As Pickersgill notes in exploring the DSM from a sociological perspective, "...diagnostic entities are powerful things, shaping society and individual subjectivities; it is, then, precisely for this reason that we should concern ourselves with what they *are* and with what they *do*" (2014, p. 524).

In bringing together sociological and psychotherapeutic approaches, it is then interesting to look at how each explores the complexities of the individual as inextricable from the social. Chodorow (2014) sees psychoanalysis as the human science of subjectivity: adding the individually particular to the study of what is culturally and socially shared, by theorizing and investigating personal meaning and social reality. Highlighting the interconnections and dissonances between disciplines, she describes the complex relationships between personal and cultural meanings, and the ways in which individual lives play out in society—the agency within the structure. Yet most importantly, she highlights the artificial nature of this seemingly fundamental theoretical distinction, suggesting that perhaps if central sociological theorizing had turned more towards Cooley and Parsons (or even Freud), there would not be such a division to reconcile (Chodorow, 2014).

Other theorists take this idea further, approaching the distinction between structure and agency, the socio and the psycho, from a more critical point of view. Seeing both psychological and sociological theorizing as having developed in specific histories and locations, it becomes apparent that each is firmly grounded in certain

[3] It is important to note that there is a diversity of opinions regarding the DSM among mental health professionals, with some seeing the diagnostic categories more as "convenient fictions" (see Pickersgill, 2014).

Western traditions around what it means to be an individual, and what it means to be part of society—even defining "society" in a peculiarly limited and Western way. Connell (2007) highlights this dichotomy as essentially a Western concern, a certain way of making sense of the place of the person and the role of the social group, shaped by a particular geopolitical and social history. In contrast, located differently, the distinction between the individual and society is neither real nor important: "Indigenous knowledge exists as indigenous understandings of who we have become, who we are now, as much as who we once may have been. The universal question 'Who am I?' in an indigenous framework becomes 'Who are we?'" (Tuhiwai Smith et al., 2016, pp. 136–137). Agency itself can thus be conceptualized in a myriad of ways, and highlighting a separation between the social and psychological (re)produces the theoretical hegemony within these disciplines, the very particular viewpoint which positions the interior and exterior worlds as in opposition (Go, 2016; Brossard & Sallée, 2020).

Psychotherapy, Sociology and the Importance of Context

Context is thus key in understanding both sociological and psychotherapeutic theory, from grand narratives of social structures, to micro level understandings of personality and action. Sociology and psychology both draw on research and theorization historically centered in the West, and assumptions of universality are both simplistic and dangerous: the idea that any single theory or practice, be it sociological or psychological, can be applied unproblematically everywhere (Durie, 2007; Tudor, 2012a), across all ethnic groups and cultures, disregarding the reality of indigenous belonging, as well as experiences of power and loss. Freudian theory is an interesting example of this, with his work frequently being translated across languages, cultures and time periods, with little regard for his original social and historical location: giving universal value to a very particular way of understanding[4] (Brossard & Sallée, 2020).

In illustrating the limitations of universality, Tudor uses the example of personality disorders within psychology, as defined and redefined through the DSM. He suggests that this view of a set number of disorders (and indeed, what counts as disordered), is based firmly in the essentialism of universality: the idea that "...there are unchanging universal qualities, attributes or, in this instance, categories of personality, which pre-date existence; and on an assumption of cultural neutrality, i.e., the (supposed) neutrality of theory across culture(s) and, therefore, the (universal) applicability of theory" (Tudor, 2012a, p. 119). While such theorization can be

[4]Rogers (1959) suggests that Freud himself was less focused on universal applicability, and viewed his theories as dynamic, working to revise them over his lifetime. He continues: "But at the hands of insecure disciples (so it seems to me), the gossamer threads became iron chains of dogma..." (Rogers, 1959, p. 191).

methodologically tidy, fitting neatly within heavily Western conceptualizations, it is inherently limited, ignoring the reality of cultural and linguistic difference, and the vast variations in intellectual and therapeutic traditions and paradigms around the world. As Rogers suggests, while theorization is valuable and important, a clear understanding of context is essential: "...every theory deserves the greatest respect in the area from which it was drawn from the facts and a decreasing degree of respect as it makes predictions in areas more and more remote from its origin" (Rogers, 1959, p. 193).

Within psychotherapy itself, theory is frequently divorced from context, highlighting an implicit assumption of sameness for human experience and development across the world, regardless of race, ethnicity, gender or culture. The dominant theorizing around mental functioning, developmental stages and pathological states are deeply rooted in Western models of what it means to be a person (Tudor, 2012a, drawing on Akhtar, 2004). Much research into human psychology and behaviour draws on sampling "...from a thin slice of humanity" (Henrich et al., 2010, p. 63), while making wider claims towards universal applicability and generalization.[5] Basic concepts within psychotherapeutic training then draw on this unspoken implication of neutrality: from models of separation and individuation, normal and disordered behaviours, self-object relations, and transitional objects, to understandings of self-esteem, attachment, and the universality of affect (De Vaus et al., 2018; Tudor, 2012a; Röttger-Rössler, 2014; Walker, 2004). What is seen as scientific, objective and neutral is inescapably inflected by its origins, having developed through (and as a result of) colonialism and neo-colonial expansion (Burns, 2008).

This is not to say that the psychological theories underpinning psychotherapeutic treatment have no value, but that, as Tudor stresses, ... "the further we are, geographically, culturally, and intellectually from the source and the ground of a particular theory, the more we need to question and test its application and applicability" (2012, p. 120). This is particularly true when applying theories across sociopolitically and historically divergent contexts, translating theories from the Global North to the Global South, from colonizing to colonized countries, discounting the experiences and the well-established knowledge of minority and indigenous groups. An interesting example of the limitations in such transfers of knowledge can be seen in the idea of the mental health "treatment gap" in the developing world: using Western perspectives on mental health (and distress) and the appropriate ways to deal with this, assuming a sameness in the origins of distress, and potentially overriding local, contextual understandings of individuality and approaches to well-being (Jansen et al., 2015).[6]

---

[5] Henrich et al. (2010) highlight that broad claims are routinely published in the world's top journals (which are themselves based in the West), using samples drawn entirely from Western, Educated, Industrialized, Rich, and Democratic (WEIRD) societies, with results then used to generalize a wider human experience.

[6] Jansen et al. (2015) refer to Ventevogel's critique, suggesting that the idea of this treatment gap potentially contributes to a Western, biomedical approach to the alleviation of psychological and

Neither is sociology immune from this metrocentrism: the tendency within the social sciences to take the theories and practices developed in (and for) the particularities of Anglo-European modernity and apply them uncritically around the world (Go, 2016). In recent decades, a number of key critical theorists have highlighted the provincial nature of "mainstream" sociological theorizing: categories, theories and research which were initially formulated to explain and meet the needs of the Western the white male élite in specific contexts in the nineteenth century (Connell, 2007; Go, 2016; Meghji, 2020). Connell (2007) makes a distinction between countries in the centre (the metropole), and those on the periphery: those central, Northern countries then "…have special privilege. They are not exploited from the outside or politically managed as colonies. The standpoint is one of power" (Go, 2016, p. 6). This critical turn is not new in sociology, emerging as Indigenous, de-colonial, feminist and Southern sociologies, yet remains "alternative", set apart from the mainstream theoretical landscape (Go, 2016).

Refining this further, Bhambra (2017) stresses the continuing methodological whiteness which characterizes much social science research. Applicable to both sociology and psychotherapy, this approach fails to acknowledge the role of race and power in everyday social structures and individual experiences, positioning whiteness as a universal experience and the unnoticed lens through which social scientists and researchers seek to make sense of the world. The histories of imperialism and colonialism, which remain very much in the present in Aotearoa New Zealand and around the world, must then be recognized in order to move away from this limited and limiting perspective: working through the discomfort that comes with accounting for the power imbalances between the colonizers and the colonized, Northern and Southern, white and non-white (Bhambra, 2017; Connell, 2007; Tudor, 2012a; Go, 2016).

Sociological critique can then add a further reflective dimension to psychotherapy as a practice, recognizing that the central ideas within psychological and psychotherapeutic theory are not an uncomplicated "truth" about humanity, but are products of, and are implicated in perpetuating the unjust power relations around the world (Burns, 2008; Barsness & Strawn, 2017). Modern psychotherapy practice is largely shaped by and biased towards Western theorists and "universal" models, omitting the lived experiences of most of the world. As Burns queries, "…in the other 90% of the world's population, is there no worthwhile philosophy or theory of personality, of the person, that has emerged over the millennia of multiple sophisticated civilisations?" (2008, p. 20). This has significant implications for psychotherapy in non-Northern societies, countries on the periphery, such as Aotearoa New Zealand. Unquestioning adoption of theories which are presented as objective and neutral, free from cultural or moral underpinnings, only reinforces hierarchies of worth and can perpetuate its own form of violence and disregard (Barsness & Strawn, 2017). Alternative understandings and experiences are thus marginalized

---

social suffering, in contexts where much distress can be attributed to social adversity such as poverty, war, and violence.

or even pathologized, and psychotherapy is constructed and played out on Northern terms in a Southern context (Burns, 2008).[7]

A different way to explore sociological and psychotherapeutic theorizing could instead focus on context. Go describes a Southern standpoint, a social situatedness rooted in race, gender, geopolitics and global social hierarchy: a social and human science from below. This would privilege a way of looking at the world that starts not from the standpoint and history of the metropole, but the positioning of marginalized, peripheral groups (Go, 2016). This acknowledges that the sameness of being human is difference: the significant diversity in experience and understanding around the world, rather than building a unifying truth. Connell (2007) and Go (2016) suggest exploring theories elsewhere, closer to home: sociologists and psychotherapists who are grounded in local context, seeking to conceptualize the world otherwise.

This way of *seeing therapy otherwise* could work to bring together psychological and sociological concerns and understandings, locating the individual as simultaneously unique and separate, and inseparable from context. Tudor (2012) suggests that Southern psychotherapies can provide a radical rethinking of a person's place in the world, theorizing in and on different ground from the Western intellectual tradition, as an "anti-oppressive, post-colonial psychosocial therapeutic practice"[8] (p. 127). Such an approach would not oppose the established body of psychological knowledge, but rather the idea that this is universally applicable knowledge. The perspectives of metropolitan centers remain of interest and value, yet it is key to recognize that these are not the only locations which produce valuable social scientific thought (Durie, 2011; Tudor, 2012a).

From Clinical Sociology in Context to Sociotherapy

The following section outlines clinical sociology as research and practice outside of the New Zealand context, before connecting to the heart of the paper: the value of Māori understandings of socio- and psycho-therapy as applied in sociotherapeutic practice in Aotearoa (see Knight, 2021). Bringing together psychotherapy with the

[7] Cohen highlights that while issues of race and culture are acknowledged in contemporary mental health training, and cultural awareness and sensitivity are encouraged, "...without a simultaneous engagement with critical theories on colonialism, race, ethnicity and culture, there remains the tendency to lose sight of the discourses and practices of power which continue to operate at the very heart of the Western mental health system... the imposition of Western psychiatric ideas and practices on the Global South [are part of] an ongoing system of ideological oppression of Indigenous populations, rather than an aspect of medical enterprise confined to the past." (2020, p. 40–41)

[8] In discussing "post-colonial" realities, it is important to note that colonization does not have a fixed end point, and the impacts and structures created and re-created by colonial processes continue today (Mutu, 2019). As Moana Jackson states: "Colonisation is a process of dispossession and control rather than a historical artefact, and now it takes on new forms" (2021).

practical applications and understandings of sociology illustrates the significant overlaps between the two, as more critical, inclusive methodologies are produced and practised. More broadly, applied and clinical sociology is concerned with utilizing the tools of sociology to make practical, positive change to people's lives, through applying multidisciplinary theory to action (Glass, 1991; Fritz, 2021a). Viewing sociology as clinical and practical illustrates how it can be applied from macro to micro levels, without reinforcing artificial theoretical distinctions and divisions—understanding that all humans are inherently social and best understood in context (Wan & Wan, 2020; Cavanagh, 2021). Rather than seeking to adjust people to the "realities" of the world, a psychotherapy informed by clinical sociology could recognize the power of sociocultural and historical situations and institutions, and how these shape individual lives (Straus, 1979).

Sociologically informed therapy is not a new idea, and has been suggested by multiple theorists as a "sociotherapy", primarily within a Western theoretical framework in North America and Europe, over the past century. It is distinguished from the practice of psychotherapy by its focus: rather than looking inwards, sociotherapy seeks to look inwards and outwards simultaneously, at the intersection of history and biography. Certain iterations of the sociotherapeutic process were directed at active intervention, with some suggesting behavioural modification or even social engineering or re-socialization as falling within the boundaries of sociotherapy (see Bain, 1936; Whiteley, 1986; Kannenberg, 2003). Given the "social" aspect of sociology, sociotherapy is often conceived of as group work, but some theorists and practitioners highlight that sociological understanding is valuable at both individual and group levels. Cavanagh (2021) highlights that sociotherapy covers a range of theories and interventions, and she divides approaches to sociotherapy into three main groups: functionalist/systems-based approaches; socialization theories targeting dysfunctional behavior through active intervention; and psychoanalytic/psychosocial sociology.

One of most theoretically well-developed sociotherapies falls within the functionalist approach: Grounded Encounter Therapy (GET) as theorized by Swan in the United States (Swan, 1985, 1988; Cavanagh, 2021). Swan proposes GET as a way for sociology to be used clinically, to practically address problems in everyday life using a sociodiagnostic and sociotherapeutic approach (Swan, 1988). This model focuses on context, and the power of understanding context for both the individual and the therapist:

> Theory and therapy are "grounded" when we allow both the problems, their explanations, and the strategies and techniques for treatment, to emerge from an Encounter. Encounter is the process through which the parties are engaged in a process of social interaction in which disclosure and discovery lead to an understanding of the social context out of which the problems emerged. Grounding and Encounter, therefore, stand in contrast to more psychotherapeutic approaches which assume a definition of the nature of the problem. (Swan, 1988, p. 77)

This form of group therapy takes a dynamic approach, grounding the content of sessions in the relevant social context in a process of discovery.[9] Swan highlights that social meanings are not objective facts, and uncovering how changing meanings shapes behaviour can have powerful impacts on the client. GET draws on the experiences and knowledge of the clients as well as of the therapist, rather than seeking to impose a theoretical explanation for the client's troubles: each therapy is thus unique to each client, being grounded in their experiences and positionality (Swan, 1988).

As Cavanagh (2021) notes, while the grounded and broad focus of GET provides an interesting alternative to traditional psychotherapeutic approaches, GET illustrates its own limitations. As conceived of by Swan, this form of sociotherapy occurs in group work, with the sociologist as the facilitator who guides participants: "The assumption is that they are stuck, and need the sociotherapist's help to become unstuck" (Swan, 1988, p. 83). This presents a similarly prescriptive, diagnostic model to other Western psychotherapies, positioning the therapist as the expert, the authority who can solve the problems of the patient, set within the same Western, capitalist and patriarchal frame (Cavanagh, 2021).

More recently, Cavanagh (2021) has outlined a critical, dynamic and context-informed approach to sociotherapy, as a psychosocial form of practice, informed by Disch's feminist and critical interdisciplinary approach to therapy (1979, cited in Cavanagh, 2021). From Cavanagh's perspective, a more nuanced form of sociotherapy would be firmly intersectional, focusing on key social issues of power, culture, socio-political history, race, gender and class: a therapeutic practice informed by sociology, "…based on a dialectical understanding of the client-subject in society" (Cavanagh, 2021, p. 1). Such a sociotherapy is distinct from psychotherapy in its emphasis on sociological context, recognizing the blurred nature of the boundaries between the self and the other, and the individual and the social (Cavanagh, 2021; Akman, 2016; Hall, 1990; Mills, 1959). This broader positioning applies to both the client and the sociotherapist, with each therapist informed and affected by their past history, gender, ethnicity, religion, class and wider context: "these are not dead and buried, but are living, breathing influences which shape one's understandings in numerous and unconscious ways, how one makes sense of one's present experiences in the world" (Barsness & Strawn, 2017, p. 229). Chodorow highlights that the therapist's consulting room is always a micro reflection of wider society, culture, and politics, as is the relationship between the client and the therapist, or even the transference-countertransference field (Chodorow, 2014).

Cavanagh (2021) highlights the Western focus of current psychotherapeutic theorizing, and looks to move sociotherapy away from diagnosis of pathologies, exploring instead the diversity of human strategies for adaptation and survival, and moving towards social change. As she states:

[9]For qualitative researchers, it is notable how there is significant overlap between GET and the Grounded Theory of Glaser and Strauss.

> It is a mistake to reduce human suffering to individual "disorders" distinct from modern societal configurations. It is worrisome that sociology, a discipline devoted to the study of modern life—including, but not limited to, advanced capitalist formations, liberal democracy, law, state policy, health care, bureaucracy, technology, labor, housing, poverty, addictions, urbanization, policing, incarceration, settler-colonialism, racialization, gender, sexuality, and so on, should be marginal to psychotherapeutic practices intended to treat people who suffer in uniquely modern ways (Cavanagh, 2021, p. 8).

Sociologically informed therapy works to locate and understand individuals as part of—shaped by and shaping—their social contexts. Individual distress is acknowledged as having a complex etiology, with suffering never arising in a social vacuum. Sociotherapy highlights the inextricably personal in the political, with very private distress caused by the very public problems of everyday life: such as increasing demands for productivity, higher costs of living, inaccessible medical care, lack of affordable childcare, gender-based discrimination and inequality, institutionalized racism, erasure of Indigenous culture and knowledge, and the pervasiveness of gender-based violence (Cavanagh, 2021). In the New Zealand context, indicators of inequality clearly show how the wider context of colonization and continued discrimination negatively impact the Māori population: with Māori having a lower life expectancy, higher suicide rates, lower rates of participation in higher education, higher rates of incarceration and lower median weekly earnings than the Pākehā population (Marriott & Alinaghi, 2021).

Sociotherapy and Sociopolitical Therapy in Practice

The practice of sociotherapy can take many forms, and there are examples of practical applications of sociotherapy around the world: this brief chapter outlines only a few.[10] In Poland, sociotherapy is a recognized method for assisting young people who are deemed at risk: a group psychological and pedagogical method which focuses on interpersonal dynamics rather than intrapsychic factors. Sociotherapists work within school settings or specialist facilities, and provide a targeted service from assessment, through intervention and then evaluation. Sociotherapy is seen as located in-between psychotherapy, psycho-education and interpersonal training, and is well regarded in this setting (Soroko & Jankowiak, 2020).

In Rwanda, sociotherapy has been used as a form of community support since 2005, providing an alternative paradigm in a context where individual suffering is understood as a form of social distress, against a background of significant trauma (Jansen et al., 2015). As a deliberate break with individualistic approaches to mental health, in this context, sociotherapy focuses on "...restoring a disrupted social fabric and reshaping communities in a way that previous social divisions that contributed to

[10] There are many more examples and applications in non-Anglophone settings, particularly French-speaking contexts including France and Quebec (Fritz, 2021b).

the past violence and its related suffering are transcended (Jansen et al., 2015, p. 4). As applied in Rwanda, East Congo and Liberia, Dekker highlights the importance of social interventions such as group sociotherapy being prioritized in such post-conflict areas (Dekker, 2018). With a strongly context-based approach that acknowledges the severe social disruption and trauma, sociotherapy participants are not seen:

> ...as individuals with private problems. The participants are treated as group members who experience problems because of unresolved matters of a social nature. When every group member is acknowledged to have been caught up in war conflict, everyone will have the space in which to think about his/her own position in the conflict and decide whether or not to talk about this (Dekker, 2018, p. 21).

This community-based practice of sociotherapy is grounded in connection, seeking to facilitate and represent social change through respectful, structured participation: a contextualized, grass-roots way of working that is characterized by inclusion.

A similar therapeutic process, the *Testimonio*, was introduced in Chile in the 1970s, working to assist people who have suffered violence and trauma as a result of state terrorism. Described by Aron (1992) as a bridge between sociotherapy and psychotherapy, the *Testimonio* is a practical, clinical method to alleviate mental distress, and an act of social and political therapy through personal testimony, aimed at reducing the suffering of the wider community (Aron, 1992). By publicly presenting a personal account of painful experiences, the *Testimonio* seeks to highlight the reality and lasting consequences of injustices and trauma: "...by re-framing that objective reality, the *Testimonio*'s subjective account of what has occurred contributes significantly to the community's knowledge and mental health. It is a form of sociotherapy, healing wounds of social trauma inflicted by the terrorist state" (Aron, 1992, p. 176).

In Australia, clinical sociology as applied to community mental health was pioneered by Neville Yeomans in the 1950–1960s, notably through Fraser House in New South Wales (Spencer, 2009). Fraser House, a Therapeutic Community–based psychiatric unit, focused on the practice of sociotherapy and relational connection, exploring ways to assist the person as located within their social network. In establishing the unit, Yeomans drew on Australian Indigenous social cohesion processes in creating a sense of "cultural locality": people connecting through the importance of their contexts and their connection to place (Spencer, 2009).

Re-centering Psycho/Socio Therapy in the Context of Aotearoa New Zealand

Exploring practices of psychotherapy within Aotearoa New Zealand with a critical, clinical sociological lens then provides an important perspective on approaches to psycho/social change, recognizing Māori ways of engaging with interpersonal relationships and social context. Māori knowledge, learnings, and values have been passed down across generations, stemming from a Mātauranga Māori worldview, providing insight into Māori experiences and understandings of the world (Hikuroa, 2017; Knight, 2021). Importantly, Māori understandings of psychotherapy in Aotearoa illustrate the lived reality of how the social and the personal intersect and overlap, and the interweavings between the personal and the political, which can be better understood outside of Northern theoretical frameworks. With professionalized psychotherapy being invisibly framed by Western theories and knowledge, talking therapies, therapists and counsellors in Aotearoa thus frequently "...exist in a tension between developing local concepts for local problems, and the continual absorption and cultural colonisation of our social ways of framing our national and cultural experience by unconscious emulation of those world centres" (Burns, 2008, p. 11).

A turn towards the sociotherapeutic can make these tensions and complexities more visible, highlighting the importance of local, contextually appropriate experiences and practices (Burns, 2008). Tudor suggests that Southern psychotherapies openly recognize local inequalities of "wealth, health and power" and their far-reaching consequences for Māori (Tudor, 2012a), as Western theoretical dominance is not merely historical coincidence but is rather an expression of underlying political power (Burns, 2008). The historical dynamics of colonization, as reflected in social and institutional structures around power, privilege and prejudice, are very present in contemporary New Zealand society, and inflect the way in which psychotherapy is taught and practised (Fay, 2018).

Psychotherapy in Aotearoa New Zealand is a regulated practice and profession, and forms part of the history of mental health service provision within the social services of the country (Tudor, 2011). Set against the rapid neoliberal reforms of the 1980s, occupational professionalism was key for sectors such as psychotherapy, psychology and social work, and each sought to define and regulate their spheres of work (Miller, 2014). In 2003, the Health Practitioners Competence Assurance Act (HPCAA) replaced existing occupational statutes for medical practitioners and other helping professions—from nurses to midwives, opticians to psychologists. The new Act "...provided a framework for the regulation of health practitioners with the purpose of protecting the public where there is a risk of harm from the practice of the profession. It included mechanisms such as scopes of practice and standards to ensure that practitioners are competent and fit to practise their professions for the duration of their professional lives" (Miller, 2014, p. 107). Psychotherapists advocated to be included under the jurisdiction of the Act,[11] and since 2007, the title "psychotherapist" has been protected: restricted to those registered with the Psychotherapists' Board of Aotearoa New Zealand (PBANZ) (Miller, 2014; Tudor, 2012b).

This move towards professionalization was controversial, highlighting divisions between approaches to psychotherapy practice, the ideals of occupational registration (as advocated for by the New Zealand Association of Psychotherapists (NZAP)) and wider regulation of the field of psychotherapy as a whole (Tudor, 2012b). Miller

[11] Counselling in New Zealand has followed a different path, well described in detail by Miller (2014).

(2014) suggests that the ideology of professionalism allowed dominant groups within the field to push for professional security and standardization, as subject to bureaucratic control and oversight, potentially at the expense of what makes therapy valuable (but is not easily measured): not standardization, but contextual sensitivity, responsiveness and a meaningful therapeutic alliance (Miller, 2014; Tudor, 2012b). While professionalization comes with key safeguards, it can also codify a particular form of theory and practice as standard and "correct". Such institutionalization can appear supportive in theory, but in practice, simplistic standards can develop at the expense of contextualized, local knowledge, minimizing the importance of Kaupapa Māori in contemporary Aotearoa (Burns, 2008; Morice et al., 2019; Miller, 2014).

Professional psychotherapy in New Zealand has worked to incorporate and acknowledge Kaupapa Māori to some extent: since the 1980s, there has been increasing visibility of Māori language, health perspectives, and psychological frameworks in mental health practices (Durie, 2011). NZAP pledged to honour Te Tiriti o Waitangi in 1993, acknowledging the bicultural partnership of Aotearoa New Zealand (Bowden, 2000). HPCAA highlights cultural competence as key for New Zealand practitioners, with a focus on how non-Māori can demonstrate cultural competence and sensitivity within this bicultural context, rather than allowing space for Māori expertise and ways of working for Māori (Miller, 2014). However, in 2007, Waka Oranga was formed as a professional association of Māori Psychotherapy Practitioners in Aotearoa New Zealand and NZAP's Te Tiriti o Waitangi partner (Morice et al., 2019). Importantly, Waka Oranga focuses on widening understandings of health and mental health in a culturally relevant way, in order to counterbalance the dominant Western approach to therapy with a more nuanced awareness of social and cultural factors, where Kaupapa Māori is central (Mikahere-Hall et al., 2019).

Repositioning and redefining therapy and therapies to make sense for the diversity of experiences in Aotearoa illustrates the importance and power of seeing psychotherapy otherwise, as grounded, local (Tudor, 2012a) and sociologically informed. This wider conception of what therapy can mean is key for Māori and non-Māori alike, opening up ways of understanding the everyday impacts of marginalization and the often-unnoticed cultural biases in theory and in everyday life (Burns, 2008).

Like Burns (2008), as a non-Māori sociologist exploring psychotherapy myself, I do not claim to understand lived Māori experiences of marginalization in Aotearoa, nor the depth or nuance of Indigenous knowledge. I share the concern that the mainstream psychotherapeutic frameworks in New Zealand are largely theoretical constructs which are presented as a universal truth, yet developed elsewhere: "...by northern powerful societies that speak and write about *their* problems from *their* point of view, and in terms of *their* political process and cultural practices in relation to those issues, and how to deal with them" (Burns, 2008, p. 12). This disparity is felt doubly by Māori: for non-Māori, living in a bicultural society is a matter of choice, and non-Māori largely do not have to engage meaningfully with Te Ao Māori. For Māori however, the dominance of Western culture means that they do not have the option not to engage, and each individual positions themselves between and within these two worlds (Morice & Fay, 2013; Hall, 2013). The dominant discourses within mental health thus struggle to capture the lived experiences of Māori (Mikahere-Hall, 2017), and Māori engage with psychotherapy services less frequently as a result: the primary users of psychotherapy in New Zealand being the middle class, educated, employed Pākehā population (Krawitz & Watson, 1997).

Seeing Mental Health Otherwise: Sociotherapy and Kaupapa Māori

Māori leaders, scholars and practitioners have thus questioned the applicability of Western research paradigms and positivist methodologies within Aotearoa's unique cultural context (Tuhiwai Smith, 2012; Mikahere-Hall, 2017). More diverse, holistic and sociological conceptions of mental health and illness can provide space for marginalized groups to explore what health means in context, while also recognizing the inescapable power of sociocultural factors (Mikahere-Hall, 2017; Fay, 2018). As Bowden (2000) suggests, psychotherapy in Aotearoa has the potential to see therapy in a different way, building a distinctive bicultural theory and practice which positions the individual within the social, rather than separating individuality from cultural connection.

Critical, feminist and liberation psychotherapies, along with sociotherapies, share some of this theoretical and practical reorientation, locating identity firmly within the context of social relationships and structures and using social analysis as a therapeutic tool (Krawitz & Watson, 1997). Breaking with the psychotherapeutic focus on the intrapsychic, such approaches focus on broader context and history to recontextualize mental distress: naming and acknowledging the lived realities of poverty, sexism, racism, marginalization, oppression, social trauma and loss (Durie, 2011; Tudor, 2012a; Krawitz & Watson, 1997). As highlighted by Ranginui Walker, in Aotearoa, the wider context of British imperialism and land dispossession by force has created an inherently unequal world for Māori, where land loss is linked directly with loss of mana and personal distress (Walker, 1996, p. 30). Using a sociopolitical lens, beginning with context first for Māori and Pākehā alike, seeks to avoid psychologizing such key social issues: recognizing "...how easy it is to become absorbed by the complex intricacies of people's inner lives and to lose touch with larger external realities..." (Enns 1993 cited in Krawitz & Watson, 1997, p. 475).

The role of Waka Oranga[12] is particularly important, as it works to highlight the positioning of the Western medical model, and the ways in which culture impacts mental health (Morice et al., 2019; Mikahere-Hall et al., 2019). Waka Oranga brings

[12]The name refers to "Waka", sea-ferrying craft or canoes which brought the migrating Polynesian inhabitants to the shores of Aotearoa. "Oranga" comes from "ora", a state of health and well-being. "Oranga" refers to survival, well-being, livelihood and welfare—everything needed for a healthy sense of "ora" (Mikahere-Hall et al., 2019).

together Māori and non-Māori practitioners, who seek to illuminate the value of traditional Indigenous knowledge and theory in understanding mental health in New Zealand, working to uphold and honour Māori wisdom and ways of being (Mikahere-Hall et al., 2019). Drawing on the wisdom of Kaumatua Haare Williams, practitioners within Waka Oranga work to create a space where tikanga Māori and tikanga Pākehā come together, re-centering Indigenous practices around social and mental health, and recognizing that Western psychotherapy also retains value (Morice et al., 2019). As described by Morice et al.: "The Māori (re)awakening that occurs through our own de-colonising experiences, complemented and supported by our Pākehā allies through their own consciousness-raising processes, has created a rich and fertile opportunity for cross-cultural engagements to emerge..." (2019, p. 36).

This move away from monocultural psychotherapy is reflected in the increasing number of counsellors, psychologists and psychotherapists who are asserting the appropriateness of Kaupapa Māori in their work (Hall, 2013). A Māori psychotherapeutic framework looks to meet the needs of Māori, making psychotherapy meaningful for Māori through acknowledging that the Māori world and Māori experiences are real and valid (Morice et al., 2019; Hall, 2013). Waka Oranga provides a valuable summary of their approach, illustrating the nuance and complexity of Kaupapa Māori: how the values of traditional knowledge can be held within the development of new knowledge (Mikahere-Hall, 2017). On their website, Waka Oranga highlights the following fundamental principles as a framework for effective and ethically sound psychotherapy practice within Te Ao Māori:

> *Manaakitanga* acknowledges the mana of others as having equal or greater importance than one's own, through the expression of aroha, hospitality, generosity and mutual respect. In doing so, all parties are elevated and our status is enhanced, building unity through humility and the act of giving.
>
> *Whanaungatanga* underpins the social organisation of whanau, hapu and iwi and includes rights and reciprocal obligations consistent with being part of a collective. Whanaungatanga is the principle which binds individuals to the wider group and affirms the value of the collective while affirming the special contribution of the individual. Whanaungatanga is inter-dependence with each other and recognition that the people are our wealth.
>
> *Kaitiakitanga* embraces the spiritual and cultural guardianship of Te Ao Māori, a responsibility derived from whakapapa. Kaitiakitanga entails an active exercise of responsibility in a manner beneficial to resources and the welfare of the people. It promotes the growth and development of Māori in all spheres of livelihood so that Māori can anticipate a future of living in good health and in reasonable prosperity.
>
> *Kotahitanga* is the principle of unity of purpose and direction. Kotahitanga is demonstrated through the achievement of harmony, balance, and moving as one. All are encouraged to make a contribution, to have their say and then together, consensus is reached.
>
> *Rangatiratanga* is the expression of the attributes of rangatira (weaving the people together) including humility, leadership by example, generosity, altruism, diplomacy and knowledge of benefit to the people. Rangatiratanga is reflected in the promotion of self determination for Māori as an expression of the rights defined by mana atua, mana tupuna and mana whenua.
>
> *Wairuatanga* is reflected in the belief that there is a spiritual existence alongside the physical. Wairuatanga is expressed through the intimate connection of the people to maunga,

> awa, moana and marae and tupuna and atua. These connections are affirmed through knowledge and understanding of atua Māori and must be maintained and nourished towards the achievement of wellness. Wairuatanga is central to the everyday lives of Māori and is integral to our worldview. (Waka Oranga, 2022)

These key dimensions highlight a broader, more encompassing framework where psychological health is inseparable from wider understandings of social wellbeing, from the sociological. Durie suggests that good health is found in the balance between four essential dimensions: *te taha wairua* (spiritual health), *te taha hinengaro* (emotional and psychological health), *te taha tinana* (physical health) and *te taha whānau* (a healthy family and social environment) (Durie 2010; cited in Miller, 2014). An individual cannot be understood as distinct from the group and the wider environment, and the bond between people and the earth, often unexplored in Western psychotherapeutic frameworks, is closely related to identity and personal psychology. In many contexts, indigenous knowledge is closely bound to place, and such knowledge of the natural world is necessary for human survival (Tuhiwai Smith et al., 2016): the very real present-day effects of land loss for Māori illustrate this power of the connections between the land and people as shaping individual, social and environmental well-being (Durie, 2007; Walker, 1996). The breaking of connections to whenua, hapū, and iwi through dispossession then have profound impacts on the protective factors of cultural identity and health (Knight, 2021). Hall highlights this importance of understanding both whakapapa and whānau in the context of Aotearoa, and how Māori approaches to psychotherapy start from the position that everything both seen and unseen has a whakapapa, a genealogy (Hall, 2013). From this broader perspective, wider sociopolitical and historical forces have influenced the choices available to whānau: an understanding of whakapapa as a whānau social systems construct emphasizes that therapeutic interventions must grow from what is socially and culturally appropriate (Hall, 2013).

As Krawitz and Watson (1997) describe, the tendency of traditional psychotherapy to focus on the psychological rather than the social or cultural reflects a particularly Eurocentric process of analysis and understanding. Cultural supervision for psychotherapists is an attempt to overcome this, as seen in NZAP and Waka Oranga's aspirational approach, providing space for each practitioner to explore the relationships between individual psychology and the wider social and cultural worlds that help to form it: both for themselves and their clients (Morice & Fay, 2013). As a practice and safeguard, cultural supervision is not just for Pākehā, and not only about Māori—it is a way to move towards cultural competence, to recognize one's limitations and biases (Morice & Fay, 2013), to acknowledge the complexity of Aotearoa's colonial history, and to work from a place of cultural humility[13] (Tervalon & Murray-García, 1998). Such an approach draws together the sociological and psychotherapeutic as re-conceived outside of the metropole,

[13] Tervalon and Murray-García (1998, p. 123) define cultural humility as "...a lifelong commitment to self-evaluation and self-critique, to redressing the power imbalances in the patient-physician dynamic, and to developing mutually beneficial and nonpaternalistic clinical and advocacy partnerships with communities on behalf of individuals and defined populations."

recognizing the inextricability of the individual from their social and cultural context, and the ways in which the sociocultural and the psychological co-exist and co-determine each other (Morice & Fay, 2013).

This reframing, this wider understanding of individuality and what makes up a person, highlights the limitations of dualistic Western frameworks of therapeutic interventions. Using the example of whakamā, a complex feeling of dis-ease, collective embarrassment and shame, Bowden (2000) illustrates how personal troubles are not just connected to public issues, but are themselves collective: rather than seeing mental distress as purely within the psyche, it can be seen as arising from the social, the interconnections between people. Whakamā is not guilt or unease for something a person has done, but rather a feeling intimately connected to the wider context of colonization (Stephens, 2020). Interactions with psychotherapeutic services in Aotearoa can thus contribute to whakamā, amplifying this pain, when Western practices are invisibly accepted, distancing the personal from the political and not engaging with Māori ways of thinking (Knight, 2021). As Bowden describes: "We must speak of the spiritual and the physical and the psychodynamic as being colours within the same thread rather than separate threads that are woven together. It is when we speak of *'the spiritual'* and *'the psychodynamic'* as if they were separate phenomena that we rely on a dualism that denies the cultural reality. We do the same with *'thinking and feeling'* and *'body and mind'*. The *mana* is already inherent in the *mauri*" (2000, p. 13).

Looking Forward: (Socio)therapeutic Possibilities and Learnings from Aotearoa New Zealand

This chapter has explored the intersections between sociology and psychotherapy, and the limitations of universality and theoretical bias - looking towards a critical sociotherapy as a possibility in providing an inclusive and sociologically informed approach to therapeutic work. A sociotherapeutic perspective foregrounds an "...acknowledgement that world history has taken a heavy toll on the social lives of millions... with a critical interest in an aftermath that is characterised by growing material inequality and constant violation of self-esteem" (Dekker, 2018, p. 221). In Aotearoa, the work of Waka Oranga highlights how professionalized psychotherapy can broaden its theoretical base and become more meaningful, by including a sociopolitical viewpoint, grounded within Kaupapa Māori to challenge traditional, individualistic approaches to research and practice (Krawitz & Watson, 1997; Hall, 2013). Sociotherapy can shift towards inclusive inquiry and practice, where local and indigenous knowledge systems collaborate within research and psychotherapeutic practice (Allen et al., 2009).

In acknowledging the limitations of current mainstream frameworks for understanding and shaping therapeutic work, it is important to draw out the contradictions in working with theory developed elsewhere, the value of Kaupapa Māori, and the ways in which the complex history and social fabric of Aotearoa presents both problems and possible solutions (Burns, 2008; Akman, 2016). For (mixed) Pākehā, such as myself, exploring this complex space requires sensitivity and a recognition of my own biases: seeking to learn about Mātauranga Māori as a non- Māori scholar, with respect and humility (see Tuhiwai Smith et al., 2016). Working to be aware of my own history and privilege, I hope to avoid perpetuating the same monocultural, Western frameworks over and over again (Barnes, 2013): something which continues to challenge me as a sociologist and psychotherapist. As Rogers (1959) looks to the cultural and personal soil from which theories spring, Go (2016) highlights the value inherent in seeing sociology and psychotherapy otherwise: stressing that the more theoretical and research standpoints we have, the better and richer our understanding of the world will be.

By positioning sociology and psychotherapy together rather than in opposition, exploring the whakapapa within social systems, the arbitrary divisions between the personal and the political fade from importance (Bain, 1936; Hall, 2013). Theoretical binaries, the opposing relationships between structure/agency, individual/society and transference/countertransference can be seen from another perspective, as mutually co-constructed, and inseparable in terms of meaning (see Stolorow et al., 1987). Stuart Hall (1992) speaks of identity bridging the gap between inside and outside, stitching the subject into structure; but perhaps these unifying stories we tell ourselves about belonging, bringing together our human complexities, have hidden the fact that there was no gap to begin with.

As in Calhoun's work (2014), this chapter illustrates some of the disconnects and integrations that exist between the disciplines, and particularly how the histories and locatedness of these disciplines have shaped our contemporary understandings. Tudor (2012) highlights the importance of privileging Southern psychotherapies (as plural, not singular) in our work as social scientists and therapeutic practitioners, providing new starting points which are specific and contextual. Mātauranga Māori, as both the pursuit and application of learnings and knowledge by incorporating culture, values and world view, has a unique place in addressing social issues in Aotearoa (Hikuroa, 2017). This broader perspective can recognize the social in the individual and the individual in the social, illuminating how "Patterns and structures can be collective, deeply emotional, and subjectively meaningful all at the same time. Culture is patterned emotion. Emotion is culture experienced" (Alexander, 2014, p. 18).

Working through these frameworks in Aotearoa offers us the opportunity to become decolonizers—being open to non-Western bases for theory, sharing power, equalizing privilege and actively working to challenge ingrained assumptions around superiority, inferiority and "truth" (Fay, 2018). While the status quo is sometimes portrayed as being the neutral option, as Krawitz and Watson (1997) suggest, not speaking is in itself a political statement, maintaining the invisible hierarchy around the unimportance of non-dominant groups. Rather than superficially acknowledging cultural difference or including token cultural content, (socio)-therapy in New Zealand can be built around Indigenous knowledge and pedagogy, a scaffolding for care developed around a Māori frame of reference (Morice & Fay,

2013, drawing on Ranginui Walker and Linda Tuhiwai Smith). Growing from the work of many scholars and practitioners, and bringing together both Indigenous and Western ways of knowing (Wilson et al., 2022), such approaches to therapy could create a new way of talking, a socio/psychotherapeutic frame in Aotearoa that connects people, and allows them to look inwards and outwards, without feeling alone.

He aha te mea nui? He tāngata, he tāngata, he tāngata.
What is the most important thing? It is people, it is people, it is people.

References

Aron, A. (1992). Testimonio, a bridge between psychotherapy and sociotherapy. *Women & Therapy, 13*(3), 173–189.

Akman, K. M. (2016). Sociotherapy as a contemporary alternative. *Bangladesh e-Journal Sociology, 13*(2), 9–1.

Alexander, J. (2014). Preface. In L. Chancer & J. Andrews (Eds.), *The unhappy divorce of sociology and psychoanalysis: Diverse perspectives on the psychosocial.* Palgrave Macmillan.

Allen, W., Ataria, J. M., Apgar, J. M., Harmsworth, G., & Tremblay, L. A. (2009). Kia pono te mahi putaiao—Doing science in the right spirit. *Journal of the Royal Society of New Zealand., 39*(4), 239–242.

Alpert, H. (1939). Emile Durkheim and sociologismic psychology. *American Journal of Sociology, 45*(1), 64–70.

Asay, T. P., & Lambert, M. J. (1999). The empirical case for the common factors in therapy: Quantitative findings. In M. A. Hubble, B. L. Duncan, & S. D. Miller (Eds.), *The heart and soul of change: What works in therapy* (pp. 23–55). American Psychological Association.

Bain, R. (1936). Sociology and psychoanalysis. *American Sociological Review, 1*(2), 203–216.

Barnes, A. (2013). *What can Pākehā learn from engaging in kaupapa Māori educational research?* Working Paper 1. New Zealand Council for Educational Research.

Barsness, R. E., & Strawn, B. (2017). Relational psychoanalytic ethics: Professional, personal, theoretical, and communal. In R. E. Barsness (Ed.), *Core competencies of relational psychoanalysis: A guide to practice, study, and research.* Routledge.

Bhambra, G. K. (2017). Brexit, Trump, and 'methodological whiteness': On the misrecognition of race and class. *The British Journal of Sociology, 68*(S1), S214–S232.

Bowden, R. (2000). Psychotherapy as a container for bi-cultural practice in Aotearoa. *Psychotherapy in Australia, 7*(1), 11–15.

Brossard, B., & Sallée, N. (2020). Sociology and psychology: What intersections? *European Journal of Social Theory, 23*(1), 3–14.

Burns, E. (2008). How can a "southern theory" perspective contribute to New Zealand counselling? *New Zealand Journal of Counselling, 28*(2), 10–24.

Calhoun, C. (2014). Foreword. In L. Chancer & J. Andrews (Eds.), *The unhappy divorce of sociology and psychoanalysis: Diverse perspectives on the psychosocial.* Palgrave Macmillan.

Cavalletto, G., & Silver, C. (2014). Opening/closing the sociological mind to psychoanalysis. In L. Chancer & J. Andrews (Eds.), *The unhappy divorce of sociology and psychoanalysis: Diverse perspectives on the psychosocial.* Palgrave Macmillan.

Cavanagh, S. L. (2021). Sociotherapy in the time of COVID-19: A critical position paper on the importance of sociology. *Journal of Applied Social Science, 5*(2), 211–225. https://doi.org/10.1177/1936724421998275

Chancer, L. (2014). C. Wright Mills, Freud, and the psychosocial imagination. In L. Chancer & J. Andrews (Eds.), *The unhappy divorce of sociology and psychoanalysis: Diverse perspectives on the psychosocial*. Palgrave Macmillan.

Chodorow, N. J. (2014). Why is it easy to be a psychoanalyst and a feminist, but not a psychoanalyst and a social scientist? Reflections of a psychoanalytic hybrid. In L. Chancer & J. Andrews (Eds.), *The unhappy divorce of sociology and psychoanalysis: Diverse perspectives on the psychosocial*. Palgrave Macmillan.

Cohen, B. M. Z. (2020). A postcolonial critique of mental health: Empire and psychiatric expansionism. In R. Moodley & E. Lee (Eds.), *The Routledge international handbook of race, culture and mental health*. Routledge.

Connell, R. (2007). *Southern theory: The global dynamics of knowledge in social science*. Sydney, Allen & Unwin Australia. Polity Press.

Dam, L. (2022). Be(com)ing an Asian tangata tiriti. *Kōtuitui: New Zealand Journal of Social Sciences*. https://doi.org/10.1080/1177083X.2022.2129078

Dekker, C. (2018). *Handbook training in community-based Sociotherapy: Experiences in Rwanda, East Congo and Liberia*. African Studies Centre Leiden.

Delahunty, C. (2021). Becoming tangata tiriti, in *E-Tangata*. Retrieved January 20, 2022, from https://e-tangata.co.nz/reflections/becoming-tangata-tiriti/

De Vaus, J., Hornsey, M. J., Kuppens, P., & Bastian, B. (2018). Exploring the east-west divide in prevalence of affective disorder: A case for cultural differences in coping with negative emotion. *Personality and Social Psychology Review, 22*(3), 285–304.

Durie, M. (2007). Counselling Māori: Marae encounters as a basis for understanding and building relationships. *New Zealand Journal of Counselling, 27*(1), 1–8.

Durie, M. (2011). Indigenizing mental health services: New Zealand experience. *Transcultural Psychiatry, 48*(1–2), 24–36.

Fay, J. (2018). Decolonising mental health services one prejudice at a time: Psychological, sociological, ecological, and cultural considerations. *Settler Colonial Studies, 8*(1), 47–59.

Fritz, J. M. (2021a). Introduction. In J. M. Fritz (Ed.), *International clinical sociology* (2nd ed.). Springer.

Fritz, J. M. (Ed.). (2021b). *International clinical sociology* (2nd ed.). Springer.

Glass, J. (1991). Foreword. In J. G. Bruhn & H. M. Rebach (Eds.), *Handbook of clinical sociology*. Springer.

Go, J. (2016). Globalizing Sociology, Turning South. Perspectival Realism and the Southern Standpoint. *Sociologica 2*.

Hall, A. (2013). Ko Rangitoto, Ko Waitematā: Cultural landmarks for the integration of a Māori indigenous psychotherapy in Aotearoa. *Ata: Journal of Psychotherapy Aotearoa New Zealand, 17*(2), 139–157.

Hall, S. (1992). The question of cultural identity. In S. Hall, D. Held, & T. McGrew (Eds.), *Modernity and its futures* (pp. 273–325). Polity Press.

Hall, C. M. (1990). Identity empowerment through clinical sociology. *Clinical Sociology Review, 8*:1, 7.

Hikuroa, D. (2017). Mātauranga Māori—The ukaipo of knowledge in New Zealand. *Journal of the Royal Society of New Zealand, 47*(1), 5–10.

Henrich, J., Heine, S., & Norenzayan, A. (2010). The weirdest people in the world? *Behavioral and Brain Sciences, 33*(2–3), 61–83.

Huft, J. (2022). The history and future of the sociology of therapy: A review and a research agenda. *The American Sociologist, 53*, 437–464. https://doi.org/10.1007/s12108-022-09534-3

Jackson, M. (2021). Decolonisation and the stories in the land in *E-Tangata*. Retrieved January 20, 2022, from https://e-tangata.co.nz/comment-and-analysis/moana-jackson-decolonisation-and-the-stories-in-the-land/

Jansen, S., White, R., Hogwood, J., Jansen, A., Gishoma, D., Mukamana, D., & Richters, A. (2015). The "treatment gap" in global mental health reconsidered: Sociotherapy for collective trauma in Rwanda. *European Journal of Psychotraumatology, 6*.

Jutel, A. (2021). Diagnosis: A social and political phenomenon. In *Routledge international handbook of critical issues in health and illness*. Routledge.
Kannenberg, R. L. (2003). *Sociotherapy for sociopaths: Resocial group*. PESI Healthcare.
Knight, K. (2021). *From whakamā to whakamana: He aha tēnei? Kaimahi and tāngata whaiora recounts of whakamā in mental health contexts of Tāmaki Makaurau*. A thesis and portfolio of clinical research submitted in partial fulfilment of the requirements for the degree of Doctor of Clinical Psychology at the University of Auckland, Aotearoa, New Zealand 2021.
Krawitz, R., & Watson, C. (1997). Gender, race and poverty: Bringing the sociopolitical into psychotherapy. *Australian & New Zealand Journal of Psychiatry, 31*(4), 474–479.
Marriott, L., & Alinaghi, N. (2021). Closing the gaps: An update on indicators of inequality for Māori and Pacific people. *Journal of New Zealand Studies, NS32*(2021), 2–39.
McDonald, M., & O'Callaghan, J. (2008). Positive psychology: A Foucauldian critique. *The Humanistic Psychologist, 36*(2), 127–142.
Meghji, A. (2020). *Decolonizing sociology: An introduction*. Polity.
Mikahere-Hall, A., Morice, M. P., & Pye, C. (2019). Waka Oranga: The development of an indigenous professional organisation within a psychotherapeutic discourse in Aotearoa New Zealand. *Ata: Journal of Psychotherapy Aotearoa New Zealand, 23*(1), 23–34.
Mikahere-Hall, A. (2017). Constructing research from an indigenous Kaupapa Māori perspective: An example of decolonising research. *Psychotherapy and Politics International, 15*(3), 1–14.
Miller, J. H. (2014). Professionalism interrupted? Professionalism's challenges to local knowledge in New Zealand counselling. *Current Sociology, 62*(1), 100–113.
Mills, C. W. (1959). *The sociological imagination* (Vol. 46, p. 355). Oxford University Press.
Morice, M. P., & Fay, J. (2013). Cultural supervision and cultural competence in the practice of psychotherapy and applied psychology. *Ata: Journal of Psychotherapy Aotearoa New Zealand, 17*(1), 89–101.
Morice, M. P., Mikahere-Hall, A., Woodard, W., Pye, C., Fleming, A. H., Armstrong, V., Poutu Fay, A., & Poutu Fay, Z. (2019). Waka Oranga: Personal reflections. *Ata: Journal of Psychotherapy Aotearoa New Zealand, 23*(1), 35–48.
Mutu, M. (2019). 'To honour the treaty, we must first settle colonisation' (Moana Jackson 2015): The long road from colonial devastation to balance, peace and harmony. *Journal of the Royal Society of New Zealand, 49*(sup1), 4–18.
Owen, I. (1993). Towards a sociology of psychotherapy. *Counselling Psychology Review., 8*(1), 6–9.
Parsons, T. (1958). Social structure and the development of personality: Freud's contribution to the integration of psychology and sociology. *Psychiatry, 21*(4), 321–340.
Pickersgill, M. D. (2014). Debating DSM-5: Diagnosis and the sociology of critique. *Journal of Medical Ethics, 40*(8), 521–525.
Rogers, C. (1959). A theory of therapy, personality, and interpersonal relationships, as developed in the client-centered framework. In S. Koch (Ed.), *Psychology: A study of a science: Formulations of the person and the social context*. McGraw-Hill.
Röttger-Rössler, B. (2014). Bonding and belonging beyond WEIRD worlds: Rethinking attachment theory on the basis of cross-cultural anthropological data. In H. Otto & H. Keller (Eds.), *Different faces of attachment: Cultural variations on a universal human need* (pp. 141–168).
Smelser, N. J. (2014). Sustaining an unlikely marriage: Biographical, theoretical, and intellectual notes. In L. Chancer & J. Andrews (Eds.), *The unhappy divorce of sociology and psychoanalysis: Diverse perspectives on the psychosocial*. Palgrave Macmillan.
Soroko, E., & Jankowiak, B. (2020). Shaping social and psychological competencies or intervening in a crisis? Sociotherapists' experiences of helping adolescents in Poland. *International Journal for the Advancement of Counselling, 42*, 349–365.
Spencer, L. (2009). The expanding role of clinical sociology in Australia. *Journal of Applied Social Science, 3*(2), 56–62.

Stephens, T. (2020). Whakamā: fighting the taniwha of shame. *The Spinoff*, July 13 2020. Retrieved January 20, 2023, from https://thespinoff.co.nz/atea/13-07-2020/whakama-fighting-the-taniwha-of-shame
Stolorow, R. D., Brandchaft, B., & Atwood, G. E. (1987). *Psychoanalytic treatment: An intersubjective approach*. The Analytic Press.
Straus, R. A. (1979). Introduction: The reemergence of clinical sociology. *American Behavioral Scientist, 22*(4), 477–485.
Swan, L. A. (1985). Grounded-encounter therapy: A sociodiagnostic and sociotherapeutic approach. *Mid-American Review of Sociology, 10*(2), 93–109.
Swan, L. A. (1988). Grounded encounter therapy: Its characteristics and process. *Clinical Sociology, 6*(1), 76–87.
Tervalon, M., & Murray-García, J. (1998). Cultural humility versus cultural competence: A critical distinction in defining physician training outcomes in multicultural education. *Journal of Health Care for the Poor and Underserved, 9*(2), 117–125.
Tudor, K. (Ed.). (2011). *The turning tide: Pluralism and partnership in psychotherapy in Aotearoa New Zealand*. LC Publications Limited.
Tudor, K. (2012a). Southern psychotherapies. *Psychotherapy and Politics International, 10*(2), 116–129.
Tudor, K. (2012b). Ebb and flow: One year on from the turning tide: Pluralism and partnership in psychotherapy in Aotearoa New Zealand. *Psychotherapy and Politics International, 10*(2), 171–178.
Tuhiwai Smith, L., Maxwell, T. K., Puke, H., & Temara, P. (2016). Indigenous knowledge, methodology and mayhem: What is the role of methodology in producing indigenous insights? A discussion from Mātauranga Māori. *Knowledge Cultures, 4*(3), 131–156.
Tuhiwai Smith, L. (2012). *Decolonizing methodologies: Research and indigenous peoples*. Zed Books.
Waka Oranga. (2022). *Māori psychotherapy*. Retrieved October 11, 2022, from https://nzap.org.nz/waka-oranga/maori-psychotherapy/
Walker, K. (2004). Practitioner beware! A critical reflection on the theoretical assumptions that inform practice. *Australian Journal of Career Development, 13*(2), 40–43.
Walker, R. (1996). *Ngā pepa a Ranginui: The Walker papers*. Penguin.
Wan, P. M., & Wan, A. H. (2020). *Clinical sociology: Moving from theory to practice*. Springer.
Whiteley, J. S. (1986). Sociotherapy and psychotherapy in the treatment of personality disorder: Discussion paper. *Journal of the Royal Society of Medicine, 79*(12), 721–725.
Wilson, D., Mikahere-Hall, A., & Sherwood, J. (2022). Using indigenous kaupapa Māori research methodology with constructivist grounded theory: Generating a theoretical explanation of indigenous women's realities. *International Journal of Social Research Methodology, 25*(3), 375–390.

Zarine L. Rocha is a sociologist and researcher, the Editor-in-Chief of *Sociology Compass* and Managing Editor of *Current Sociology*. She is an Honorary Research Fellow at the University of Auckland, and an Affiliated Researcher at the Department of Sociology, National University of Singapore. Zarine specializes in issues of mixed race/mixed ethnic identity, narratives of belonging, multiculturalism and diversity, and clinical/applied sociology in Asia and the Pacific, and has worked as a researcher in academic institutions and international organizations, including at the United Nations Research Institute for Social Development, the United Nations Environment Programme and the World Economic Forum. She has published widely on issues of identity and belonging, race and ethnicity, and applications of sociology.

Applied Sociologists Within Applied Social Research in Aotearoa New Zealand

Charles Crothers

Introduction

An ambition of many sociologists is to be socially useful, to ensure that their work has some social *impact*. The level of commitment to this goal and how it is accomplished depends on the sector of knowledge production sociologists are located within. This chapter attempts an overview of the various modes of social knowledge production in Aotearoa New Zealand (ANZ) and how 'applied sociology'[1] is embedded in these (see Crothers, 2010c). The chapter draws on my own work and history in developing sociology as a discipline in New Zealand, and the extensive connections and networks I have within this comparatively small country and sociological community. It outlines the role of applied sociology within the main academic, governmental and other public and private institutions of the country, highlighting key individuals and projects which have been particularly influential, before outlining two key types of practical contributions that have developed in New Zealand: Social Impact Assessment and Programme Evaluation.

As elsewhere, while some academic sociologists in New Zealand have some level of engagement with applied sociology, the main heavy lifting is consigned to non-academic or 'applied' knowledge production. There are many challenges: the complexities and difficulties in providing good applied sociological advice can be quite different to the challenges offered by academic work. In academic work, understanding the real world may not necessarily be as important as framing arguments in relation to contemporary academic debates; incisive understanding of a social system in order to offer good advice concerning change (or continuance) is not necessarily the goal in academic work. However, this challenge of applied

[1] "Clinical sociology" is not a term commonly used in Aotearoa New Zealand but is seen as a particular form of applied sociology.

C. Crothers
Auckland University of Technology, Auckland, New Zealand

© The Author(s), under exclusive license to Springer Nature Switzerland AG 2023
Z. L. Rocha, K. L. Davidson (eds.), *Applied and Clinical Sociology in Aotearoa New Zealand*, Clinical Sociology: Research and Practice,
https://doi.org/10.1007/978-3-031-36581-2_5

sociology is often not recognised and it is unfortunately often assigned a lesser status.

There are some immediate difficulties in carrying out the task I have set myself here. A crucial blockage is lack of information, as while academic knowledge production can be monitored through well-established systems such as bibliographical data-systems but also the Performance-Based Research Fund (PBRF)[2] processes, annual institutional accounting and through highly visible institutional websites, there is almost no *systematic* source of information on applied sociology in Aotearoa. Moreover, applied sociology in non-academic contexts has very little visibility.[3] This information deficit throws considerable reliance onto my particular knowledge, which is where personal limitations (age, background, location etc) intrude. The account provided in this chapter is partial (partly because of space limitations) and needs to be expanded to include the 'Applied Social Research'[4] (ASR) system as a whole, rather than its artificially-limited focus on applied sociology.

In applied sociology, disciplinary labels tend to be quite irrelevant: for example, the occupational classification used by the census has no category of 'sociologist' (although see Table 2). Nor in the 'market' of knowledge production is there any obvious terminology that is frequently deployed. In Government circles 'Policy research and evaluation (PRE)' is often used, and an emerging common contemporary label is 'Insights' while 'Analytics' has grown in use as a term to refer to the utilisation of data in models.

The main purpose of *sociology* as a discipline, and those who hold identities as *sociologists*, is to produce theory and empirical evidence which aid the understanding of society and perhaps (particularly emphasised for some sociologists) can be pressed into use in monitoring social trends and effecting change.[5] To effect change can involve indirect and direct paths: sometimes described as the 'Enlightenment' and the 'Social Engineering' modes (Weiss, 1977). The two differ in being orientated towards general (for example, the public) or specific clients. The 'Enlightenment' mode can be very powerful and usually involves the vivid presentation of the social condition of a particular group, whereas 'Social engineering' usually requires 'translation' into 'social technology': programmes which deliver appropriate material and nonmaterial resources to groups of people. However, the development of such programmes is seldom amongst the skill-sets of sociologists, although they need to be acquired by most applied sociologists.

There is no official control over identification as a 'sociologist', beyond being able to win recognition as one (usually through having an appropriate advanced

[2] See https://www.tec.govt.nz/funding/funding-and-performance/funding/fund-finder/performance-based-research-fund/

[3] The Social Wellbeing Agency (SWBA) hosts a depository of some 10,000 government social research reports but only three are tagged with 'Sociology'.

[4] ASR refers to applied research which draws on any of the various social science disciplines.

[5] There is some overlap with criminologists, who increasingly see themselves as sitting separately alongside sociology.

qualification—being a 'sociology graduate'[6]). Academic sociologists have a disciplinary identity within the profession (occupation) of university teaching/research, but there are few readily available routes for becoming a *professional* applied sociologist. Indeed, applied sociologists are usually 'social (science) researchers', 'policy analysts' or some similar generic professional title, and they seldom have received training or mentoring to become applied sociologists.

Sociological knowledge production is achieved through several modes:

- Mainstream academic sociology
- Other cognate academic fields of study (e.g., Social Policy)
- University research centres
- 'Independent' research centres
- Government department (and other) research units
- Consultancies
- NGO research and policy analysis units/roles.

To some extent these different modes of knowledge production form an Applied Social Research system with each mode having a particular role. Although the relations amongst the various social research enterprises is best described in network terms, in principle, mainstream academic sociologists sit at the most prestigious level of the system, responsible for training personnel, providing ongoing training/support, getting involved in 'public sociology'/social criticism and other applied research, and ultimately validating what passes as valid knowledge.[7] However, the more applied aspects of knowledge production are often seen as below their dignity, and they do not always 'descend' into close engagement with 'real world' issues and policy/decision-making from the more theoretical concerns they rightly must attend to.

Various research centres pursue academic and/or applied research (sometimes including a capacity to mount large-scale and/or long-term projects), while smaller social research units or even sole practitioners may be linked to particular organisations. Consultancies/practitioners provide much of the in-the-field research work, but also ideas for social change. Unofficial brokers and translators mediate between components (e.g. providing media coverage, funding, and diffusion of results). Even where an agency contracts out its social research it must retain a sufficient capacity to commission and then utilise the results of social research. However, it is a very loosely fitting system,[8] partly because of commercial sensitivities amongst

[6]As distinct from those doing undergraduate 'filler' courses and Sociology undergraduate majors.

[7]Occasionally, although not to my knowledge in New Zealand, sociological associations attempt to pass judgement on the state of knowledge on a particular topic—although this is always a somewhat fraught exercise.

[8]Of its own volition, mainstream sociology often takes aboard an agenda which includes dealing with key issues of the day and endeavours to give voice to suppressed concerns. Its alertness to social hurt is sometimes (hopefully) in advance of the slower mobilising of government research and eventually policy responses: for example, the small poverty studies of the late '80s and early '90s.

competing research firms and researchers and partly because the field has few aggregating mechanisms. Applied sociology fits (almost indistinguishably) within this applied social research arena.

An underlying assumption about most applied social research is that it operates mainly within the state arena. Indeed, some Government social research is legally mandated: for example, through the Local Government Act, Health and Disability Act, Public Service Act, Resource Management Act and some programme-specific legislation (Crothers, 2010b). In comparison, evidence-informed advice to capitalism tends to be mainly left to market researchers and others more related to Business Schools and those with university education gained from them. There are some instances, though, of 'corporate sociologists' (e.g. Jeannin, 2017).[9]

As with all social phenomena, the applied sociology arena is shaped by societal and political changes (see Clayworth, 2014; Preston, 2018). In New Zealand, early ASR work in the 1930s was rather episodic (see Robb et al., 1996; Robb, 1987).[10] The first era (the 1950s) when social research became common was in a rather conservative and bureaucratically ordered world where social research (SR) was seldom deployed although research units began to be developed in the larger 'Social' State Departments. The subsequent Neoliberal period of 'Rogernomics' and 'Ruthnomics'[11] (mid-'80s to mid-'90s) emphasised the language of economics, materialities and the dourness of economic necessity. 'Audit' seemed an appropriate term for much of the research carried out, and often ideology was so prevailing that it was assumed ideas developed overseas (e.g. Neoliberalism) were applicable locally without any local scrutiny (Crothers, 2010a).[12] Since at least the turn of the Millennium, social policy in NZ (and in much of the Western world) has been seen through a 'third way' evidence-influenced frame, in which there is also considerable emphasis on community-based and controlled developments but with a particular emphasis on feasibility.[13] The policy and evaluation research implications of this approach was rehearsed in NZ by two conferences hosted by the Ministry of Social Development (MSD), including The Social Policy Research and Evaluation Conference 2003 (Pole, 2003). Alongside this there was an investment in SR offered by the Minister of Social Development (and former academic sociologist) Steve Maharey to provide $10 M for Building Research Capacity in the Social Sciences (BRCSS). Unfortunately this capacity-building was considerably subsumed by academic social scientists and the long-term effect on ASR was minimal. The

---

[9] I am unaware of any Aotearoa New Zealand sociologists embedded in the corporate world.

[10] A Bureau of Social Research was set up within the DSIR in the late 1930s studying living standards but had a short life.

[11] In this period NZ public policy took a strong neoliberal direction under first a Labour and then a National government: the terms are derived from the names of the two Ministers of Finance who were most responsible for driving this neoliberalism. While quite strong neoliberal policy impulses have continued since, this was the period of most heightened neoliberalism.

[12] If nothing else, the small scale of NZ prevented properly competitive markets arising.

[13] While the Key Government (2008–2017) reverted to a more neoliberal stance it included broader approaches such as 'social investment'.

'third way' was in part a continuation of the neoliberal approach but also extended a strengthening of the social fabric through community development.

This framework was partly continued but also partly replaced by the National Party/Bill English's 'social investment' approach which prioritised the funnelling of government interventions towards the children of 'problem' families so that the long-term mal-consequences could be limited through early targeted interventions. In this approach, much importance was placed on analyses derived from linked databases: in particular, the IDI.[14] Finally, the contemporary sixth Labour Government approach has taken a 'Social Wellbeing' lens with social goals being put in place, and measures of social progress developed, to offset solely economic objectives (see Piercy et al., 2017). One interesting and unexpected consequence has been the Treasury's deepening involvement in social research under the rubrics of Living Standards and Wellbeing. Another adroit bending to ideological winds was the renaming of the Social Investment Agency to the Social Wellbeing Agency. Also, the current (2023) Government has seemed to place much emphasis on policy development which may have given impetus to more contract research being commissioned. (For the record of payments to consultants, see Table 3 in the appendix) The 'evidence-based policymaking' movement continues its importance.

The Government in power and its guiding ideology can thus be seen as having influenced AS during each relevant period. It is more difficult to pin down the theoretical, methodological and institutional changes which may have re-shaped the social research community. Certainly one important change has been increasing inclusion of and sensitivities to Māori, Pasifika and Asian communities and knowledge, and growing openness to community inputs. Qualitative in-depth understandings tend to be more valued in some quarters, while quantitative approaches are seen as even more centrally important in others—albeit left for economists and psychologists to tackle. Although these different policy and methodological strategies imply significantly different ways in which the social research community might be arranged, in practice things have continued along a slower change trajectory.

This chapter then provides an historical and contemporaneous account of applied sociological knowledge activity in ANZ for each of the modes listed above. Emphasis is placed on ways and means in general rather than specific historical detail, so that this account provides mere glimpses of the history of AS in New Zealand.

Literature Review

Firstly, this chapter provides some review of the literature on applied sociology in general, which is considerable, although seldom precise or widely-grounded. I present a cursory review, drawing attention to NZ studies. In particular, there are

[14]Integrated Data Infrastructure (IDI) hosted by Statistics NZ, which provides a partially linked warehouse of 'social bookkeeping' data.

studies of the extent to which social researchers endeavour to communicate their findings to policy-makers and (symmetrically) the extent to which policy-makers scan the literature or read any proffered research-based advice (see Löfgren & Cavagnoli, 2015; Löfgren & Bickerton, 2022). However, research into the production of knowledge by consultancies or government researchers is seldom broached. At the time of writing, a major study into evaluation culture in ANZ, funded by a Marsden grant is underway (Cumming et al., 2021).

Governments are sometimes accused of abandoning leadership to instead run the country steered by the findings of focus groups. Yet this point should not be taken jocularly. The measuring of public opinions and practices indeed plays a crucial role in running modern states.[15] This political need is largely met by applied social research, albeit filtered through the views of policymakers and their political advisors (on Ministerial advisors, see for example Eichbaum & Shaw, 2005).

Applied sociology (and clinical sociology in other contexts) describes practitioners who use sociological theories and methods (outside of academic settings) to produce progressive social change through planned interventions (Price & Will, 2015). More specifically, applied sociology is the translation and development of sociological analysis (or more generally sociological training) into practice to answer research questions posed by specific (and sometimes general) clients.[16] A wide range of data-sources and data-analysis approaches can be deployed, with an early list suggesting: 'evaluation research, program evaluation, cost/benefit analysis, systems analysis, community ethnography, public opinion polling, and market analysis' (DeMartini, 1979: 333). The experiences of academic, applied sociologists and policy-makers are distinguished in several ways (see Crothers, 2006), as detailed in Table 1.

In a useful case study of the 'two-community model" in the New Zealand housing policy and research communities, Löfgren & Bickerton (2022: 95) found that "...although the two-community model prevails, the actual relationship between academia and policy professionals is more complex once you begin to probe into the minds of the policy professionals and cannot be reduced to two separate tribes". In studies of academic social researchers, Blewden et al. (2010) and Witten and Hammond (2010) found much claimed applied activity.

A US survey filling the empirical gap concerning applied sociologists was carried out by the American Sociological Association in 2007 (Spalter-Roth, 2007) based on the responses of 600 PhD sociologists employed in applied, research, and policy positions. Given the inclusion of only PhDs and those still retaining contact with the ASA means that the survey covers a more elite portion of the applied sociology workforce. The analysis focuses on posited correlations between professional

[15] Their essential role might particularly be revealed by case studies of Covid-related social research and social research on the consequences of the Christchurch earthquakes.

[16] Many definitions of applied sociology assume that while available sociological material is indeed fitted to applied circumstance, that it is applied rather than creatively generated (as I will argue in this chapter it often is).

Table 1 Some key differences between applied sociologists and academic sociologists

Factor	Applied Sociologists	Academic Sociologists
Outputs	Utility of their work to non-academic audience/stakeholders	Publishing in academic journals
Time orientation	Narrow constraints on time and the specificity of their work outputs	Free to choose their research topic; longer time-frame with which to develop their scholarship
Standards	Adhere to scholarship 'only to the extent necessary to achieve usable results'	Adhere to 'absolute norms' of rigorous scholarship
Validity criterion	More concerned with 'external validity', that is, the extent to which their conclusions speak directly to their specific client's topic area	'Internal validity'—to making a contribution to the academic literature, and the judgements of their peers
Drivers/motives	Practical payoffs	Theoretical contributions, 'discoveries'
Criteria in judging the success of their work	Client's adoption of their proposed solutions, and their ability to influence their stakeholders' decision-making	Work does not always lead to specific actions

characteristics, such as how use of specialized knowledge, autonomy, ethical norms, and basic research, are related to overall job satisfaction and satisfaction with economic security. The study confirmed these linkages.

However, space limitations preclude further exploration of the literature. The remainder of this chapter works through each of the modes of knowledge production.

Mainstream Academic Sociology Departments

While many NZ academic sociologists have engaged in applied sociology, it is not a prevalent activity. While applied concerns were built into the establishment of sociology in NZ, over time such commitments seem to have gradually faded. One example of this is that the Sociological Association of Aotearoa New Zealand (SAANZ) issued various public statements in its early days but has not done so recently. The following account briefly describes applied sociology in each of the departments, in order of their founding (more generally see Crothers, 2017; 2020; 2021).

Historically, NZ Sociology has been organised in separate Departments (albeit with attached fields of study) although more recently Sociology and other former disciplines are now programmes within broader (and larger) Schools.[17] There are a

[17] The process of School formation seems seldom studied.

variety of ways academic sociologies can be involved in applied sociology. From time to time departments develop an orientation or climate which is more or less orientated towards applied sociology. Some appointments and their teaching may be quite applied (e.g. Sociology of Health offered as a mainstream sociology course). Being within Schools alongside more applied social researchers can nudge sociologists into more applied-compatibility, since Sociology departments/Schools over time have variously housed demography, social policy, social work, criminology and women's/gender studies and social research methods.[18] Some research projects are also likely to have applied aspects—for example, the community surveys often deploying students which were so-often mounted in the earlier decades, and many current research projects will also require some engagement with communities (Crothers, 2018). To get funding for research projects, recourse may necessarily be made in some instances to research funding tied to applied aspects. A recent teaching innovation (e.g. Tolich & Shephard, 2014) has been to further train students by setting up placements in the community. Other programmes have also offered internships from time to time and have offered papers providing applied sociological content.

Academics are often approached by the media for expert comment and this can be an important way in which the public exposure of sociology is increased. 'Op eds' offered to the media are an example of a staff-initiated variant of this. However, neither of these modes of engagement with the public tend to include many sociologists since it affords little academic recognition and may actually be seen as detrimental to careers (since other sociologists are the more preferred audience). Serving on government advisory committees and similar, or providing expert evidence submissions to these is another applied route.

Applied Sociology Around the Universities

Applied sociology was built into the foundation of NZ academic sociology, albeit often through piecemeal efforts which were not particularly based on fresh empirical research. The main institutions are outlined below.

Victoria University of Wellington

The School of Social Science was established at Victoria University College in 1949 with a special grant from the government underwriting the 2-year postgraduate diploma for training professional social workers. Jim Robb was appointed, later

[18]Practitioners of these cognate fields are not considered in this chapter unless they seemed to have a more determinant allegiance to mainstream sociology.

becoming a Professor (see Kirkman, 2012). His extensive experience in London provided a good foundation for when he was later involved with the establishment of the New Zealand Marriage Guidance and other similar enterprises, including providing support for Homosexual Law Reform. With John McCreary (appointed in 1953 to teach in the School of Social Sciences and who later became the Professor of Social Work) they carried out a series of surveys using the group of social work students, some at the behest of the Departments of Health and Social Security and/or local stakeholders. The Department's link with applied concerns continued—variously involving Social Administration, Social Work, Social Policy, Applied Social Studies—although these were all eventually excised. While Jim was a role model for 'Public Sociology', his colleagues have not carried on his involvements. Allan Levett (Crothers and Dwyer, 2010) brought in several American approaches to policy development in the NZ Labour Party and developed survey work on political networks.

University of Canterbury

Canterbury University's Richard Thompson was intensely opposed to NZ's 1960s sporting contacts with apartheid South Africa and channelled his anti-racism involvements into the long-standing Citizens Association for Racial Equality (CARE) which he cofounded in 1964.[19] A later Professor, Bill Willmott, was committed to fostering a distinctive New Zealand sociology that engaged critically with contemporary issues and state policy. From at least the mid-1970s the Canterbury department consolidated its cross-disciplinary orientation, engagement with contemporary political debate and its links with community organisations. There was a focus in the teaching of first year sociology to make students aware of critical analyses of both other cultures and local political, cultural and economic practices. To further this, community activists would be invited to lecture in order to make connections between lecture topics and efforts at community social change. Later, during the late 1990s and early 2000s, Professor David Thorns guided the building of a Social Science Research Centre (SSRC), which was multi-disciplinary and included applied social researchers from government and private businesses. It housed various externally funded research projects and visiting academics.

[19] Thompson reports that he was later excluded from consideration as a professor at CU because of his protest involvements.

University of Auckland

Early University of Auckland staff in the 1970s included Dr. Ranginui Walker, who went on to become one of NZ's leading Māori scholars, and other applied sociologists including an urban planner and a local clergyman. There were many community surveys and there had also long been a limited range of service teaching (Engineers, Planning, Real estate students) which provided some links to non-sociology students. Auckland sociologists debated other writings—e.g. stringent criticism of 'pop sociology' work on "Theory K" which attempted to produce management guidance for New Zealand firms based on a range of case studies.

In the early 1980s, Macpherson and Crothers were involved at the behest of sociology-graduate area commander Superintendent Jim Morgan in providing evidence that would support developing conceptions of community policing based on extensive surveys in South Auckland. The ensuing discussion at Police HQ with all the insignia-laden regional commanders with a supportive Police Commissioner was an interesting experience, which did assist in propelling the NZ police forward deploying this approach. Claudia Bell's (1996) very visible sociology thesis on rural New Zealand was transformed into a widely popular book *Inventing New Zealand,* and sequalae on the public symbolism of small town New Zealand became a TV program. Professor Maureen Baker came from Canada in the late 1990s, bringing with her a comparative interest across Canada, Australia and New Zealand. She carefully produced a series of small empirically-based studies and texts on family and family policy. Professor Peter Davis was appointed to the department in 2004 and brought with him a quite 'alien' quantitative tradition in research and an interest in agency-theory born of long experience in the health sector and in his previous positions in Public Health at the University of Otago, Christchurch and, earlier, the University of Auckland Medical School (see Davis, 2004). As the funding environment opened up and a succession of large financial research grants was obtained he set up the Centre of Methods and Policy Application in the Social Sciences (COMPASS). In turn this supply of grant moneys allowed the hiring of research-only specialist personnel.

Professor Tracey McIntosh, another Auckland sociology graduate and now staff member, has been heavily involved with university administration on matters of equity and, later, in running *Ngā Pae o te Māramatanga*, the Māori Centre of Research Excellence in which capacity she produced journals and edited books on ethnic identity. In 2012 she was the co-chair of the Children's Commissioner's Expert Advisory Group on Solutions to Child Poverty, and still sits on a number of governance boards, particularly in the area of social harm reduction including the Robson Hanan Trust: Rethinking Crime and Punishment and *Te Waka Moemoea: Being the Change Trust* while also being the Science advisor to MSD.

Robert Webb has been active in the running of the Māori Association of Social Scientists (MASS) and in criminological research and critique.

Waikato University

A key part of the founding of Waikato University in the mid-1960s was Vice-Chancellor Llewellyn's conviction that the university should be an integral part of the Waikato and Hamilton community. Links included public lecture series and staff involvement in community groups, as well as more academic enterprises such as the School of Social Sciences' interdisciplinary longitudinal study in the 1970s on the social and economic impacts of the construction of the Huntly thermal power station, funded by the Ministry of Works and Development. Again, there were community surveys and other applied studies.

Massey University

Massey University's well-regarded Merv Hancock was President of the New Zealand Association of Social Workers (NZASW) (1964–65), and while on MU staff, actively supported the establishing of sociology in universities as a discipline critical to social work and important in its own right. Thirty years after he was President of the NZASW, he became President of SAANZ in 1995.

By the late 1970s, growing internal class sizes and distance education created a need for new staff. Appointment of blind sociologist Peter Beatson led to the enrolment of a modest number of blind and partially sighted students.[20] The writing of extramural study guides helped develop material which met the felt need to address New Zealand sensitivities and experiences—for teaching material that 'spoke' to New Zealand students. Local research blossomed too: for example, in 1988, Christine Cheyne obtained a grant from the Commission for Justice, Peace and Development to investigate sexism in the Catholic Church. Public commentary was provided on the Commission of Inquiry into Pornography alongside submissions to the relevant authorities on various relevant topics.

In the 1980s, staff in the Department used block-mode face-to-face teaching to provide courses on key features of New Zealand society for the Senior Inspectors' Qualifying Course at the Police College in Porirua. These 1980s developments occurred under the continued leadership of Graeme Fraser (see Spoonley, 2003) who by the late 1980s combined his role as head of sociology with that of Assistant Vice-Chancellor adding over time many other administrative and research advisory body positions. The department strengths were in areas such as gender and sexuality, class and the critique of neoliberalism, racism and ethnicity, and public policy.

[20] Peter's seeing-eye dog had to become an honorary member of the Department's staff so she could attend lectures and staff meetings if necessary!

Lincoln University

Lincoln University has never had a sociology department, but its sociological interests go back to the 1930s. The Agricultural Economics Research Unit (AERU) added sociology with the appointment of Research Sociologist John Fairweather in 1984 who led research over three decades into the effects of the policy changes which New Zealand agriculture had undergone following the withdrawal of farm subsidies in the mid-1980s. During this period, though, the impacts of the structural reforms of the era led to a marked decline in the AERU's core funding, the end of funding for a long-running series of farmer surveys, and a dramatic reduction in staff numbers. Related work on rural employment relations continued including from 2000 another Ministry of Agriculture project on the shortage of farm labour and related topics such as employment needs and farmer stress.

Auckland University of Technology

AUT has always been something of an applied (and multi-disciplinary) outpost of the AU department. Sociology was seen as one of the four foundations and was carefully built on in subsequent teaching years (see Crothers, 2004). Sociology was also implicated in the development of criminology as a new undergraduate major in 2007, which has expanded to become more important than the social science parent. Some social research methodology training was provided at post graduate level with courses on policy development and different modes of applied social research methodology.

University of Otago

Otago University was the most recently established sociology programme, but more informal engagements can be traced back to the 1920s and the University still hosts several sociologists across other departments. While its programme is not particularly noted for applied aspects, an internship programme is an interesting development.

From time to time overseas-domiciled sociologists have explored applied sociology themes in New Zealand: one example has been an interest in the Accident Compensation Commission (ACC) (Vosburgh and Kronick, 1980: this group had strong NZ connections).

In sum, applied sociology has been favoured from the early days at Victoria University of Wellington, for a more extended period at Canterbury University and intermittently at Massey University, Lincoln University and Auckland University of Technology. These differences in receptiveness to applied sociology arise in considerable part because of both size (at least in terms of social science complements) but also because of the non-mainstream applied ideology of the latter two universities.

Other Academic Sub-types of Sociology

Sociologists are also strung across a variety of Schools, many applied—such as Schools of education, health, and sports, etc. Adherents to these more specialist sociologies often have not had mainstream sociology training and may have little association with mainstream sociologists. Their teaching is often aimed at the training of practitioners and their research at the operation of practitioner activities and so tends to be inherently more applied, although such sociologists nevertheless often contribute substantially to academic work. All these specialties are present in NZ (for more detail, see collection in Crothers, 2016).

University Research Centres

At various times, research centres of varying lifespans have been set up to carry out (large-scale/long-term) research projects or to facilitate these. These may have a capacity for carrying out fieldwork and providing a platform for consideration of methodological developments (e.g. COMPASS's development of the Socio-economic Index (SEI) scale for measuring the status of occupations) or wider reflections and cumulation. Peter Davis set up the University of Auckland's COMPASS[21] around 2000 and this is still continuing (albeit with little attachment to the School of Social Sciences), while the former Canterbury Social Science Centre set up by David Thorns did not last long. In addition, some research programmes which receive medium-term funding may set up appropriate medium-term research entities to house them. Only a few NZ sociologists have been involved with large-scale projects so most have not had much need of support from research centres. One exception was Louise Humpage (see 2015) in her work on attitudes to the welfare state which drew on support from COMPASS.

An interesting personal account of working on a major project has been provided by Mike Lloyd (1991) who was catapulted into working with the longitudinal Christchurch Health and Development Study (CHDS)[22] after being trained in a postgraduate methods course that had left him ill-equipped for this very quantitative environment. He was able to adapt sufficiently to gain some useful skills and

[21] A research team undertaking quantitative social science research with particular policy relevance.

[22] The CHDS followed the health, education, and life progress of 1265 children born in the Christchurch urban region in mid-1977, with frequent rounds of interviewing.

findings from the experience. Rosemary Du Plessis (1992) provides a case study in the politics of research programmes, pointing out that with her involvement in a large-scale project on women's employment, complex issues of intellectual property and control arose. There are also some more descriptive accounts of applied sociology units (see, for example, Butcher, 2009 on the Asia NZ Foundation platform of surveys).

'Independent' Research Centres (IRCs)[23]

Another avenue for knowledge production is through 'think tanks' and IRCs which may from time to time employ sociologists or deploy a sociological frame of understanding. Many NGOs (e.g. Mental Health Foundation) include a research function and sociologists may get drawn into these (although few examples come to mind). There are some voluntary organisations which have been research-focused. The Society for Research on Women was heavily populated with sociologists (mainly women) and carried out large-scale studies (e.g. a Survey on Urban Women). More recently, the Child Poverty Action Group (including amongst its volunteers sociologist Gerry Cotterell) often produced documentation of people experiencing various particular types of difficulty. Some interest groups invest in social research as a weapon in moral battles over issues such as homosexuality, abortion, euthanasia or marijuana, with the data from these becoming potential data platforms for subsequent sociological analyses. Some iwi also have research units and another research area where sociologists have been involved in the (distant) past are the several Parliamentary research units providing advice to the MPs of political parties.

Government Department (and Other) Research Units

Since the 1950s various government departments have built-up (and occasionally reduced!) research units, some with staffing including sociologists. "For large departments and agencies this development tends to follow a natural growth path reflecting the organisation's needs and the information and advice needs of the government. This path usually begins with the analysis of administrative information and the search for relevant research findings from outside the organisation, and grows in particular areas such as qualitative research. For large entities this has

[23] There have been few NZ equivalents to investigative journalists such as Pilger although some social issues journalists (e.g. Simon Collins from the *NZ Herald;* Gordon Campbell earlier from the *NZ Listener* and Max Rashbrooke now with VUW—see Rashbrooke, 2016) have written interesting material.

meant the development of specific research, evaluation, statistical and analytic capabilities" (Preston, 2018: 6). Preston goes on to point out that "Within departments, the research units with the longest life spans are those associated with delivering core social services, particularly public education, public health, social security and the justice system" (Preston, 2018: 64). All such units face a trade-off between using external versus in-house research, although at least a minimum of the latter is needed to oversee the former. They usually have an immense ability (if they choose) to mobilise very considerable resources to support social research.

In earlier eras, any sociologists would be employed within the overall 007 clerical class as investigating officers (or similar) and would carry out a range of research-related tasks from their desks. More recently they are engaged across the Public Service as Policy Analysts (PAs) which includes a variety of tasks and includes staff with a variety of training. Some further research training may be available (e.g., see Forbes & Keegan, 2016). Data on how PAs are distributed across the public service is available (see Table 2) and there is also census data: there are some 3500 PAs and their growth flows and ebbs according to Government policies. Necessarily, the vast majority of PAs are located in Wellington, at the seat of Government. For some 35 years (from around 1980), regular meetings (and/or other activities) were held by the Association of Social Science Research (ASSR), set up by sociologist Tom Dwyer. In the Central government some other coordination arrangements have been in place from time-to-time most notably MSD-supported SPEAR (coordinated by Raewyn Good) and for a period MSD hosted the *Social Policy Journal of NZ* (SPJNZ), although there are some difficulties in running 'open' research-support while keeping Ministers at arms-length. The 'Policy Project' attempts to provide learning support for policy analysts, but does not seem to extend to more specific social research method skills. Recently a cross-agency Research and Evaluation Managers forum has been supported by the Ministry of Education, which might also provide some reach across the various sectors. Applied sociology is also conducted within Local government, with Auckland Council's Research, Investigation and Monitoring unit (RIMU) particularly prominent. An alliance of the larger local governments sponsors a large quantity of life survey reports every other year.

Again, earlier engagements have not been sustained. In the mid-1970s a substantial cohort of sociology graduates from Canterbury University (including Waghorne and Thorns) with a few from VUW: (such as Tait, Crothers, Dwyer and Toynbee) descended on Wellington taking up jobs across various departments and also the Labour Party Policy Research Unit (LPRU). They sensed they were in a powerful position to leverage data which would provide insights into society. One result was the drawing up of a manifesto, (Tait et al., 1981) presented at a Wellington SAANZ conference proclaiming that the future of Sociology in NZ lay with Applied Sociology! Somewhat in the manner of chain migration, some departments have been more prone to employ sociologists—e.g. Department of Internal Affairs, Statistics NZ, Ministry of Works and Development, Ministry of Social Development and earlier the Department of Scientific and Industrial Research (DSIR) and the Labour Party Research Unit. However, there is little to distinguish the work of sociologists from other researchers in these settings.

Table 2 Policy analysts: data source—PSC Workforce data

Unit	2020	Percent of policy analysts	Percent of total	Annual change (%)
Crown Law Office				
Department of Conservation	49.0	2.03	1.59	113.04
Department of Corrections	55.0	0.56	1.79	30.95
Department of Internal Affairs	197.0	8.27	6.41	2.60
Department of the Prime Minister and Cabinet	76.6	41.14	2.49	6.54
Education Review Office	6.0	2.88	0.20	3.45
Inland Revenue Department	64.0	1.35	2.08	4.92
Land Information New Zealand	16.9	2.34	0.55	181.67
Ministry for Culture and Heritage	49.0	37.40	1.59	35.73
Ministry for Pacific Peoples	13.7	20.33	0.44	95.43
Ministry for Primary Industries	261.0	7.77	8.49	45.00
Ministry for Women	290.3	59.03	9.44	58.03
Ministry for the Environment	16.7	47.19	0.54	36.79
Ministry of Business, Innovation and Employment	318.0	6.80	10.34	25.20
Ministry of Defence	42.8	27.30	1.39	78.33
Ministry of Education	110.0	3.16	3.58	48.65
Ministry of Foreign Affairs and Trade	529.0	46.69	17.21	33.59
Ministry of Health	61.0	5.14	1.98	−75.30
Ministry of Housing and Urban Development	86.9	28.75	2.83	
Ministry of Justice	43.0	1.08	1.40	−64.17
Ministry of Māori Development	88.4	25.75	2.88	32.73
Ministry of Social Development	78.0	0.98	2.54	−12.36
Ministry of Transport	95.2	56.40	3.10	50.63
National Emergency Management Agency	45.1	70.36	1.47	
New Zealand Customs Service	34.0	2.66	1.11	21.43
Office for Māori Crown Relations—Te Arawhi				
Oranga Tamariki-Ministry for Children	52.0	1.12	1.69	
Pike River Recovery Agency				
Public Service Commission	85.6	52.26	2.78	21.59
Social Wellbeing Agency				
Statistics New Zealand	3.0	0.27	0.10	−50.00
The Treasury	307.0	53.47	9.99	36.81

N = 3074

In the new Millennium there was an increased presence of sociologists in the public sphere of government at higher levels (than before) and from outside academia: some notable examples include Steve Maharey (Minister of Social Development), Paul Spoonley, Graeme Fraser (especially on the Health Research Council), Geoff Fougere (through the National Health Committee[24]), Rosemary du Plessis (for example, with Ministry for Research), Peter Davis, Christine Cheyne (Ministerial advisor in the Prime Minister's office), Rose Barrington (whose last posting was with the Ministry of Transport, see Barrington and Gray, 1981 and Davey and Crothers, 2013) and Phil Harington (Lotteries Board). This was a broad move supported by a sympathetic post-1999 Labour-led government with which there was a substantial overlap of personnel. Several SAANZ conference themes in the early 2000s were on the relationship of sociology to policy (although not all that much of the material in such conferences was on this topic).

Some methodologies become particularly fashionable in the public services from time to time: one particularly popular at the time of writing is behavioural economics (see Hampton & Adams, 2018).[25] When DSIR was split into component units, the New Zealand Institute for Social Research and Development was set up involving several sociologists under the directorship of Peggy Koopman-Boyden, but it was under-funded and closed after a few years.

Consultancies and Independent Practitioners

There are a variety of social research consultancies in NZ, some run by self-employed sociologists or including sociologists amongst the staff. Larger and more established consultancies may have their own capacity for carrying out fieldwork, including surveys. Others may be only very sporadically involved in consultancy work. The range of consultancies also varies from those providing routine services to those on the cutting edge who have developed their own research programmes. Although some consultants can amass enough discretionary space to do more self-directed work, most consultancy work is under the direction of clients who are paying the bill. Consultancies are brought in to supplement in-house expertise and capacities.

[24]The National Health Committee was originally a creature of National's health reforms, charged with drawing up a list of treatments that would be publicly funded. It failed in this task but gradually repurposed itself as a health system think tank. This gained further momentum after Labour's 1999 election victory. Labour also incorporated into it the Public Health Advisory Committee which took on some of the role that the Public Health Commission had previously had (and Fougere latterly came to chair). When National returned to office in 2008 they essentially disestablished the Public Health Advisory Committee.

[25]Behavioural economics (in distinction from more classical models) studies the effects of psychological, cognitive, emotional, cultural and social factors on the decisions of individuals or institutions.

Various issues arise with consultancy work, particularly the running of a business. Getting ethical clearances can be difficult although such services may be supplied by the client, through guest appearances with a University Ethics Committee or by utilising Martin Tolich's Aotearoa Research Ethics Committee.[26] Potential government contracts are supposed to be advertised on the Government procurement system, GETS. Consultants operate under time as well as spending constraints, but above all they have the particular constraint of needing to come up in a timely manner with clearly presented and valid results and sometimes innovative solutions to difficult client concerns. Their work may be shelved by the client or at best appear in the grey literature (as a report on a website), although a little is published academically. Given the political nature of government programmes sometimes research/evaluation is undoubtedly designed to 'park' an issue. Thus, recommendations arising from research are not always followed.

There are some commonalities across ASR but there is also an array of approaches each with their own texts, vocabularies and organisational arrangements. Two of the most prominent of these are Social Impact Assessment (SIA) and Programme Evaluation (PE). Others include social indicators, environment scanning etc. Many applied sociology researchers cleave to professional roles within one or other of these genres. There is no particular unique 'applied sociology' outside these multi-disciplinary approaches, but sociologists have been prominent in some. The NZ situation broadly replicates that of other similar jurisdictions, with a particular point that NZ sociologists have been internationally prominent in some areas of applied sociology, especially SIA.

Social Impact Assessment

SIA internationally has seen a major NZ contribution (see Taylor et al. 2004; Taylor & MacKay, 2016), along with that from other 'settler dominions' where there is still considerable natural resource development and infrastructure construction activities, thus requiring SIA, often mandatorily. SIA is a component of environmental impact assessment (EIA), and involves a combination of social research, social monitoring and social development activities. The local foundation for SIA arose in the era of "think big" industrial development of the 1970s, and this impetus continued into the neoliberal era of project planning by private developers under the Resource Management Act 1991. This Act mandated SIA for hearings involving large development projects. Those involved in SIA extended this bread and butter work into broader social considerations of planning, sustainability, resource management and social change in New Zealand. SIA has been carried out from different work auspices, including central government, universities, regional and local government, private sector firms and self-employed researchers: often combinations have been fruitful.

[26] https://aotearoaresearchethics.org/

Other social scientists, particularly human geographers and anthropologists, have also been active in SIA. In the early 1970s a number of large-scale infrastructure projects, which had been part of the government's post-war development strategy, were beginning to wind-down. The social cohesion of the construction workforce and its temporary settlements (single industry boom towns) were also of policy concern. In the late 1970s, an extensive monitoring programme was set up to cover the impacts of the Huntly power station construction. At that time the New Zealand Government began to plan a second round of large-scale infrastructure programmes under a policy known as "Think Big" to provide employment but also increase NZ's self-sufficiency in energy resources. SIA projects exploring likely outcomes were developed for these, and research into mobile workforces was also conducted.

In Canterbury, a group of early SIA practitioners, including Nick Taylor (PhD in environmental sociology from CU, also Colin Goodrich from CU) began working out of the Joint Centre for Environmental Studies (later the Centre for Resource Management: CRM), at Lincoln University. As well as carrying out major field investigations, the group were particularly interested in establishing SIA in New Zealand as a theoretically-based enterprise, influenced by the strands of environmental sociology, (rural and small town) community studies and development theory set within a world systems framework. Building up the methodological basis for SIA practice was also invested in, including systematising procedures for data collection and analysis. SIA courses and teaching resources were developed, with the teaching of SIA beginning in the Sociology Department at the CU in 1983, while in-service training was also offered. Eventually a co-authored book on social assessment theory, methods and practice was published by the Centre for Resource Management in 1990 and this has been expanded and updated since.

At the national level the New Zealand Social Impact Assessment Working Group was set up following a series of workshops in Wellington in 1984, and became in 1990 a formal professional organisation: the New Zealand Association for Social Assessment (NZASA). The key annual event is the conference, most focusing on a single theme—e.g. transport in 2013. Several international conferences have also been hosted. NZASA was more recently recast as the New Zealand Association for Impact Assessment (NZAIA) signposting a broader mandate. The Association publishes *Impact Connector* which is a series of articles and opinion pieces by practitioners and academics working in the field of impact assessment, with each issue having a theme (generally a type of impact assessment).

A Social Policy Unit and associated Research Section in the Ministry of Works and Development (MWD) and the Department of Internal Affairs (community development) were important early (but long since dismantled) bases for the development of policy responses and practical interventions in assessing the social impacts of major projects, and related topics such as the changing provision of rural services. As neoliberal restructuring developed, remnants of the social policy section of the MWD went to the State Services Commission working specifically on managing the impacts of state-sector 'restructuring' (labour shedding) in sectors such as forestry and mining as well as on the project wind-downs of construction work from the "Think Big" era.

In the early 1990s a small Social Science Unit in DSIR which theorised around technological change was expanded. It later became a short-lived Crown Research Institute. With shifting funding priorities, SIA researchers in this area suffered from funding cuts, forcing individuals to seek employment opportunities elsewhere or to establish their own private practices. The statutory requirement under the Resource Management Act provided a steady flow of work for many private sector SIA practitioners who have applied their expertise, for example, to exploring the social implications of hydro-scheme and irrigation development proposals, waste management facilities, mining applications, transport corridors, shopping malls and retail precincts, prisons, stadia developments and modifications to ports and airports. Other legalisation has also required or prompted SIAs, particularly for developments associated with casinos, fisheries, deep-sea mining operations, marine reserves and national parks.

Programme Evaluation

Another major arm of ASR in NZ is programme evaluation (for a set of locally-orientated essays see Lunt et al., 2003). Evaluation studies stretch back quite far into the history of the ANZ welfare state, and have become ever-more expanded. By the 1980s, Australasian organising of professional programme evaluation began, and ANZ branches of the Australasian association developed and then the Aotearoa New Zealand Evaluation Association (ANZEA) in 2006. There are regular conferences, a newsletter and a journal[27] and the association is particularly concerned to develop appropriate local (and indigenous) approaches to evaluation. Within the association are the Mā te Rae—Māori Evaluation Association and ANZEA Pasifika Fono which are concerned with mobilising evaluation as a tool for transformation for Iwi Māori and Pacific peoples respectively. ANZEA has a board comprising academics, government staff and applied practitioners which provides some linkages amongst evaluators across work locations. Some data is available about members of the association—three quarters are women and half domiciled in Wellington. The profession has a relatively young age structure (compared to many occupations) with a modal age-category 45–54. Forty per cent are employed in Central Government (apparently including many Education Review Office field staff), 20% are independent consultants, with around 10% each in local government, not-for-profit, corporate consulting and academia.

There has been substantial involvement by government agencies in evaluation research (and standards governing this), with government from around 2010 establishing its own central evaluation unit (Social Policy Agency now SWBA).

[27] *Evaluation Matters—He Take Tō Te Aromatawai* is an international, inter-disciplinary, peer-reviewed journal published annually by ANZEA and the New Zealand Council for Educational Research (NZCER) and the association also co-sponsors then *Evaluation Journal of Australasia* (*EJA*).

Other agencies (including nongovernmental ones) are also active in the domain. The Ministry of Education hosts a Cross-agency Research and Evaluation Managers forum but it has yet to be effective.

Market Research/'Insights'

It is only market research firms (and indeed only some of these) which have the capacity to carry out large scale social research. There is much change in marketing market research and it is now portrayed as not needing 'market' as a qualifier, and the terminology of 'insights' is instead used. Another new development is the further offering of data analysis and conceptualisation services which were not usual in earlier market research, which tended to stop with the provision of a report and/or an accompanying briefing. Market research is a full-scale industry with a very active representative association (Research Association New Zealand (RANZ) with some 650 on its membership listing and over 30 firms) and even then some operate outside the RANZ framework. Several sociology graduates have been in leading positions within market research firms but it is not an area where many can be found, perhaps because of quantitative skill deficits.

Social Indicators

Another line of development of applied sociologists has involved Social Indicators (SI). In 1974 a SI unit was set up within the Department of Statistics including sociologists Margaret Shields (Crothers and de Joux, 2015), Paul Brown, Denise Brown and David Tait. They drew up listings of variables of available data, published a compendium of these and then carried out a SI survey. In 1976 a seminar to consolidate this work was held under the auspices of the Social Sciences committee of the UNESCO Commission, which brought together various sociologists (Crothers, Davis, and Swain) and geographers who were more concerned with territorial indicators. However, this first wave of the SI movement faltered while NZ was distractedly plunged into coping with the deleterious social outcomes of Rogernomics.

However, SI was too good a conception to die, and there was a reversion around the turn of the century. In 2000 I pulled together a set of trend indicators and published these in the *Social Policy Journal of New Zealand* (Crothers, 2000). The Minister of Social Development (sociologist Steve Maharey), enthused by the social indicator work he'd seen in a trip to the UK, pushed the then-Agency into developing a 'Social Report', steered to some extent by an advisory group. This report drew on a range of indicators and was carefully developed and evaluated to ensure consistency and thoroughness. It was issued yearly over the next decade until being shut down when there was a change of government. The Social Report was designed to provide an 'early warning' of the development of social issues in relation to particular groups and deployed some useful visual aids to assist with interpretations.

Conclusion

Applied social research thus faces many challenges that arise from the difficulties which festoon society. Usually at the behest of sponsors, researchers provide advice on impact and how to overcome or at least ameliorate social difficulties—or more rarely, advice about further possibilities which might be pursued. The field in which ASR operates is poorly developed institutionally in NZ although there are some structures present. The several professional sub-fields are competitive arenas and there is little overview of the overall social research enterprise—as in some overseas jurisdictions.[28]

Academia, mainly organised in terms of water-tight disciplines, is poorly articulated within applied social research. Disciplinarity makes little sense in applied sociology—and in fact makes little sense in academia! In Aotearoa New Zealand, applied sociology arises in some sectors of academia but is mainly embedded in several professional fields. Academic sociologists are little engaged with these, and sociology graduates finding their way to jobs are little assisted either by prior training or ongoing support (Crothers, 2017). SAANZ conference attendance by applied sociologists is sporadic. There is almost no teaching support, although there has been from time to time in decades past. Yet applied sociology has a large store of practical knowledge about what is happening on the ground and what works, and mechanisms need to be organised to promote better access to this knowledge stock.

In contrast, the several applied sociology associations—New Zealand Association for Impact Assessment (NZAIA) and Aotearoa New Zealand Evaluation Association (ANZEA) and also the Research Association New Zealand (RANZ)—provide much support: particularly in indicating standards which should pertain in their work and providing some training to bring members' skill-sets up to these standards. They provide other professional opportunities (conferences, journals) and advocate for their brand of social research.

Inevitably some strains and gaps open up. One is the limited quantitative skills of many applied sociologists (see Cotterell & von Randow, 2010). Yet, how can one understand modern societies without using census/survey data and the like (although ethnographic grounding is needed in any research)? The lack of up-take of quantitative options is ironic just when governments are extensively turning to such data. This leaves the field to economists and psychologists because they are quantitatively trained: unfortunately they are trained and tend to use powerful statistics which are difficult to comprehend and the ethnographic grounding is likely not present.

I would like to conclude this chapter on a personal note. The 2015 SAANZ conference, organised by Maxine Campbell, was held at the University of Waikato and celebrated applied sociology with keynote addresses and panels on experiences of

[28] For example, the UK Chief Research Officer. Social research related to Covid seemed well organised and coordinated because of the UK's SR coordinating institutions. See Burnett & Duncan (2008).

social change by sociologists across a range of historical episodes.[29] Three years later when the 2018 SAANZ conference was to be held at VUW it occurred to me that the organisers might not notice that their offices overlooked an array of downtown buildings where various applied sociologists and other researchers were accommodated and I volunteered to organise a pair of sessions putting on the roster researchers from the Social Policy Evaluation and Research Unit (Superu), MSD, Treasury, SWBA, the Department of the Prime Minister and Cabinet (DPMC) and others. I thought this would provide opportunities for academics to find out about and critique Government applied sociology research work and also perhaps forge links of advantage to the employment prospects of Postgraduate students. While the sessions went well, there was no interest from the academic sociologists attending the conference. Rather bemusedly I noticed later that on the table with attendees' name-tags there were several from the DPMC who, as always happens in Wellington, had been called away on more urgent tasks: yet how many SAANZ conferences are in part funded by DPMC?

Editor's Note: Charles Crothers sadly passed away in August 2023, before he could see this chapter published. We are grateful to him for sharing his thoughts and expertise in this piece.

Appendix

This appendix provides information relevant to applied sociology, although this information refers to ASR more generally.

Census Data: Classifications

AS are buried within various Census categories. Being a sociologist is not separately accounted for in the Stats NZ occupation classification. Academic sociologists are usually defined as University teachers. Some policy analysts may well be sociologists and there is a residual category of 'other social professionals nec' which includes many from sociology and related disciplinary backgrounds. At the 2018 census there were 7,353 policy analysts and 5568 Social Professions nec. As well as the descriptions relating to specific occupations, those relating to the higher-order unit group are also included. Although claiming of an occupation is the prerogative of respondents, the Occupational coding provides useful indications of what is involved.

[29] In 2022 SAANZ talks organised by younger sociologists also featured Applied Sociology.

Unit Group 2244 Intelligence and Policy Analysts

INTELLIGENCE AND POLICY ANALYSTS collect and analyse information and data to produce intelligence and to develop and analyse policies guiding the design, implementation and modification of government and commercial operations and programs.

Indicative Skill Level

Most occupations in this unit group have a level of skill commensurate with a bachelor degree or higher qualification. At least five years of relevant experience may substitute for the formal qualification. In some instances relevant experience and/or on-the-job training may be required in addition to the formal qualification (ANZSCO Skill Level 1).

Tasks Include

- determining organisational and client intelligence requirements
- organising, collecting, collating and analysing data, and developing intelligence information such as electronic surveillance
- compiling and disseminating intelligence information using briefings, maps, charts, reports and other methods
- ascertaining the accuracy of data collected and reliability of sources
- conducting threat and risk assessments and developing responses
- liaising and consulting with program administrators and other interested parties to identify policy needs
- reviewing existing policies and legislation to identify anomalies and out-of-date provisions
- researching social, economic and industrial trends, and client expectations of programs and services provided
- formulating and analysing policy options, preparing briefing papers and recommendations for policy changes, and advising on preferred options
- assessing impacts, financial implications, interactions with other programs and political and administrative feasibility of policies

Occupations

224411 Intelligence Officer
224412 Policy Analyst

224411 INTELLIGENCE OFFICER (Collects and analyses information and data to produce intelligence for an organisation to support planning, operations and human resource functions. Specialisations: Criminal Intelligence Analyst; Defence Intelligence Analyst

224412 POLICY ANALYST (Policy Adviser) Develops and analyses policies guiding the design, implementation and modification of government or commercial operations and programs.

Unit Group: 2724 Social Professionals

Research and study human behaviour, society and institutions from current and historical perspectives, and verbally render spoken statements, and transcribe text and recorded spoken material from one language into another.

Tasks

- Assembling historical data by consulting sources of information such as historical indexes and catalogues, archives, court records, diaries, newspaper files and other materials
- Organising, authenticating, evaluating and interpreting historical, political, sociological, archaeological, anthropological and linguistic data
- Undertaking historical and cultural research into human activity, and preparing and presenting research findings
- Providing simultaneous and consecutive verbal or signed renditions of speeches into another language
- Rendering the meaning and feeling of what is said and signed into another language in the appropriate register and style in a range of settings such as courts, hospitals, schools, workplaces and conferences
- Studying original texts and transcripts of recorded spoken material to comprehend subject matter and translating them into another language

272499 Social Professionals nec (not elsewhere classified)

Occupations in this group include:

Anthropologist; Criminologist; Geographer; Heritage Consultant; Linguist; Parole Board Member; Political Scientist; Sociologist; Transport Analyst.

(1) Government Workforce Data

Policy analyst is one of some 11 occupations on which data is provided.

(2) Government Consultancy Expenditures

OpEx focuses on day-to-day business expenses, while CapEx has a longer-term view. The left hand column gives some indication (Xx where more highly likely) of the likelihood that consultants might be carrying out social research

Table 3 Expenditure on Consultants

ASR relevance		FY2019/20			FY2020/21		
	Agencies	OPEX	CAPEX	Total	OPEX	CAPEX	Total
	Cancer Control Agency	$0.4	None	$0.4	$1.4	None	$1.4
	Crown Law Office	$1.5	$0.1	$1.6	$1.7	$0.1	$1.8
X	Department of Conservation	$12.4	$0.9	$13.3	$14.6	$2.1	$16.8
X	Department of Corrections	$20.7	$25.6	$46.3	$20.0	$24.8	$44.8
X	Department of Internal Affairs	$47.0	$29.7	$76.7	$59.2	$27.9	$87.1
X	Department of the Prime Minister and Cabinet	$2.6	None	$2.6	$7.5	$0.0	$7.5
Xx	Education Review Office	$1.3	$0.2	$1.6	$1.9	$0.4	$2.4
X	Inland Revenue Department	$111.5	$72.3	$183.8	$67.1	$44.2	$111.3
	Land Information New Zealand	$6.8	$4.0	$10.8	$8.2	$5.5	$13.7
Xx	Ministry for Culture and Heritage	$4.7	$0.5	$5.2	$11.4	$0.2	$11.7
Xx	Ministry for Pacific Peoples	$2.2	None	$2.2	$1.9	None	$1.9
X	Ministry for Primary Industries	$50.2	$3.3	$53.5	$26.9	$4.5	$31.5
X	Ministry for the Environment	$16.7	$0.2	$16.9	$23.4	None	$23.5
Xx	Ministry for Women	$0.8	None	$0.8	$0.9	None	$0.9
X	Ministry of Business, Innovation and Employment	$70.2	$38.7	$108.9	$68.9	$21.5	$90.3
	Ministry of Defence	$1.2	$1.0	$2.2	$1.1	$0.4	$1.5
Xx	Ministry of Education	$57.5	$109.8	$167.2	$63.1	$112.9	$176.0
X	Ministry of Foreign Affairs and Trade	$14.4	$4.3	$18.7	$12.2	$5.9	$18.1
X	Ministry of Health	$25.0	$17.2	$42.2	$52.8	$9.2	$62.0
X	Ministry of Housing and Urban Development	$14.7	None	$14.7	$7.9	None	$7.9
Xx	Ministry of Justice	$21.4	$7.1	$28.5	$19.3	$6.9	$26.2
Xx	Ministry of Māori Development-Te Puni Kōkiri	$18.5	$0.7	$19.3	$17.1	None	$17.1
Xx	Ministry of Social Development	$38.5	$23.4	$61.9	$42.6	$52.2	$94.8
	Ministry of Transport	$16.5	None	$16.5	$13.5	None	$13.5
	National Emergency Management Agency	$0.6	None	$0.6	$0.7	None	$0.7

	New Zealand Customs Service	$6.6	$13.4	$20.1	$6.1	$11.2	$17.4
x	Office for Māori Crown Relations-Te Arawhiti	$4.7	$0.0	$4.7	$3.5	None	$3.5
X	Oranga Tamariki-Ministry for Children	$19.6	$2.9	$22.4	$19.3	$3.9	$23.2
X	Public Service Commission	$2.1	None	$2.1	$2.2	None	$2.2
	Serious Fraud Office	$0.5	None	$0.5	$0.5	$0.05	$0.6
Xx	Social Wellbeing Agency	$1.8	None	$1.8	$2.7	None	$2.7
X	Statistics New Zealand	$6.6	$2.3	$8.9	$13.3	$1.3	$14.6
	Te Kāhui Whakamana Rua Tekau mā Iwa-Pike River Recovery Agency	$2.9	None	$2.9	$1.5	None	$1.5
x	The Treasury	$7.3	$0.9	$8.2	$8.8	$0.3	$9.1
	Total Public Service	$609.4	$358.5	$967.9	$603.4	$335.6	$939.1

Source: Official Information requests

References

Barrington, R., & Gray, A. (1981). *The Smith women: 100 New Zealand women talk about their lives*. Reed.

Bell, C. (1996). *Inventing New Zealand: Everyday myths of Pakeha identity*. Penguin Books.

Blewden, M., Carroll, P., & Witten, K. (2010). The use of social science research to inform policy development: Case studies from recent immigration policy. *Kotuitui: New Zealand Journal of Social Sciences, 5*, 13–25.

Burnett, J., & Duncan, S. (2008). Reflections and observations: An interview with the UK's first chief government social researcher. *Critical Social Policy, 28*(3), 283–298.

Butcher, A. (2009). The Asia New Zealand Foundation and its research programme. *New Zealand Sociology, 24*(2), 102–112.

Clayworth, P. (2014). Social sciences - Forerunners of the social sciences. *Te Ara - the Encyclopedia of New Zealand*.

Cotterell, G. A., & von Randow, M. (2010). Addressing the quantitative skill shortage in the social sciences. *New Zealand Science Review, 67*(4), 126–128.

Crothers, C. (2000). Monitoring The changing social conditions of New Zealanders, Social Policy Journal of New Zealand, Issue 15, December 2000.

Crothers, C. (2004). A multidisciplinary applied Bachelor's degree in the social sciences: The AUT experience. In B. Yourn & S. Little (Eds.), *Walking to different beats: Good practice and innovation in higher education* (pp. 57–76). Dunmore Press.

Crothers, C. (2006). *Mapping the social sciences: Characteristics of academic research outputs*. Building Research Capacity in the Social Sciences: Occasional paper 3, 22 pp.

Crothers, C. (2010a). New Zealand sociology in a neo-liberal era: Strands of political economy in New Zealand social science. In M. Burawoy, M. K. Chang, & M. F. Hsieh (Eds.), Facing an unequal world: Challenges for a global sociology (II) (pp. 228–243). Taipei, Taiwan: Institute of Sociology at Academia Sinica, Council of National Associations of the ISA, and Academia Sinica.

Crothers, C. (2010b). Social science research funding and agendas in New Zealand: An editorial. *New Zealand Sociology, 25*(2), 2–14.

Crothers, C. (2010c). Reproducing the center at the periphery: Antipodean traditions of sociology. In S. Patel (Ed.), *The ISA handbook of diverse sociological traditions* (pp. 346–357). Sage.

Crothers, C. (Ed.). (2014, 2016). History of New Zealand sociology. *New Zealand Sociology, 29*(4) and 31(3).

Crothers, C. (2017). New Zealand graduates with social science degrees and social scientists in the New Zealand paid workforce. *New Zealand Sociology, 32*(1), 97–103.

Crothers, C. (2018). Social research projects: Some preliminary descriptive parameters. SAANZ conference December, 2018.

Crothers, C. (2020). Kōtuitui and the social sciences in Aotearoa/New Zealand: into a new decade, Kōtuitui: New Zealand Journal of Social Sciences. *Online, 15*(1), 1–7.

Crothers, C. (2021). Social indicators in Aotearoa/New Zealand: The 2021 'state of the play'. *Aotearoa NZ Journal of Social Issues, 2*.

Crothers, C., & de Joux, M. (2015). Obituary: Dame Margaret Shields. *New Zealand Sociology, 30* (1), 172–174.

Crothers, C., & Dwyer, T. (2010). Obituary Allan Edward Levett. *New Zealand Sociology, 25*(1), 131–140.

Cumming, J., Mcdonald, J., Fa'Asalele Tanuvasa, A., Russell, L., & Aspin, C. (2021). Evaluation culture and practice in the public service. *Public Sector, 44*.

Davey, J. A., & Crothers, C. (2013). Obituary: Rosemary Barrington 1947-2013. *New Zealand Sociology, 28*(1), 171–174.

Davis, P. (2004). Saving and sharing research data: Issues of policy and practice. *Social Policy Journal of New Zealand / Te Puna Whakaaro, 21*, 211–215.

DeMartini, J. R. (1979). Applied sociology: An attempt at clarification and assessment. *Teaching Sociology, 6*(4), 331–354.

Du Plessis, R. (1992). The politics of policy orientated research: a case study. *New Zealand Sociology, 7*(1), 62–72.

Eichbaum, C., & Shaw, R. (2005). Why we should all be nicer to Ministerial advisers. *Policy Quarterly, 1*(4), 18–25.

Forbes, S., & Keegan, A. (2016). Helping raise the official statistics capability of government employees. *Journal of Official Statistics, 32*(4), 811–826. https://doi.org/10.1515/jos-2016-0042

Hampton, S., & Adams, R. (2018). Behavioural economics vs social practice theory: Perspectives from inside the United Kingdom government. *Energy Research & Social Science,* 46(1), 214–224.

Humpage, L. (2015). *Policy change, public attitudes and social citizenship: Does neoliberalism matter?* Policy Press.

Jeannin, H. (2017). Being a corporate sociologist: An insider's view. American Sociologist, first online 19 April 2017.

Kirkman, A. (2012). Professor James Harding Robb (Jim) – A public sociologist: 28 April 1920 – 23 June 2011. *New Zealand Sociology, 27*(1), 46–59.

Lloyd, M. (1991). Troubles with team research: A personal account of a sociology graduate entering a health research unit. *New Zealand Sociology, 6*(2), 177–190.

Löfgren, K., & Bickerton, S. H. (2022). The two-community model in the New Zealand housing policy community – A bottom-up perspective. *Australian Journal of Public Administration, 81*(1), 95–110.

Löfgren, K., & Cavagnoli, D. (2015). The Policy Worker and the Professor Understanding how NZ policy workers utilise academic research. *Policy Quarterly, 11*(3), 64–72.

Lunt, N., Davidson, C., & McKegg, K. (Eds.). (2003). *Evaluating policy and practice: A New Zealand reader.* Pearson Prentice Hall.

Piercy, G., Mackness, K., Rarere, M., & Madley, B. (2017). Investigating commentary on the fifth labour-led government's third way approach. *New Zealand Sociology, 32*(1), 51–75.

Pole, N. (2003). Foreword (ministerial conference on social policy research and evaluation conference). *Social Policy Journal of New Zealand, 20.*

Preston, D. (2018). *For whom the bell tolls: The sustainability of public social research institutions in New Zealand.* Superu.

Price, J., & Will, J. (2015). Applied sociology. In *International Encyclopedia of the social & behavioral sciences* (2nd ed.).

Rashbrooke, M. (2016). Keynote address: Public lecture missing in action: Income inequality and sociology. *New Zealand Sociology, 31*(5):32–55.

Robb, J. H. (1987). *The life and death of official social research in New Zealand.* VUW, Sociology working paper 7.

Robb, J. H., et al. (1996). Some thoughts on beginnings in the establishment of sociology in New Zealand: A 'Founders' retrospect. *New Zealand Sociology, 11*(2), 323–329.

Spalter-Roth, R. (2007). Sociologists in research, applied, and policy settings: Bringing professionals in from the cold. *Journal of Applied Social Science, 1*(2), 4–18.

Spoonley, P. (Ed.). (2003). Special Issue: Graeme Fraser and New Zealand Sociology. *New Zealand Sociology, 18*(1) [Watson, Ian 7-14; Hancock, Merv 15-20; Maharey, Steve, 21-23; Wood, Brennon 24-32; O'Brien, Mike 33-44; Munford, Robyn 46-54.]

Tait, D., Waghorne, M., Crothers, C., & Dwyer, T. (1981). *Applied sociology: The future of the discipline.* Paper presented to Sociological Association of Australia and New Zealand, Christchurch, November 1981, 9 pp.

Taylor, N., & MacKay, M. (2016). Social impact assessment (SIA) in New Zealand: Legacy and change. *New Zealand Sociology, 31*(3), 229–246.

Taylor, C. N., Bryan, C. H., & Goodrich, C. G. (2004). *Social assessment: Theory, process and techniques* (3rd ed.). Social Ecology Press.

Tolich, M., & Shephard, A. (2014). An evaluation of experiential learning in a sociology internship class. *New Zealand Sociology, 29*(1), 119–134.

Vosburgh, M., & Kronick, J. (1980). The family policy implications of a new social program - the New-Zealand accident compensation scheme. *Journal of Marriage and the Family, 42*(3), 683–693.

Weiss, C. (1977). Research for policy's sake: The enlightenment function of social research. *Policy Analysis, 3*(4), 531–545.

Witten, K., & Hammond, K. (2010). What becomes of social science knowledge, New Zealand researchers' experiences of knowledge transfer modes and audiences. *Kotuitui: New Zealand Journal of Social Sciences Online, 5*, 1–10.

Charles Crothers is Emeritus Professor of Sociology at Auckland University of Technology, New Zealand and Senior Research Associate at the University of Johannesburg. He completed his PhD at Victoria University of Wellington (VUW) and has worked at VUW, the University of Auckland, and the University of Natal in Durban. Charles' current areas of research include Social Theory, Methods of Applied Social Research and policy processes, the History and Current Situation of Sociology, and Settler Societies (especially New Zealand and South Africa) with a particular interest in settlements. He has been Editor of The Royal Society of New Zealand's *Kotuitui* and former Vice-President of the Research Committee on the History of Sociology of the International Sociological Association, and President of the Sociological Association of Aotearoa/New Zealand.

Clinical Sociology and the Sociology of Intersections Between Policy, Identity, Categories, and Labelling

Robert Didham

Introduction

Sonia Mazey and Jeremy Richardson ask a perfectly valid and topical question in their latest exploration of policy making in the Aotearoa New Zealand: is the policy process fit for purpose? (Mazey & Richardson, 2022). They point to many of the major unresolved and perhaps unresolvable policy issues identified by contributors to their earlier book (Mazey & Richardson, 2021), noting some of the disconnects between policy formulation and the many varied conflicting needs and outcomes. Limited progress is rightly explained as largely the result of lack of capacity (in all its many connotations). The interface between research and policy processes was further explored by Cate Roy and George Slim, in a later issue of the *Policy Quarterly* (Roy & Slim, 2022), concluding that "there are positive signs of effective engagement at the research-policy interface" (p. 65) but identifying a range of tensions, challenges and roadblocks that remain to be resolved.

Although there is a clear, although perhaps unintended, credentialist focus on qualifications rather than expertise (partly reflecting recruitment processes), the observation that the relationships between policymakers and academics are vitally important is fundamental, as indeed is the more mundane but critical objective of retention of expertise in both arenas. True depth of knowledge and capacity to build subject matter and policy expertise takes time. A lot of time. Along with recognition of the need for systematic opportunities to develop a reasonable depth of knowledge. A degree in sociology no more prepares one to be an effective clinical sociologist than a data science degree provides more than some of the essential practical fundamentals of systems implementation. The continued thirst to learn, the common

R. Didham (✉)
Te Ngira: Institute for Population Research, University of Waikato, Hamilton, New Zealand
e-mail: robert.didham@waikato.ac.nz

© The Author(s), under exclusive license to Springer Nature Switzerland AG 2023
Z. L. Rocha, K. L. Davidson (eds.), *Applied and Clinical Sociology in Aotearoa New Zealand*, Clinical Sociology: Research and Practice,
https://doi.org/10.1007/978-3-031-36581-2_6

sense to apply knowledge and the openness and trust fundamental to building an interdisciplinary relationship are prerequisites.

There is an equally clear interface between policy making and research for policy which, in a world where wellbeing and society matter, means an overt connection with clinical/applied sociology (Wirth, 1931; Fritz, 1988; Freedman, 1989; Clawar, 2008; Wan & Wan, 2020; David, 2022; Rocha, 2022). In this context, clinical sociology refers to the application of sociological theories, research/methods, and interventions to address a range of social issues and problems identified in the real world. Thus, clinical sociology can be said to extend applied sociology to include intervention, prevention, and social amelioration components to its framework.

Clinical sociology and applied sociology go hand in hand with a minor difference in focus. Applied sociology and clinical sociology are two terms that are almost synonymous, and tend to be used synonymously by practitioners, though distinguished as sub-branches of the discipline of sociological practice (Fritz, 2021, p. 3). In Aotearoa New Zealand, the preferred term among practitioners, except to some extent among sociologists in the health sector, is 'applied sociology', emphasising the linkages with sociological theory rather than the more client focussed remedial approaches implied by the term 'clinical sociology' and its association in medicine with other uses of the word 'clinical'.

Stephen Steele, in his presidential address at the 2016 Annual Meeting of the Association for Applied and Clinical Sociology (AACS) listed, and expanded upon, five aspirations he had identified for applied and clinical sociology and AACS, which can act as a framework for connecting theoretical sociology with the pressured world of social policy:

1. A sociology that uses its perspectives and tools creatively.
2. Applied sociology will more aggressively mine the human stories that make human social life.
3. Applied sociology will ethically engage action and "doing" to produce positive social change.
4. Applied and Clinical Sociology will demonstrate its value, broaden its functional appeal, and create paths to diversity. Known for its integrative nature as a problem-solution-focused being, AACS will be a model twenty-first-century organization.
5. Sociology will clarify its core and demonstrate its direct value. Support solutions to societal and client problems. (Steele, 2017)

Perhaps we should also observe that many of the practitioners of clinical sociology in the field are in fact not trained as sociologists. This is not unique to sociology. The boundaries between fields in most disciplines are becoming ever more blurred despite increasing specialisation, or rebranding of specialisations. Many of the people working in the field of clinical sociology started out, in their educational background, with degrees in as diverse fields as geography, psychology, public health science, physics, epidemiology, political science and demography, just to name a few that feature in the current crop of people working in this space, often morphing into sociologists by default as legislative requirements encourage a more overt social science perspective. This has been thrust to the fore, as is clear from the recent wellbeing report from The Treasury (2022), which is a direct outcome of new requirements under the Public Finance (Wellbeing) Amendment Act 2020 for reporting on wellbeing at (at least) 4-yearly intervals.

Given the diversity of backgrounds and the even greater diversity of topics being addressed for identification and understanding of issues, policy formulation, policy implementation and analysis of outcomes, the playing fields on which the analytical work is done need to be as level and well-defined as possible. One of the major prerequisites is a strong and coherent underpinning framework of concepts and classifications so that people can converse effectively across and within the information system(s). This is a toolbox that clinical sociology requires, and must provide, as a pre-requisite. Sectoral siloes remain a challenge—what has perceptively been categorised as 'islands of expertise' (Shaw & Heap, 2022)—the combination of the pressure of time constraints and conflicting agendas do nothing to discourage this.

The information systems, however, do not work on a level playing field. This can be seen in the rapidly growing awareness of implicit inequalities and inequities that have been historically embedded into data collection systems and into subsequent reporting. Calls to address these injustices have been long seen as, at best, inconveniences, and at worst, irrelevances. Redressing outcomes of colonialism and identifying pathways to decolonisation (Smith, 2012; Kukutai & Taylor, 2016) now render these historical concerns urgent. The unpacking and understanding of these issues comprise the core province of sociology. This aspect is vitally important for making sense of the framing of knowledge structured around the trichotomy of the actors, the acted upon and the contexts, especially if one is dealing with a growing recognition that the system is systemically and systematically racist (Came, 2014; MacDonald, 2018).

This chapter looks at some aspects of the frames within which clinical sociology and clinical sociologists operate, rather than at the actors within the system. These are frames which are applicable to both praxis and practice (van Hulst & Yanow, 2016), therefore also relevant to both theoretical and applied sociologists—a requirement if they are to avoid talking past each other. Moreover, underlying assumptions and classifications provide the underpinnings of effective policy formulation and implementation. Policy interventions serve to define, address and monitor perceived inequalities, inequities and social injustices. These interventions are often couched around a single monolithic topic, with titles such as Māori housing strategy, or Pacific health strategy, with limited attention to the multiplicity of intersecting dimensions because of prescribed space or lack of attention to the environmental, social, demographic and cultural contexts that impinge on their scope. Clinical sociology has a key role to play in identifying and integrating these important elements.

Public policy sets the frameworks within which society is viewed, usually within the constraints of a political agenda. This is not always consistent with how society operates. Nor can it always be, because, by the very nature of public policy, society is construed organically as a body, the anatomy of which is secondary to the objective of the policy. One of the consequences of this is that society has been frequently in the past something to be "done to" rather than "done for", as Jan Fritz has noted (Fritz, 1988, 2021). In recent years in Aotearoa New Zealand there has been a shift, under such slogans as "by and for XXX" or "for all New Zealanders", all too often bordering a little too closely on a racialised construct. An increasingly urgent need is to go beyond these slogans and look at the sociology within and between the analytical dimensions.

Indeed, at least within the policy agencies, we do see progress in this direction. Designers of local policies and interventions are not blind to the issues. Public policies designed to address real and perceived immediate social needs, for example among Pacific populations in Aotearoa New Zealand, have often exhibited a tendency to inadequately take account of the cultural and social diversity within the populations of interest. This is primarily because of the tendency to treat populations monolithically, and these policies have tended not to consider the way in which other populations of interest intersect with these populations.

Policies of organisations sitting under the public policy umbrellas do not always consider internal diversities, though increasingly this will be untenable. Recent work and prospective directions by key agencies are reflected in the long-term insights briefings. Agencies are required under the Public Service Act 2020 (Schedule 6, clauses 8 and 9) to publish think pieces on the future that affect New Zealand society and wellbeing at least once every 3 years. These briefings are designed to identify and define pathways for addressing known issues. Typical are those published or in the process of development by the Ministry of Pacific Peoples (2022), Ministry of Housing and Urban Development, and The Treasury (2022). A briefing in progress is being prepared jointly by four agencies with a common set of goals for young people and families, illustrating that de-siloisation is possible, if not yet easy (Ministry of Business, Innovation and Employment, Ministry of Education, Ministry of Social Development and Ministry for Women, 2022). Produced independently of ministers and in consultation with the public, the outcomes of the insights briefings thus far demonstrate a keen awareness of the need to focus on within-group diversity and a maturing attention to the sociological underpinnings of their concerns. This approach will continue to be essential for the effective operation of these organisations if they are to deliver to their mandates. However, an opportunity exists for there to be more direct coordination between different organisations, within government and between government and academia and non-government organisations. This will identify both commonalities and interlacing interdependencies.

This is where common sets of definitions and classifications becomes critical. For example, any attempt to understand Māori health, where 'Māori' is defined by ethnicity, implicitly requires an understanding of Pacific, European and Asian health at the broad level if only because many of the causal components of health concerns are, in each case, not independent of each other.

Nor do the communities live separately. At least in part, the levels of multiple ethnicity suggest that there are shared causalities as well as unrecognised diversities. Ethnicity must for reasons of data availability also act as a surrogate for ancestry/

descent, which is of similar if not more relevance, especially if the interest includes iwi-level concerns. Many of the health issues have persistent genetic and epigenetic dimensions, especially in metabolic and heart diseases, that sit alongside the public and private health concerns which derive from socio-economic and cultural environments, to the extent that the simplistic notion that ethnicity is a purely social construct continues to be questioned (Hartigan, 2008). Unpicking and unpacking realities requires a thorough knowledge of the sociology, demography, geography and history of each grouping of ethnicities within Aotearoa New Zealand, along with the diversity within these groupings—always keeping in mind that the labels and content of many of the groupings, while convenient, are not entirely appropriate, having their roots in colonial history or overly broad geographic basis for definition. We see this problem with diverse macro-groupings of ethnicities such as 'Asian' and 'African', as Kumanan Rasnathan has observed (Rasanathan et al., 2006).

The application of a clinical sociological lens adds value in identifying thematic and theoretical implications in the data, in conjunction with the other lenses brought to the table. Age structures, ethnic composition, location, housing quality, employment, birthplace and family histories all impinge on health, as do other dimensions such as gender, sexual orientation, education, access to services and institutional racism. In this chapter the Pacific population is used as an exemplar to suggest some of the ways in which clinical sociology has helped, or could help, recognise missed opportunities, and contribute to addressing perceived inequalities, iniquities and inequities. This population serves as a prime illustration of the way in which many of the assumptions and prejudices can play out in the data to the unintended detriment of both Pacific people and other communities with shared histories.

Notably, the Fijian Indian population, which in terms of classification is treated as Asian for a range of valid reasons, but in some data collections people who give this as one of their ethnicities are miscoded as Fijian to the detriment of the analytical validity of both Pacific and Asian data. This is a well-known example of a population where we need to consider limitations and inconsistency in data collection and recording. Furthermore, if collection has a tickbox in the ethnicity question for 'Indian' but fails to record country of birth or parental, linguistic or cultural connections, then the person can only be aggregated into 'Indian' and effectively lost to the population of interest, which is 'Fijian Indian'. The sociological, demographic and health implications run very deep.

Similarly, a significant proportion of the Pacific population also identifies as Māori and is 'lost' to Pacific if the data is prioritised, distorting both Pacific and, potentially, Māori measures—in this case also the mixing between people of Māori and different ethnicities within the Pacific grouping varies greatly, so communities are differently affected.

Labelling

In the literature, the population within the Pacific grouping of ethnicities is referred to as Pacific or as Pasifika, though not quite synonymously depending on context, as explained below. In the current New Zealand Standard of Ethnicity (Statistics New Zealand, 2005) the descriptor used is the 'Pacific Peoples Ethnic Group', which does acknowledge internal diversity by the use of the word 'peoples' but contrasts with other labels used for these level 1 categories in a slightly uncomfortable way. Of the two principal descriptors, the term 'Pacific' has a greater time depth and is associated with an externally imposed perspective, growing out of the older "Polynesian" and "Pacific Islander" labels as the sources of the population diversified and the locally born populations grew. For an admittedly crude dichotomous approach, we can consider terminology in terms of the various morphs of the emic/etic paradigm, originally coined by Kenneth Pike (1954) but used in a variety of flavours throughout anthropology, sociology, psychology and linguistics (Galperin et al., 2022). The term 'Pacific' is intrinsically linked to a colonial etic view (Sibley et al., 2011; Beals et al., 2020). The hallmarks of this etic view are stereotyping and othering. One of the consequences of this historical context is that the complexities of the interlacing of the diverse communities within the group are frequently overlooked.

The term 'Pasifika', partly as a reaction, emerged in Aotearoa New Zealand out of this context for two key reasons. Political dimensions of decolonisation gained traction, associated with emerging, and essentially emic, literature as Pacific voices were increasingly being heard. The more sociologically salient aspect, which is a consequence of a growing cohesive sense of shared ambitions and identity among, especially, the younger locally born generations, is the recognition of the power of group size and shared emerging common goals. Increasingly too, younger people are tending to identify with this sense of a wider group cohesion, especially in cultural areas such as literature and performing arts, alongside embracing diversity implicit to the intersectionality of the fonofale model, developed by Fuimaono Karl Pulotu-Endemann in 1984 (Pulotu-Endemann & Bush, 2000; Pulotu-Endemann, 2021), where many dimensions other than ethnicity intersect—dimensions such as language, religion, sexuality, gender, community, neighbourhood. 'Pacific' is more commonly used when the emphasis is on the ethnic dimensions of identity which sit within the wider socio-cultural dimensions encompassed by 'Pasifika'. In other words, the eye of the sociologist is in the process of displacing, or at least sitting alongside, the eye of the accountant.

A core problem is that too often the labelling of populations carries with it embedded prejudices, accompanied by colonial baggage and implicit 'othering' that inhibits effective policy formulation. Political and social contexts may also result in individuals changing their ethnic identifications to facilitate outcomes based on their perceptions of expectations (Didham, 2016). Admittedly, there is some level of "non-meaningful measurement error" (Mok, 2019, 142) in all data, especially when imputation of responses or recording/processing errors occur, but in general the good data is sufficiently dominant and robust to enable effective analysis. A much larger problem looms when output strategies intrude to attempt to systematically reduce the number of responses provided by an individual by some method of prioritisation (Didham & Callister, 2012). In these cases, the critical requirement is to ensure that in any derived rates the numerators and denominators are actually compatible (Didham, 2005), recorded with similar accuracy, and are measuring the same thing. This becomes very important if analysing survey data such as Growing Up in New Zealand and then deriving measures from other sources as explanatory evidence (Yao, 2022).

Ethnicity is a characteristic of an individual and cannot be easily ascribed to any social unit consisting of individuals (Callister et al., 2007). For the purpose of this chapter, families, extended families and households are defined in what is the most common way for census data: for example, a 'Pacific family' is a family in which at least one member identifies with an ethnicity within the Pacific grouping of ethnicities. This can be applied at any level required: 'Tongan family' is a family in which at least one member is of Tongan ethnicity. Families would be counted in every relevant category, so that a family containing people with at least one Samoan and at least one Tongan ethnicity would be counted as both Samoan and Tongan. The understanding of the complex sociological relationship between individual characteristics and typological ascription to families remains largely unresolved.

The Pacific Population in Aotearoa New Zealand

First a necessarily brief overview of the context within which Pacific data and Pacific people in Aotearoa New Zealand live. Historical injustices remain very fresh and relevant to much of the way in which the Pacific communities see themselves inside and are seen from outside—not just associated with events such as the Dawn Raids in the 1970s when people who had overstayed their visa permits were rounded up. Embedded alongside these memories are the consequences of prejudices and attitudes visited upon the populations by colonial history.

There has been a Pacific presence in Aotearoa New Zealand for well over 150 years (Mallon et al., 2012). However, much of this population's presence remained essentially invisible, or at best partly visible, for the first 80 years or so. For example, despite considerable contemporary public interest and debate (surrounding, for instance, the Daphne and Lulu affairs—see, for example, Graves, 1986 for an overview), early censuses tended to exclude much of the indentured labour, so that the Vanuatuan indentured labourers exploited by the flax industry in the 1870s were notable for their absence in census records in 1871. The *Evening Post* on 31 May 1870 noted the "arrival at Auckland of a vessel from the South Sea Islands, bringing a party of Kanakas [sic]—nominally coming of their own free will—to work at a flax mill under engagement for a term of years ..." which confirms that they met the criterion for inclusion in census.

Nonetheless, it was following the Great Depression, but largely interrupted by the Second World War, that migration started increasing significantly. The Pacific population in Aotearoa New Zealand increased from 1109 people in 1936 to 50,434 by 1971 as skilled and semi-skilled labour shortages hit hard in some industries. Although migration from the Pacific nations increased following the Second World War, most of the Pacific migrants were from within the Polynesian triangle, with relatively small numbers from the rest of the Pacific. The sex ratio balance of male and female migration shifted with changes in labour requirements and changing sociology both in Aotearoa New Zealand and in the home countries. The total Pacific population in Aotearoa New Zealand in 1961 was 16,743 people with a sex ratio of 109 males per 100 females. The 1960s and 1970s were a period of rapid growth with the population reaching 74,106 people by 1976 with a lowered sex ratio (103 males per 100 females) as female labour migration increased and the babies born to migrants contributed to a growing locally born population.

One of the consequences of the rapid growth of this largely Auckland based population was the emergence of strong transnational communities, associated with specific industries and locations. These communities tended to be regarded as generally hard working, industrious, but exploited and temporary labour resources. An unwelcome consequence of rapid growth was a climate of xenophobic racism, culminating in the Dawn Raids (Anae, 2020), for which the Crown has recently apologised (Ardern, 2021).

The relationship between labour and Pacific migration continues today, with arrangements such as the RSE Scheme (Bedford et al., 2017). Seasonal workers are largely not counted in the New Zealand resident population because of labour contracts lasting for less than 12 months, but their presence does have relevance for services such as health provision. Increasingly there are calls for widening the scale and scope of labour migration from the Pacific (Smith et al., 2021), not least of which is in response to climate change. However, the New Zealand born component is increasingly the driver of growth rather than migration, with deep sociological changes occurring within family and social structures and expectations.

The population is diverse and complex. The 2018 Census of Population and Dwellings recorded 381,642 people with one or more ethnicities within the Pacific grouping of ethnicities, of whom 66.4 % were born in Aotearoa New Zealand. This diverse population makes up 8.12% of the Aotearoa New Zealand 2018 Census Usually Resident Population. While two-thirds (66.4%) of the Pacific population are born in New Zealand, this percentage varies dramatically among the communities encompassed by this grouping. Communities with longer histories of settlement in New Zealand include Niuean, with 83.0% locally born, and Tokelauan, at 78.5%, respectively, born in New Zealand. Partly this reflects significant historical inflows and their small remaining source populations.

The Niuean population in New Zealand is nearly 19 times that of Niue. Similarly, the Tokelauan population in New Zealand is more than 6 times that of Tokelau. For Niue and Tokelau, the relationship between New Zealand born and migrant parts of their diaspora is socially and economically fundamental to the survival of cultural and linguistic heritages.

The three largest communities, Samoan (182,721 people of whom 66.7% are New Zealand born) and Tongan (82,392 people, 64.4% New Zealand born), and Cook Island Māori (80,532 people, 83.1% New Zealand born, and New Zealand citizens by right) each have had a long-standing presence in this country extending for more than a century, and are associated with large source populations and ongoing migration flows. The New Zealand based Samoan population is almost as large as Samoa's population, while the Tongan population in New Zealand is about 80% the size of Tonga's population. The Cook Island Māori population in New Zealand is 5 times larger than the diverse populations living in the Cook Islands.

The links between Aotearoa New Zealand and the respective Pacific nations remains strong. Although both Samoa and Tonga have globally spread diasporas, the New Zealand based communities remain critical to the 'home' countries economically for remittances and support, and increasingly so (Brown, 1995; Connell & Brown, 2005; Gibson et al., 2006; Cunningham 2022). The Pacific population in New Zealand continues to increase as a proportion of both the New Zealand population and the global ethnic populations.

The Pacific population in New Zealand is a significant proportion of the population. In the 2006 Census, 6.9% of the population with specified ethnicities recorded at least one ethnicity within the Pacific grouping of ethnicities. By 2018 this had increased to 8.1% of the total usually resident population. As expected of a young population structure, people aged under 15 years are increasingly likely to be Pacific, increasing from 12.0% of New Zealand children in 2006 to 13.9% in 2018.

Family, Neighbourhoods and Well-Being

This is where sociology intersects history, demography, psychology and public health. The predominantly young Pacific population is also aging, with an increase among the 65 years and over ages from 2.1% of the population in 2006 to 2.8% 12 years later in 2018. Population aging, and the aged population, will increase as more of the larger Pacific cohorts currently in the younger ages survive beyond 65 years of age. Given the preferences among Pasifika for multigenerational housing solutions, this will have implications for housing futures (Stats NZ, 2023). The Pacific population is currently a young population, among whom just 5.3% of the Pacific population is aged 65 years or older.

These percentages are important. In the 2018 Census there were 715,161 people aged 65 years and older. However, only 20,205 of these identified with at least one Pacific ethnicity, 86% of whom were born overseas. Nearly half (48.8%) were Samoan, with Cook Island Māori and Tongan accounting for 17.1 and 17.9% respectively. An important aspect that affects the sociology of aging is location. Auckland dominates for most groups. Less visible at a national level are Niuean and Tokelauan because there are few people in the older age groups in Auckland, but in the case of Tokelauan, for example, over half of Tokelauans live in the Wellington region. Such differences in location can affect the capacity within and between communities to maintain social connectedness, to cope with loneliness and to prevent health issues within particular groups. In short, sociology without geography has limitations.

Importantly for the Pacific population, of the 103,293 people who live in an extended family, 70,260 people are members of a three-or-more-generation extended family, representing around a third (32.3%) of all Pacific people coded in households. However, in sharp contrast to the rest of the population, this peaks at 45.2% for those aged 80–84 years, indicating that older Pacific extended family members tend to be cared for at home and remain as part of the household. These families typically include children, parents and grandparents, in many cases along with other family relatives. Of course, from a sociological viewpoint, the definition of family as reflected here is based on being located within a dwelling. For Pacific, as with many other parts of the population, this definition contrasts sharply with definitions of family used by the members themselves, who are much more likely to operate closer to a whanau-type of concept of family or may extend for some to encompass the whole ethnic community, on the basis that 'family and collective need has priority over individual need' (Pasikale & George, 1995, p. 68).

There is a relationship between cultural requirements in a home and the physical limitations of suburban housing. In general, houses in which extended families find themselves are inadequate for needs and home ownership is a greater challenge (Goodyear, 2017). Moreover, in an environment where suburban housing is designed on the assumption that one size fits all and the population is residentially highly mobile, spaces may be repurposed so that garages and streets become communal spaces (Macpherson, 1997). Modifications to the functions of spaces in this way have served as symbols of dysfunction because of racial prejudices implicit in the eyes of outsiders looking in. In contrast, a sociologist should immediately see that this is a positive adaptation provoked by an inadequate environment, and has in fact been recognised in some recent initiatives in culturally appropriate housing led by the Penina Trust, a trust dedicated to Pacific community wellbeing in South Auckland (Tokalau, 2023). Significant for Pacific communities is a place to call home, with space defined in a much different sense than purely geographic. It aligns more closely with the Māori concept of tūrangawaewae (Mead, 2003; Cram et al. 2022), one of belonging, extending beyond back to ancestral origins and across to multiple social contexts.

Cultural Continuities and Transformations

Communication pathways within societies and between social communities must remain open. The intergenerational transfer of knowledge and its maintenance is part of the cohesive fabric of human society. Knowledge in this context encompasses all forms of knowledge, however acquired through formal education systems or belonging to so-called (and perhaps euphemistically) 'traditional knowledge', all too often regarded as of lesser status in a colonialised world, but increasingly recognised globally as of major importance to health and wellbeing (Dow et al., 2023). In the case of Pasifika, as with all communities and heritages, oral literatures, languages, arts, environmental knowledge, whakapapa, and cultural practices are fundamental dimensions of identity. The continuance of this knowledge becomes difficult if brain chains (a useful term coined by Friesen & Collins, 2017) are broken.

Of significant interest is the asymmetrical nature of knowledge transference. In a recent report by the Retirement Commission, the contrasting values placed on extended families by younger and older generations was highlighted:

> When asked what it was like to live intergenerationally, the overwhelming response from matua was the feeling of contentment, happiness and being able to live with their children and grandchildren. This feeling of contentment is reciprocal too, with younger members of those living in the same households, also reporting happiness and contentment, to have the presence of their grandparent(s) within the home. The aspirations of Pacific matua living in intergenerational households may not always be shared by younger generations. Younger participants shared their desire for more independence, privacy, and bigger living spaces. This difference of aspirations is further accentuated when younger family members enter a relationship with 'those outside their culture'. Building a family home in their Pacific home countries may be a goal for Pacific matua, but not for their children and grandchildren. (Rohorua et al., 2022, p. 10)

The flows of knowledge between generations are not the same in scale, content, or value when seen from below (the perceptions of younger generations) or from above (the aspirations of the older generations). This asymmetric aspect is a feature of many migrant communities because each generation has very different histories and inhabits quite different, if intersecting, spaces. The youngest children value, and are valued by, grandparents, but teenagers and young adults have different aspirations. The interesting aspect is the reference to "outside their culture" because interethnic partnering is an important component of social realities, but one which complicates any analysis which ignores the sociology of change. Of key importance is an understanding of neighbourhood social capital (Aminzadeh et al., 2013).

Extending the observations about the functional reassignment of existing spaces (Macpherson, 1997), and placing them alongside changing cultural change among younger people, it could be suggested that there is an urgent need to reframe the topical debates on youth crime and social disorder among cohorts moving between childhood and adulthood (Webb et al., 2022; Bellringer et al., 2022). This discussion demands integrated solutions, through family-focussed agencies, public health suppliers as well as police and justice systems. This is where cross-agency policy formulation requires the services of skilled clinical sociologists with the support of other relevant professional analysts in order to ensure that interpretation of evidence is appropriately based on facts rather than on embedded discriminatory prejudices implicit in the language used to describe concerns.

Language and Religion

There are other consequences too of change as young children grow up and form alliances and connections with their peers beyond the family circle, many of which are precursors to interethnic partnering (Callister et al., 2005), symbolic ethnicity (Gans, 1979, 2017) and emerging identities. Policies may not be nuanced enough to instigate action. This is not to suggest necessarily that the prior research has not been done—it often has been, but then research gets lost sight of during the reporting phases, reaching the policy interface as little more than diplomatic shadows. The work of the clinical sociologist, involving the support of evidence, may be seen as too technical, too controversial or simply contrary to preconceptions and prejudgements of the gatekeepers. Usually persistence will succeed, if only tangentially. Two dimensions of identity can serve as illustration—language and religion.

Language is both a taonga and a primary component of identity for any community, but of special importance when language loss affects the well-being and cultural transfer across generations, especially among migrant communities. Unfortunately, this importance is often under-recognised, although a forthcoming report on Pacific housing in New Zealand has retained a small section on language retention across families and extended families (Stats NZ, 2023) which draws on ongoing work (Didham, 2023). The observation about the difference in attitudes of young adults contrasting with those of young children and grandparents noted above (Rohorua et al., 2022) is not unrelated to a question raised by research led by Elsie Ho into language maintenance and cultural continuance among Asian children as they moved from a highly diverse and engaged environment at kindergarten level to older youth environments where language capability was no longer an imperative. The first part of the study—on the younger ages—was completed (Ho et al., 2017) and well received. The other, more concerning aspect (why languages were being lost as children age) has not yet been picked up, although work is ongoing in this space.

Family and community are central in preventing language loss. Loss of heritage languages reduces the capacity for older generations to communicate with younger generations, and also breaks the chain in transmission of traditions and traditional knowledge. While this has been recognised internationally as a public health concern for youth wellbeing (Chandler & Lalonde, 1998; Hallett et al., 2007), it is an element in the isolation of older generations who are more likely to have lost their ability speak English or have not had the opportunity or necessity to learn. New Zealand has the second highest suicide rate in the OECD and Pacific people have triple the risk of suicide attempts compared with the general population (Teevale, et al. 2016). The relationship between wellbeing and language is equally a topic of concern for Māori (Durie, 2017). The emergence of formal and informal language nests for some Pacific languages, modelled on the kohanga reo approach applied to Māori, is a recognition of the importance of the language to well-being, as is the program of Language Weeks, which now includes many of the Pacific languages spoken within New Zealand.

The social dimensions of language and wellbeing are as important to sociology as they are to health. Among the Pacific communities the situation is varied. For example, in 2018 it was shown that over all half (51%) of people of Pacific ethnicities in New Zealand spoke only English. Recency of migration, group size, family living arrangements, age, sex and communal proximity all matter. Relatively recent migrants tended to have lower percentages speaking only English, as we see among Tuvaluan and i-Kiribati, at 36.8 and 38.4% respectively speaking only English. This contrasts with people with longer migration histories, such as Cook Islanders (74.2% speak only English) and Niueans (71.1% speak only English). In the case of Niueans, this is of particular concern because of the severely endangered status of the language and the fact that New Zealand is home to the great majority of the Niuean world population.

Conversely, people who do not speak English tend to be either new migrants or are older overseas born. In general, fewer than 5% of the New Zealand born Pacific people do not speak English, dominated by young pre-school children where English is rarely spoken in the home. Among the overseas born the percentages are generally higher, with 17.6% of overseas born Tongans and 16.6% of Samoans not speakers of English. These details are of special importance for policies related to health and elderly care. A question which forms part of ongoing work is where and how are languages being lost, retained or acquired, because of the insights this can provide into social change and support requirements.

The other dimension of identity cited here is religious affiliation. Most literature on Pacific populations within New Zealand and across Pacific nations identifies the centrality of religion in daily life and as a locus of communal cohesion (Macpherson & Macpherson, 2001; Lilo et al., 2020). In most studies the role of religion and spirituality is seen as positive and protective (O'Brien et al., 2013) and it is demonstratable that religion plays a much greater role socially among Pasifika than among the population at large. Above all, places of communal meeting are often also places of worship. However, from the perspective of a sociologist, this premise is accepted, generally unquestioned, on the assumption that attendance relates to faith whereas the social function may be the dominant element.

Along with language, religion among Pasifika provides a primary locus of cultural transmission and sense of belonging. Initially emerging from a colonial past, Christian-based religions have been increasingly indigenized across the Pacific, centred around strong church-based networks, along with newly emerging religions. Strikingly, whereas 48.2% of the New Zealand population stated they had no religious affiliation, only 22.9% of people of Pacific ethnicities did so. By contrast, 53.5% of Māori, a population with a similar age structure, affiliated with no religion. The connections between language, religion and identity run deep, with the breaking of these connections seen as negative. However, the relationship between this and the lived realities of youth and the social contexts within which they live beyond the ethnic communities is a central driver (Joseph, 2005).

In general, adherence to a religion reflects migration histories as well as the colonial history of missionary activities across the Pacific. For example, Roman Catholicism ranks ahead of other religions for overseas born Samoans, but

Presbyterianism ranks first among overseas born Cook Islanders and Niueans, and Methodism ranks first among overseas born Tongans and Fijians.

The children and grandchildren of Pacific migrants tend to retain the religions of their elders, though the rate of changes to religious affiliations across generations varies. If we look at the New Zealand born for these ethnicities and religions, we find, for example, that Methodism still ranks second behind 'no religion' among Tongans but drops to fourth for Fijians.

Focussing on categories that are most common at a total population level can lead to missing details important to the communities of interest. Among the religions with smaller numbers of adherents, the Mormon religion has maintained strong appeal among Pacific communities. In 2018, 48.6% of Mormons identified as being of one or more Pacific ethnicities, of whom 16.6% also identify as Māori. The prevalence of this religion among tangata whenua and tangata moana is noteworthy, even though it accounts for only a small percentage of the ethnic groups at 3.4% for Māori and 7.3% for Pacific. As early as 1951 over 80% of Mormons in New Zealand were Māori and in 2018, 45.4% of Mormons identified as Māori. Together, Māori and Pacific account for 86.0% of New Zealand's Mormons.

Most studies point to spirituality and adherence to a faith but 'no religion' is less often considered because Pacific people who state in census that they have no religion are predominantly young adults born in New Zealand. Thus, differentiating by birthplace is key to reaching a more holistic view of social realities. Studies have identified that religious faith can play a protective role (Teevale et al., 2016; Tautolo et al., 2020), but often these studies look at the family unit level rather than under the hood at the individual actors. People within families may affiliate with different religions or may have no religious affiliation yet accompany family members to religious functions. Differences in affiliations among people within families is often the locus of tension. Other intersections may also be relevant to the sociologist: an ambiguous relationship seems to exist between religion, familial support and wellbeing for gender diverse people (Henrickson, 2007).

Birthplace also matters. People who affiliated with no religion in the 2018 Census returned the highest number of respondents for the total Pacific ethnic group as well as for people of Samoan, Cook Island Māori, Tongan, Niuean and Fijian ethnicities. Given the dominance of religion in the Pacific nations, one might erroneously conclude that we are observing a loss of faiths. However, when we look at those born overseas (predominantly the older age groups), 'no religion' ranks seventh overall but with considerable variation: Samoan (seventh), Cook Island Māori (second), Tongan (fifth), Niuean (second) and Fijian (sixth). A question that remains to be investigated is whether there are differences in affiliations between those in the home countries who migrate compared with those who do not, or indeed if there are differences by choice of migration destination—the characteristics of those who migrate to New Zealand may be different from those who migrate to other places.

Interestingly, among overseas born Fijians, Islam ranks fifth, ahead of 'No Religion', (for the New Zealand born Fijians, Islam ranks seventh with No Religion first) but this may be largely the result of miscoding of Fijian Indians, as discussed in the next section below. However, as a cautionary note, this requires further investigation because Islam also ranks thirteenth for Niueans, twelfth for Samoans, Tongans and Cook Islanders, indicating that it may not be valid to assume this is simply the result of miscoding, but an indication of an emerging Muslim community.

The Fijian Question

The data on Fijians and Fijian Indians is highly problematic, and a clear case where clinical sociology can contribute. These data issues matter immensely to both the Fijian communities and to the Fijian Indian (Girmitya) communities. Fijian as a label is a special case. The mandate of the Ministry of Pacific Peoples relates to i-Taukei, indigenous Fijians, and this is the population referred to as 'Fijian' in the collection of ethnicity. The Fijian Indian population, by contrast, defined as Asian, sits within the mandate of the Ministry of Ethnic Affairs. These mandates are defined by ethnicity and not by geography.

Fiji is, after New Zealand and Papua New Guinea, by far the most populous country among the south Pacific nations, with a current population of around 900,000 people (population estimates for Fiji vary markedly between sources), of whom an estimated 54% are indigenous Fijians. The Fijian ethnic population in New Zealand is growing but is currently relatively small, with 19,722 people in 2018, of whom 41.2% were born in New Zealand. This definition excludes non-indigenous groups such as Fijian Indians unless they also have identified as of Fijian ethnicity.

The difficulty stems from the way people describe themselves—the ethnicity questions are often answered in terms of citizenship or nationality. The Constitution of the Republic of Fiji acknowledges that all iTaukei, Fijian-Rotumans and Fijian Indians are Fijian by 'citizenry':

> WE, THE PEOPLE OF FIJI ... RECOGNISING the descendants of the indentured labourers from British India and the Pacific Islands, their culture, customs, traditions and language ... DECLARE that we are all Fijians united by common and equal citizenry (Government of Fiji, 2013).

Moreover, many Fijian Indians assert themselves as belonging to the Pacific, feeling uncomfortable being seen as belonging within Asian grouping of ethnicities, and more specifically with being included in the Indian grouping. People who identify as "Fijian Indian" are self-identifying as such. They have not indicated that they identify as 'Pacific' nor are they identifying as 'Indian' because they have deliberately eschewed the "Indian" tickbox which is included on many collection instruments. While the Fijian constitution is a legal definition of belonging applicable in Fiji relating to a nationality rather than ethnic construct, people from Fiji bring with them this context, which does have an impact on how people perceive themselves and respond to an ethnicity question. It is a quandary indeed but is one of the problems with any classification that is used in many different contexts. Moreover, if Fijian Indians were counted as Pacific then they are no more visible at an aggregated level than they are in Asian—it is no solution in any situation where the data cannot be dissected at a more granular level.

Either way there is a problem. Fijian Indians have high levels of diabetes and heart disease which results in poor health and premature death. Measuring the long term implications requires a good understanding of the population at risk as well as the factors that are driving changes in the incidence and severity of these health issues. The 2018 Census reported 15,132 people who identified specifically as Fijian Indian, but careful analysis of the data, taking into account other details such as being born in Fiji and being recorded as of 'Indian' ethnicity, shows that the true number is at least 75,348 (Narayan et al., 2022). This is more consistent with what is known about migration histories which, along with births in New Zealand, suggest that the Fijian Indian population in New Zealand is significantly larger than indigenous Fijian counts. In this case both a health lens, to look at the epidemiology and epigenetics within the health data, and a sociological lens, to examine the nature, size and demography of the implied population at risk is necessary to lay the groundwork for detailed solutions. How a population is counted and how it is labelled becomes of vital practical importance.

Conclusion

Clinical sociology then is multidisciplinary. Sociology provides theoretical frameworks and paradigms, but when translated into a clinical/applied context the theory must interface with competing theories from a large number of other disciplines, both within social, psychological and health sciences. The term 'clinical' is connected with reclining (Wirth, 1931), conjuring an image of society as an object of inquiry in a supine dysfunctional state. The work of the clinical sociologist does indeed often focus on the dysfunctional because of the imperative to fix a perceived problem, but a more productive approach is to understand the organism first. This allows a prior assessment that the perceived problem is in fact a problem, providing the opportunity for increased efficiency and effectiveness. The primary question raised by Mazey and Richardson (2022) is important because if the policy process is not fit for purpose, in the words of William Wordsworth ([1807] 1990, p. 150), by "getting and spending, we lay waste our powers" without effective solutions. Fashions in policy and progressing in fits and starts have been a feature of much of the analysis and intervention surrounding Pacific people in New Zealand, but progress is very clear. Wellbeing is currently to the fore, as is health, education and housing. There are more nuanced surveys either being conducted or coming online. These include longitudinal studies such as Growing Up in New Zealand as well as the General Social Survey and, in development, Living in Aotearoa and a post-censal Disability Survey both going into the field in 2023. Integrated data tools continue to develop, providing the basic data for detailed research.

Evidence is primary for clinical sociology, so data comparability is crucial. Currently, the collection of ethnicity is undergoing a review. There are two objectives. The first is to determine whether or not the principles underpinning the 2005 Standard of Ethnicity remain valid, which will entail addressing concerns that have emerged since 2005 about completeness, relevance and placement of some categories. The second objective is to establish an agreed mandated standard which will be applied across most of government where possible, obliging departments to collect, record and report ethnicity on the basis of this standard.

The key critical development will be the implementation of this mandated set of classifications to ensure that data is collected systematically and that the analytical outcomes based on data are as comparable to each other as possible. While this is the ambition of the current review of ethnicity standard and classification, it is likely to be some years before this could be implemented across the data system and likely will not enable backward compatibility with historical data in at least some cases. Crucial to the outcome is the development of mechanisms with the capacity for comparability across time because time-series are a fundamentally, though often under-recognised, analytical resource.

Even with these basic precursors in place, much work will need to be done in the clinical sociology space. Clinical sociology is hard because it is not a skill that is taught, as Charles Crothers observes in this volume, but one that is learnt on the fly in the field. This assumes a high level of multidisciplinary knowledge, or at least the flexibility and capacity to work within multidisciplinary teams. It is an emerging and increasingly valued field within policy and practice in Aotearoa New Zealand.

References

Aminzadeh, K., Denny, S., Utter, J., Milfont, T., Ameritunga, S., Teevale, T. & Clark, T. (2013). Neighbourhood social capital and adolescent self-reported wellbeing in New Zealand: A multilevel analysis. *Social Science and Medicine, 84*, 13–21.

Anae, M. (2020). *The platform: The radical legacy of the Polynesian panthers*. Bridget Williams Books.

Ardern, J. (2021). Speech to dawn raids apology. *New Zealand Government*. https://www.beehive.govt.nz/speech/speech-dawnraids-apology

Beals, F., Kidman, J., & Funaki, H. (2020). Insider and outsider research: Negotiating self at the edge of the emic/etic divide. *Qualitative Inquiry, 26*(6), 583–592.

Bedford, R., Bedford, C., Wall, J., & Young, M. (2017). Managed temporary labour migration of Pacific Islanders to Australia and New Zealand in the early twenty-first century. *Australian Geographer, 48*(1), 37–57.

Bellringer, M., Pearson, J., & Iustini, L. (2022). Pre-teen gang involvement is associated with teenage gambling behaviour: Exploratory findings from a longitudinal cohort study of Pacific youth in New Zealand. *Asia Pacific Journal of Public Health, 34*(1), 72–78.

Brown, R. (1995). Hidden foreign exchange flows: Estimating unofficial remittances to Tonga and Western Samoa. *Asia and Pacific Migration Journal, 4*(1), 35–54.

Callister, P., Didham, R., & Potter, D. (2005). *Ethnic intermarriage in New Zealand*. Official statistics research series volume 1. Statistics New Zealand.

Callister, P., Didham, R., Newell, J., & Potter, D. (2007). "Family ethnicity": Knitting a jumper using two woolly concepts. *Social Policy Journal of New Zealand, 32*, 32–48.

Came, H. (2014). Sites of institutional racism in public health policy making in New Zealand. *Social Science and Medicine, 106*, 214–220.
Chandler, M., & Lalonde, C. (1998). Cultural continuity as a hedge against suicide in Canada's first nations. *Transcultural Psychiatry, 35*(2), 191–219.
Clawar, S. (2008). Clinical sociology. In *The Blackwell encyclopedia of sociology* (pp. 1–3). Wiley.
Connell, J., & Brown, R. (2005). *Remittances in the Pacific: An overview*. Asian Development Bank.
Cram, F., Hutchings, J., & Smith, J. (2022). *Kāinga tahi, kāinga rua*. Bridget Williams Books.
Cunningham, J. (2022). *International labour migration and the children left behind: Gearing the voices of young people traversing transnational parenting in Tonga*. PhD thesis, University of Wollongong.
David, G. (2022). What's phase 2? Crafting the value proposition for applied and clinical sociology. *Journal of Applied Social Science, 16*(2), 371–381.
Didham, R. (2005). *Understanding and working with ethnicity data*. Statistics New Zealand.
Didham, R. (2016). Ethnic mobility in the New Zealand census, 1981–2013: A preliminary look. *New Zealand Population Review, 42*, 27–42.
Didham, R. (2023). Language maintenance, language loss and dimensions of identity among ethnic communities in Aotearoa New Zealand. *New Zealand Population Review*.
Didham, R., & Callister, P. (2012). The effect of ethnic prioritisation on ethnic health analysis: A research note. *New Zealand Medical Journal, 125*(1359), 58–66.
Dow, R., Warran, K., Letrondo, P., & Fancourt, D. (2023). The arts in public health policy: Progress and opportunities. *The Lancet Public Health, 8*, e155–e160.
Durie, M. (2017). Indigenous suicide: The Turamarama declaration. *Journal of indigenous wellbeing – Te Mauri – Pimatisiwin, 2*(2) Article 5.
Evening Post. (1879, May 31). Pasifika labourers arrive in Auckland. *Evening Post* (1870). https://nzhistory.govt.nz/page/pasifika-labourers-arrive-auckland. Evening Post May 31, 1870.
Freedman, J. (1989). Defining clinical sociology. *The Development of Clinical and Applied Sociology, 7*(1), 53–56.
Friesen, W., & Collins, F. (2017). Brain chains: Managing and mediating knowledge migration. *Migration and Development, 6*(3), 323–342.
Fritz, J. (1988). The history of clinical sociology. *Clinical Sociology Review, 1*(1), 72–95.
Fritz, J. (2021). *International clinical sociology* (2nd ed.). Springer Nature.
Galperin, B., Punnett, B., Ford, D., & Lituchy (2022). *An emic-etic-emic research cycle for understanding context in under researched countries. International journal of cross-cultural management*. On-line first. https://doi.org/10.1177/14705958221075534
Gans, H. (1979). Symbolic ethnicity: The future of ethnic groups and cultures in America. *Ethnic and Racial Studies, 2*(1), 1–20.
Gans, H. (2017). Another look at symbolic ethnicity. *Ethnic and Racial Studies, 40*(9), 1410–1417.
Gibson, J., McKenzie, D., & Rohorua, H. (2006). How elastic are remittances? Estimates from Tongan migrants in New Zealand. *Pacific economic bulletin, 21*(1), 112–127.
Goodyear, R. (2017). A place to call home? Declining home ownership rates for Māori and Pacific peoples in New Zealand. *New Zealand Population Review., 43*(1–2), 8–34.
Government of Fiji. (2013). *Constitution of the Republic of Fiji*. http://www.paclii.org/fj/Fiji-Constitution-English-2013.pdf.
Graves, A. (1986). Colonialism and indentured labour migration in the Western pacific, 1840-195. In P. C. Emmer (Ed.), *Colonialism and migration: Indentured labour before and after slavery* (pp. 237–259). Martinus Nijhoff Publishers.
Hallett, D., Chandler, M., & Lalonde, C. (2007). Aboriginal language knowledge and youth suicide. *Cognitive Development, 22*, 392–399.
Hartigan, J. (2008). Is race still socially constructed? The recent controversy over race and medical genetics. *Science as Culture, 17*(2), 163–193.
Henrickson, M. (2007). Lavender faith: Religion, spirituality and identity in lesbian, gay and bisexual new Zealanders. *Journal of Religion and Spirituality in Social Work, 26*(3), 63–80.

Ho, E., Cheung, V., & Didham, R. (2017). *Starting strong: Nurturing the potential of our Asian under-fives*. Asia New Zealand Foundation.

Joseph, T. (2005). *Cracked coconuts: An exploration of why young cook islanders are leaving cook islander congregations of the Presbyterian Church of Aotearoa New Zealand*. MTh thesis, Otago University.

Kukutai, T., & Taylor, J. (2016). *Indigenous data sovereignty: Towards an agenda*. ANU Press.

Lilo, L., Tautolo, E.-S., & Smith, M. (2020). Health literacy, culture and Pacific peoples in Aotearoa, New Zealand: A review. *Pacific Health, 3*, 1–11.

MacDonald, L. (2018). *Silencing and institutional racism in settler-colonial education*. PhD thesis, Victoria University of Wellington.

Macpherson, C. (1997). A Samoan solution to the limitations of urban housing in New Zealand. In J. Rensel & M. Rodman (Eds.), *Home in the islands: Housing and social change in the Pacific*. University of Hawai'i Press.

Macpherson, C., & Macpherson, L. (2001). Evangelical religion among Pacific Island migrants: New faiths or brief diversions. *Journal of ritual studies., 15*(2), 27–37.

Mallon, S., Māhina-Tuai, K., & Salesa, D. (2012). *Tagata o le moana, New Zealand and the people of the Pacific*. Te Papa Press.

Mazey, S., & Richardson, J. (2021). *Policy-making under pressure: Rethinking the policy process in Aotearoa New Zealand*. Canterbury University Press.

Mazey, S., & Richardson, J. (2022). Is the Aotearoa New Zealand policy process fit for purpose? *Policy Quarterly, 18*(2), 93–99.

Mead, H. (2003). *Tikanga Māori: living by Māori values*. Huia Press.

Ministry of Business, Innovation and Employment, Ministry of Education, Ministry of Social Development and Ministry for Women. (2022). *Preparing all young people for satisfying and rewarding working lives. Draft Long-term Insights Briefing September–October, 2022*. https://consultation.education.govt.nz/education/long-term-insights-briefing/

Ministry of Pacific Peoples. (2022). *Long-term insights briefing 2022*. Ministry of Pacific Peoples. https://www.mpp.govt.nz/assets/Reports/Long-Term-Insights-Briefing/MPP-LTIB-v3.pdf

Mok, T-M. (2019). *Inside the box: Ethnic choice and ethnic change for mixed people in the United Kingdom*. PhD thesis in social policy, LSE.

Narayan, P., Rahiman-Manuel, I., Raju, A., Satyanand, T., Gandhi, R., Kristono, G., Faatoese, A., Didham, R., Watene-O'Sullivan, C., Lehnert, K., Larsen, P., & Snell, R. (2022). Investigating the genetic underpinnings of premature cardiovascular disease among Girmit-descendants living in Aotearoa. *CAHRE National Symposium*. University of Auckland, Grafton Campus 2 September 2022.

O'Brien, L.-A., Denny, S., Clark, T., Fleming, T., Teevale, T., & Robinson, E. (2013). The impact of religion and spirituality on the risk behaviours of young people in Aotearoa, New Zealand. *Youth Studies Australia, 32*(4), 25–37.

Pasikale, A., & George, T. (1995). *For the family first: A study of income allocation within Pacific Islands families in New Zealand: The Pacific Islands component of the intra family income & resource allocation project*. Destini Incorporated.

Pike, K. (1954). *Language in relation to a unified theory of the structure of human behaviour*. Summer Institute of Linguistics.

Public Finance (Wellbeing) Amendment Act. (2020). https://www.legislation.govt.nz/act/public/2020/0029/latest/LMS254609.html

Public Service Act. (2020). https://www.legislation.govt.nz/act/public/2020/0040/latest/LMS106159.html

Pulotu-Endemann, F. (2021). Not another new bloody model of wellbeing. *AKO Journal, 2021*, 20–21.

Pulotu-Endemann, F. K., & Bush, J. M. (2000). *Making a Pacific Island difference in a mental health setting: Training workshop for people wanting to increase their understanding around Pacific Island mental health*. Auckland Healthcare Limited.

Rasanathan, K., Ameratunga, S., & Tse, S. (2006). Asian health in New Zealand – Progress and challenges. *The New Zealand Medical Journal, 119*(1244), 1–8.

Rocha, Z. (2022). Clinical sociology and mixedness: Towards applying critical race theory in everyday life. *Genealogy, 6*(2), 32. https://doi.org/10.3390/genealogy6020032

Rohorua, H., Natua, J., Tapu, M. & Koloto, M. (2022). *Report on housing and retirement among Pacific Peoples in Aotearoa.* Te Ara Ahunga Ora Retirement Commission and Ministry of Pacific Peoples.

Roy, C., & Slim, G. (2022). Two worlds: Enhancing knowledge sharing between academics and policy makers in Aotearoa New Zealand. *Policy Quarterly, 18*(4), 65–73.

Shaw, S., & Heap, N. (2022). Health workforce planning: An urgent need to link islands of expertise. *Policy Quarterly, 18*(4), 74–83.

Sibley, C., Stewart, K., Houkamau, C., Manuela, S., Perry, R., Wootton, L., Harding, J., Zhang, Y., Sengupta, N., & Roberston, A. (2011). Ethnic group stereotypes in New Zealand. *New Zealand Journal of Psychology, 40*(2), 25–36.

Smith, A., Fereti, S., & Adams, S. (2021). Inequities and perspectives from the COVID-Delta outbreak: The imperative for strengthening the Pacific nursing workforce in Aotearoa New Zealand. *Nursing Praxis in Aotearoa New Zealand, 37*(3), 94–103. https://doi.org/10.36951/27034542.2021.040

Smith, L. (2012). *Decolonising methodologies: Research and indigenous peoples* (2nd ed.). Zed Books.

Statistics New Zealand. (2005). *Statistical standard for ethnicity*. Statistics New Zealand.

Stats NZ. (2023). *Pacific housing: People, place and wellbeing in New Zealand.* Statistics New Zealand. https://www.stats.govt.nz/reports/pacific-housing-people-place-and-wellbeing-in-aotearoa-new-zealand/

Steele, S. (2017). “When you come to the fork in the road, take it . . .” aspirations for applied and clinical sociology: Paradigms to princesses. *Journal of Applied Social Science, 11*(1), 5–10.

Tautolo, E.-S., Faletau, J., Iustini, L., & Paterson, J. (2020). Exploring success amongst Pacific families in New Zealand: findings from the Pacific Islands Families Study. *Pacific Health Dialog, 21*(5), 216–225. https://doi.org/10.26635/phd.2020.627

Teevale, T., Lee, A. C.-L., Tiatia-Seath, J., Clark, T. C., Denny, S., Bullen, P., Fleming, T., & Peiris-John, R. J. (2016). Risk and protective factors for suicidal behaviors among Pacific youth in New Zealand. *Crisis: The Journal of Crisis Intervention and Suicide Prevention, 37*(5), 335–346.

The Treasury. (2022). Te tai waiora: Wellbeing in Aotearoa New Zealand 2022. *The Treasury.* https://www.treasury.govt.nz/publications/wellbeing-report/te-tai-waiora-2022

Tokalau, T. (2023). New Zealand’s first multigenerational state homes a Pasifika game-changer. *Stuff* January 15, 2023. https://www.stuff.co.nz/national/130614482/new-zealands-first-multigenerational-state-homes-a-pasifika-gamechanger

Van Hulst, M., & Yanow, D. (2016). From policy “frames” to “framing”: Theorizing a more dynamic, political approach. *American Review of Public Administrations, 46*(1), 92–112.

Wan, P., & Wan, A. (2020). *Clinical sociology. Moving from theory to practice*. Springer.

Webb, R., Suaalii-Sauni, T., Wright-Bardohl, T., & Tauri, J. (2022). Building understanding of Māori and Samoan experiences of youth justice: Navigating beyond the limits of official statistics. *New Zealand Sociology, 37*(1), 70–92.

Wirth, L. (1931). Sociology and clinical procedure. *The American Journal of Sociology, 37*, 49–66 (reprinted in *Clinical sociology review*, 1(1), 7–22).

Wordsworth, W. (1990). *Poems, in Two Volumes, and Other Poems, 1800–1807*. Ed. Jared Curtis. Cornell UP.

Yao, E. (2022). *Classifying ethnicity in multi-ethnic contexts: Implications of methodological decisions in quantitative research.* PhD thesis, University of Auckland.

Robert Didham is a demographer with Statistics New Zealand and a research associate with the Te Ngira: Insitute for Population Research at Waikato University, and an elected honorary life member of the Population Association of New Zealand. He is a specialist in ethnicity and identity, with interests in historical linguistics, Buddhology, diaspora studies and the relationship between social and biological sciences and the importance this interface has on health and inequality, and has published widely in these fields.

Sociology as Applied Within Healthcare Research and Practice in Aotearoa New Zealand

Kevin Dew

Introduction

Sociology as applied to healthcare has a rich history in Aotearoa New Zealand. Sociologists working on health-related topics can take on several labels, including medical sociologists, sociologists of health and illness, and also more generic titles like health social scientist or health researcher. New Zealand medical sociologists have also taken their trade overseas, with some making major impacts to the field of sociology as well as beyond in the places where they have dwelled. For example, John McKinlay was a very early graduate in sociology at Victoria University of Wellington who went on to become an outstanding scholar in the field of medical sociology, with his work being recognised by the American Sociological Association with a Distinguished Career Award. Evan Willis, a medical sociologist who also graduated from Victoria University of Wellington with a Master's degree received The Australian Sociological Association Distinguished Service Award, and his book *Medical dominance: the division of labour in Australian Health Care*, was voted by his peers as one of the ten most influential books in Australian sociology in 2003.

New Zealand has a complex and ever-evolving health system with funding for services coming from a mix of public funding, private insurance and out-of-pocket payments. In 1938 New Zealand established a publicly funded hospital service, the first country to do so (Blank, 1994). However, private hospitals could still operate, and primary care services provided by general practitioners (GPs) were not covered in the same way. Currently most patients attending GPs pay out-of-pocket for the service or through private medical insurance. In addition to the complexity around

K. Dew (✉)
Sociology and Social Policy Programme, Te Herenga Waka – Victoria University of Wellington, Wellington, New Zealand
e-mail: kevin.dew@vuw.ac.nz

© The Author(s), under exclusive license to Springer Nature Switzerland AG 2023
Z. L. Rocha, K. L. Davidson (eds.), *Applied and Clinical Sociology in Aotearoa New Zealand*, Clinical Sociology: Research and Practice,
https://doi.org/10.1007/978-3-031-36581-2_7

payments, the organisation of the healthcare system has changed many times since the establishment of publicly funded hospitals, with at various times the governance of hospitals being overseen by appointed officials, or elected members, and names changing according to political ideologies, such as hospitals at one stage being called Crown Health Enterprises. Given this complexity and evolution, sociological research is then imperative to try to understand the impacts of these arrangements and where calls can be made for improving the delivery of healthcare services.

In the following I will provide a brief outline of developments in sociology as applied to health care in Aotearoa New Zealand, and then work through key examples illustrating some of the relationships between health topics or issues, sociological theorisation, the practical application of sociological research approaches and the relevance of this to the delivery of healthcare.

Developments in Sociology Applied to Healthcare

Well before sociology was established as a standalone discipline in New Zealand universities there were many strains of research related to health sociology. As far back as 1887, in his book *The State: Rudiments of New Zealand Sociology*, James Pope included material on the provision of and governance of hospitals and asylums (Brickell, 2007). In the 1920s at the University of Otago, students in preventive medicine undertook research on topics that had health concerns of a sociological nature, such as on the lives of those living in poor housing and the health and safety management of a local chocolate factory (Brickell, 2007). In the 1950s a School of Social Sciences was set up at Victoria University in Wellington and research by staff and students covered topics such as factory accidents and aging.

The first sociology department in New Zealand was established by Jim Robb who taught an honours sociology of medicine course from 1968 (Kirkman, 2012). Robb also taught in the social work programme after his arrival at Victoria University in 1954 and students in this programme could work as medical social workers. With the aim of gaining a greater depth of understanding of the working circumstances of medical social workers so that sociological insights could be applied to their training, and in turn those insights be applied to their work practices, Robb undertook extensive research on medical social work. In the early 1960s he conducted interviews at 25 hospitals throughout New Zealand, which included 99 interviews with medical social workers, medical superintendents, hospital matrons and others. In addition he gathered information on medical social work from personnel at the School of Social Work at the University of Sydney, the State University Hospital, Syracuse, New York, the Regional Hospital Board, Birmingham, and the Institute of Almoners, London (Robb, 1965). The report that was produced from this research was written for and circulated "among social workers, medical superintendents, and others concerned in the employment and training of medical social workers" (Robb, 1965). The report contained a list of recommendations including ones on training, remuneration and the scope of practice of medical social work. This early work was not, to my knowledge, published in academic journals, but was a sociological inquiry with a very practical goal: firmly directed at improving the training, working conditions and practices of medical social workers, with those able to respond to this targeted in the circulation of the report.

Jim Robb continued his interest in health matters, at times publishing in academic outlets and contributing to sociological theorisation of, for example health promotion. In one article he notes the failure of health promotion programmes in preventing smoking. He argued that viewing smoking as a rite of passage for some social groups would assist in how smoking prevention programmes would be pitched. He encouraged smoking cessation programmes to target dominant social groups so that smoking would eventually no longer be viewed as a rite of passage (Robb, 1986). Prior to the establishment of a University of Otago health sciences campus in Wellington in 1977, Robb, and his colleague John McCreary, had worked with epidemiologists from the Wellington hospital since the 1960s (Robb, 1996). This research studied "the influence of culture patterns on various aspects of health" especially cardiovascular disease, with a focus on Māori across different dimensions of rurality and urbanisation and island groups in the South Pacific such as the Tokelau Islands (Robb & Crothers, 1985, p. 480).

Since the 1960s/1970s there have been a range of fields of inquiry looking at applications of sociological theorising to healthcare opened up by sociologists in Aotearoa New Zealand. The following is not exhaustive but notes some prominent areas of research and practical impacts over the past decades.

Peter Davis, who worked in various departments in New Zealand, including the Sociology Departments at the University of Canterbury and the University of Auckland, has researched a number of topics, including dental care and pharmaceuticals. One of his major research projects was on the quality of care in New Zealand public hospitals. This research was a cross-sectional survey of 6579 patients admitted to larger hospitals in New Zealand in 1998. The research team published findings on a range of adverse events in hospitals, including surgical and drug-related adverse events, and found, for example, that Māori were more likely to experience preventable adverse events than non-Māori (Davis et al., 2002; Davis et al., 2006). Recommendations from this research included the encouragement of further development for Māori health providers and support for cross cultural and cultural competence training.

Pauline Norris, a social pharmacist at the University of Otago who gained her PhD in sociology at Victoria University of Wellington, has also researched in a range of areas include breast implants, the impact of prescription charges for medications on people living in poverty, and also a study on knowledge and use of antibiotics. The latter included research with Samoan participants, finding that these participants drew on both Samoan and *palagi* [white] paradigms of illness, and worked to determine which one was relevant for the illness being suffered: such a determination was not just made by the individual sufferer but also by the family. A recommendation from this finding is that when dealing with illness in the Samoan community, family should be involved in the consultation process (Norris et al., 2009).

Rhonda Shaw, based at Victoria University of Wellington, has undertaken extensive research related to bioethical issues concerning morality and altruism, covering topics including human milk sharing, organ donation and surrogacy. The latter included research based on interviews with 20 gestational surrogates, 20 intended parents and 47 experts in the field. Included in the recommendations from this research was a reconsideration of New Zealand's policy of prohibiting payment and compensation for surrogates, such as covering loss of earnings resulting from pregnancy (Shaw & Gibson, 2022).

These sociologists are just a few of the examples of researchers applying their sociological expertise to practical issues, and a selection of the applications of their research to healthcare. There is a vast range of other research covering many areas, including women's and girls' health (Hyde, 2000; Donovan & Telfar-Barnard, 2019; Barker, 1999; Grace, 1997; Fenwick, 1980), death and dying (McManus, 2013); teams working with the chronically ill, elderly and psychiatric patients (Opie, 2000), diagnosis (Jutel, 2011), health policy (Scott et al., 1986; Fougere, 1974), mental health (Cohen, 2016), foetal alcohol spectrum disorder (Gibbs, 2019), pesticide spraying (Vallée, 2021), alternative medicine (Dew, 2003, 2021) and many more.

As can be seen, there has been a vast amount of sociological research on healthcare in Aotearoa New Zealand. In the following section I will focus on three key areas, given their sociological orientation and practical focus on contributing to a change in thinking in healthcare delivery. These areas are not only chosen for their applied interest, but also because the author of this chapter was involved in the research and so has some depth of understanding of the research and its goals.

Social Meanings of Medication Research and Pharmacovigilance

There has been a long history of sociological interest in pharmaceutical practices and medication in New Zealand (Davis, 1992). In the late 2000s I was involved in research that explored the social meanings of medications. The focus here was on household use of medications, with medications understood as whatever householders did or took for therapeutic purposes, so including alternative medicine and folk remedies, as well as prescribed and over the counter pharmaceuticals. We collected data from 55 households across Aotearoa New Zealand through household interviews, diary elicited interviews and photo-elicited interviews, the latter two where householders recorded thoughts and encounters with medications over the course of 2 weeks and took photos of anything that related to medications over that time. Through the research a number of issues were identified and written about, including the moral dimensions of therapeutic use (Dew et al., 2015), the routines and relationships established around medication use (Hodgetts et al., 2011) and the way in which the home could be viewed as a therapeutic centre in its own right (Dew et al., 2014).

In considering the moral dimensions of therapeutic use, we noted the way in which responsibility, discipline and values underpinned the consumption of medications. An analytic approach using interpretive repertoires found four dominant repertoires (Dew et al., 2015). One was a repertoire of a 'disordered society', where the consumption of pharmaceuticals was seen as a symbol and outcome of living in a society that was in an unnatural state and so required synthetic unnatural remedies. Another was a 'disordered self' repertoire where the consumption of medications was seen as a moral failing because one was not able to attain a state of health that required discipline in terms of such things as exercise and diet. A third repertoire was a 'disordering substances' one, which primarily applied to those participants who were taking anti-psychotic medications, where the drugs themselves could be disordering but could also be necessary, and a balance had to be found between the two. Finally, there was what we called a 're-ordering substances' repertoire, where medications simply and unproblematically returned one to a better state of health or maintained a particular level of health. Importantly this research showed the variable ways in which pharmaceutical use tied into one's sense of identity, and we developed the concept of pharmaceutical governance to alert us to the different roles and responsibilities that come with pharmaceutical consumption. Knowing these various responses can help us to consider how compliant pharmaceutical users might be and make sense of non-compliance.

When we looked at the routines of medication consumption, including pharmaceuticals, supplements and what might be called folk remedies, it was notable how medications tied into and could change relationships inside households (Hodgetts et al., 2011). When we asked participants to bring their medications out and we got them to pick them up and tell us about them, the act would transport people through time to recollect events and relationships: who took this medication, where did it come from, who was responsible for overseeing its use or determining when it should no longer be used? Different parts of the home became spaces for storage, or to facilitate the routine encountering of medications that needed to be taken on a daily basis. Caring across generations meant that for some householders, elderly family members were encouraged to live with their children so that medication consumption could be overseen. Through exploring the relationality of medication consumption, this analysis heightens awareness that medication consumption is a social practice and impacts on relationships and the organisation of household spaces.

Through this research on households we came to the view that it is useful to consider the home or the household as a therapeutic centre in its own right (Dew et al., 2014). Householders can bring medications into the home from many different sources: from pharmacies and health shops, supermarkets, the consultation rooms of alternative practitioners and so on. They access ideas about medications from many sources, including health professionals, the media, family members, work colleagues and friends. They then make sense of all of this inside the home, where they may experiment, closely observe and tactically manipulate advice from outside. This is so medications can align with their routines, resources and values. Interpreting the household as a therapeutic centre in this way decentralises the role of health professionals and deepens our understanding of wellness practices in all their tremendous variety.

During this research on the household use of medications the team was approached by the Centre for Adverse Reactions Monitoring (CARM) to see if we could shed light on what was something of a puzzle for them. This was the puzzle: in July 2007 a new formulation of a pharmaceutical to treat hypothyroidism was introduced into New Zealand. As this was the only formulation that was approved to be subsidised by PHARMAC, the New Zealand pharmaceutical management agency, most patients who were on the previous formulation, 70,000 of them, were switched to the new one. The new formulation was considered to be bioequivalent to the old formulation, that is, it was deemed to be no different in terms of its therapeutic effect or its toxicity. The change came about as the drug manufacturer consolidated its manufacturing operations, and although the active ingredient was the same, the colour of the tablet was changed from yellow to white. This minor alteration was not expected to cause any problems. However, to the surprise of the pharmacovigilance agency in New Zealand, the Centre for Adverse Reactions Monitoring (CARM), a sharp jump in reports of adverse reactions to the new formulation started coming in. Between 1973 and July 2007 there had been a total of only 14 reports of adverse reactions to thyroxine medications. Between July 2007 and September 2008 there were 810 reports linking the new formulation to various adverse reactions including visual disturbances, skin rashes, and joint and muscle pain, and in some cases these reactions were severe.

CARM tried to make sense of this reaction. They contacted 83 countries on the World Health Organization's adverse reactions monitoring scheme. They found that similar reactions had been reported in some countries for other brands of thyroxine, but not for this formulation. In addition, a research team I was working in was asked if we would be interested in having a look at the issue. Could we, as sociologists and social scientists, shed some light on this?

The Medicines Adverse Reactions Committee (MARC), an advisory committee to the Ministry of Health, concluded that there was no explanation for an increase in adverse reaction reports. However, due to the high level of adverse reactions, PHARMAC subsidised other brands of the medication for those who were intolerant to the new formulation, and it was reported that many who made the switch improved. So, what was going on? Several candidates for an explanation had been considered at various stages and by other researchers.

Another group of researchers had expressed interest in this issue to CARM, and provided a very particular interpretation of this event, putting it down to an irrational response from vulnerable patients (Faasse et al., 2010). They noted that there had been media coverage of this issue and suggested that combined with a distrust in PHARMAC, patients who were vulnerable to emotional distress because of their condition were encouraged by key individuals (for example, a pharmacist in Southland who appeared in early media coverage expressing his concern about patients who had bad responses to the new formulation) to see these symptoms of distress as resulting from the new formulation. In their published research the authors produced no evidence that people reporting adverse reactions to the new formulation were irrational, or that they were any more emotionally vulnerable than other people. In addition, the authors assumed that the usual level of reporting adverse reactions to medications is the correct level, an assumption that is demonstrably not the case. Even a rudimentary scan of medical and social science literature shows that there is a long tradition of patient reports of adverse reactions being dismissed, and that there is an extraordinary underreporting of adverse reactions to medications overall (Abraham & Shepherd, 1999; Mintz, 1985; Lopez-Gonzalez et al., 2009; Wiktorowicz et al., 2012). However, this version of events gained traction in clinical circles, being published in a medical journal with wide circulation. An explanation of irrational people means the issue can be safely ignored, and that we have no need to attend to our pharmacovigilance systems or anything else. Silly people will be silly people no matter what.

Turning from psychological explanations to physical explanations, there was some evidence that the assumption about the bioequivalence of the new formulation was not justified. Medsafe, which regulates therapeutic products in New Zealand and oversees drug safety activities, used an internationally accepted range for determining bioequivalence, however, some prominent organisations used a much narrower range. For example, the American Thyroid Association and others assumed a much narrower range of bioequivalence than was used in New Zealand, which was a 80–125% bioequivalence range. So, from the American point of view adverse reactions could be occurring because the new formulation did not have enough of the active ingredient (so say 80% of the old formulation) or had too much of the active ingredient (so say 125% of the old formulation). The former may cause symptoms of hypothyroidism and the latter hyperthyroidism.

But why would this be a problem in New Zealand and not elsewhere? The role of PHARMAC is central here, as in New Zealand patients could not access hypothyroid drugs from other manufacturers as PHARMAC only subsidised the one formulation, whereas in overseas jurisdictions if a patient was having problems with a particular brand they could be easily switched to another one.

Another explanation combined the psychological and the physical. Early on, Medsafe suggested that people were experiencing adverse reactions because of poor compliance. Again, with no evidence, the suggestion is that the change of formulation somehow led to a change of patient behaviour, that in turn had adverse effects. Why people would have poor compliance with the new formulation when they complied with the old formulation was not explained. However, this understanding of causation was not further raised by Medsafe after the initial suggestions.

In trying to get some understanding of this puzzle we collected data from relevant media, predominantly newspapers, from the period of the controversy, June 2008 to August 2009. Press releases from PHARMAC, Medsafe, the Ministry of Health and political parties were obtained, and the minutes from the meetings of MARC. The approach we took drew on Actor Network Theory and our objective was to provide a picture of the unfolding of events and the different actors involved (Dew et al., 2017b; Gardner & Dew, 2011).

So how did the events unfold once we followed the actors? What we found was that local newspapers published articles that provided accounts from patients about their experiences of adverse reactions. But in addition to this, later articles noted that CARM wanted to hear from people who had experienced what they thought was an adverse reaction to the new formulation, and they provided contact details for CARM. This is significant, as the role of CARM is not well known in New Zealand, and very few people indeed contact CARM in 'normal' situations. CARM usually relies on what is termed spontaneous reporting in the surveillance of medications once they are on the market. As such it does not seek out 'signals' of potential problems with medications but relies on patients and health professionals to make reports to them. Only 1–2% of reports to CARM are typically made by patients, with the vast majority coming from health professionals. But now patients were learning of this new avenue, for them, of reporting their concerns. This was further facilitated by members of parliament raising concerns and issuing their own press releases, which again provided information on how to contact CARM, and this was picked up and publicised by the press. In addition, some radio programmes picked up the story, further alerting people on this medication that any unusual symptoms they were experiencing could be caused by the new formulation.

This media attention continued over many months, and there were questions in Parliament about this and pressure placed on the different agencies to find some solution to this ongoing problem. Eventually PHARMAC relented and subsidised a different medication, Goldshield, for people who were having problems with the new formulation of Eltroxin, and with this change media coverage quickly became much less frequent, as did reporting of adverse drug reactions.

So, what might be a sociological explanation for this phenomenon? As noted, most reporting of side effects and adverse reactions to medications in a business-as-usual scenario come from health professionals, and commonly General Practitioners (GPs). Research has shown that underreporting of side effects or adverse reactions to medications may be as high as 94% (Hazell & Shakir, 2006) and that patient concerns about side effects in consultations are, with a few exceptions, downplayed, ignored or dismissed by GPs (Dew et al., 2012; Seale et al., 2007; Backstrom et al., 2000). I will return to this issue in the section on interactions in the consultation below. With such dramatic underreporting of side effects, the Eltroxin case indicates that a new mechanism for reporting adverse reactions opened up in New Zealand at that time. Information provided by the media fostered patient reporting in ways that does not usually occur, and around 40% of the reports to CARM came from patients. In other words, the media played a role in facilitating pharmacovigilance, as opposed to preying on irrational people. Pharmacovigilance agencies around the world have been trying to work out how to be more proactive, rather that reactive, in identifying adverse drug reactions. It is likely that some reports will be 'false positives', that is, there is another explanation for the symptoms a patient has experienced other than the drug they are concerned about. But currently, with New Zealand's passive reporting system, we have a woeful picture of the extent of adverse reactions to drugs. The Eltroxin case indicated one way in which this could be enhanced, a way that circumvented the limitations of reporting through GPs.

The sociological explanation suggested here, that coverage by the media, facilitated by the involvement of other actors such as pharmacists and members of parliament opened up a new pathway for the reporting of adverse drug reactions, is not meant to be exclusive and the only one, but can be combined with others to provide a fuller understanding of the phenomenon. In particular, the issue of bioequivalence noted earlier may provide the explanation for physiological pathways that caused symptoms, but the sociological explanation draws attention also to the new pharmacovigilance pathway. This application of sociology gives us insight into a mechanism that enhances pharmacovigilance in New Zealand. The case of Eltroxin provides important insights into the underreporting of adverse drug reactions and suggests that there needs to be more effort put into opening up reporting channels. Given the high level of underreporting we should perhaps be less concerned with trying to explain any increase in reporting levels as a psychological problem residing with the medication users and more concerned with how we can obtain higher levels of reporting.

Understanding Difference in Health Service Delivery

Health inequities in cancer care outcomes are well documented in Aotearoa New Zealand. In an effort to better understand inequities between Māori and non-Māori, with Māori having a 93% higher mortality rate from cancer than non-Māori (Blakely et al., 2007), an interdisciplinary research team used a number of research strategies to explore how the healthcare system itself might add to these inequities (knowing that much inequity is an outcome of social, political and economic issues that have their impact before someone enters the healthcare system). Given the topic, a treaty-based approach was taken to the research, with two principal investigators, one Māori and one non-Māori. The research team consisted of members who had expertise in sociology, epidemiology, health promotion, clinical research and most importantly Māori health research.

There were three phases to the research, one phase included audio-recordings of multidisciplinary meetings where pathologists, oncologists, cancer nurses and others discussed patients and considered treatment plans for them. Another phase involved the audio-recording of consultations between patients and medical oncologists where a treatment plan for patients newly diagnosed with cancer was discussed. And another phase involved interviewing patients who had completed an initial treatment stage for cancer. The goal was to see if we could identify anything through this process that would facilitate interventions to reduce inequity.

In the analysis of the data collected the research team would come together and consider how to interpret what we were seeing. One thing that was immediately apparent was that there were very few instances where you could point to something and say—that is clearly racist or discriminatory. Not that this was completely absent, but it was relatively rare. On the other hand, a closer sociological analysis of the data did reveal a number of issues that could have a bearing on health inequities.

In the phase looking at multidisciplinary team meetings the recordings were listened to, transcribed, and various aspects were given a very close reading using an approach called conversation analysis. In conversation analysis an effort is made to transcribe as much detail of talk as possible, and not just the words. So, for example, changes in pitch and loudness would be identified, as well as pauses and non-lexical expressions like intakes of breath. Through this close reading some features of the interaction were identified that were not at first obvious. For example, some suggestions made by members of the multidisciplinary meeting were followed up and some were not, and in the cut and thrust of the meetings some were not even heard. Chairs of the meetings were important in determining what happened here. For this phase of the research members of our research team were participants in these meetings, and in some cases chaired them. When we took the results of our analysis back to these team members they were surprised. Being in the midst of the meeting meant they had missed a great deal of what was going on. When this was shown to them this had an immediate response, with one clinical researcher changing the way she ran the meetings as a result of what she now saw. For those of us who were non-clinical researchers, this meant our understandings were being immediately translated into practice, indicating the importance of interdisciplinary work of this nature where sociologists work alongside clinicians.

Another important finding from this analysis was identifying that where no one in the meeting had met the patient, the team members often struggled to interpret the information they had to hand. This showed the importance of in-person subjective assessments, such as how fit someone seemed or how frail, that could be crucial in determining whether someone would be offered, for example, surgery to remove cancer. This finding alerted us to two issues. One is that if subjective assessment is important, it needed to be done in such a way that it did not exacerbate inequities. Clinicians need to be cognizant of their own assumptions about things such as likely social support and home life, assumptions that might play into their views about recovery and so on. The second issue was that these team meetings occurred at secondary or tertiary hospitals as these were the places where there were the facilities to diagnose and treat the cancer. So those living in provincial areas were less likely to gain access to in-person contact with team members. As such they were at a disadvantage, and with higher proportions of the Māori population living in provincial areas there was opportunity for inequities to be exacerbated.

Another way in which difference between Māori and non-Māori could be seen was through the interviews with people who had completed at least the initial stage of cancer treatment. In the research we had conducted 34 interviews, 19 with non-Māori and 15 with Māori. We asked participants to discuss a range of issues, including the nature of their interactions within hospitals, how their pathway through the healthcare system could have been made better and whether they had been treated respectfully.

Here I will just focus on one finding to illustrate what a sociological analysis can bring to the table. When we started looking at the interview data it was noticeable that there were a number of subject positions that our participants seemed to take, and after considering different approaches to analysis, I suggested that we could look at the data using an ethnomethodologically influenced approach called membership categorisation analysis. The aim of an ethnomethodological approach is to describe how we, as members of a collectivity, "create and maintain a sense of order and intelligibility in social life" (ten Have, 2004, p. 139). Using membership categorisation analysis with the interview data allowed us to consider the different kinds of categories that participants described, and the rights and obligations associated with those categories. By doing so we could get a sense of the moral order of cancer care for patients, that is, how one might expect oneself and others to act.

Obvious categories that participants talked about were health professionals and patients, but what became of interest was the way in which the rights and obligations assigned to these categories could vary for different participants. In terms of this analysis, being a cancer patient was a category, one that had rights and responsibilities. For a cancer patient they would have a right to advice from oncologists and others, and a right to treatment. They would also have responsibilities, primarily to agree to the treatment being offered and to make oneself available for it. But for some Māori patients they operated with the categories of both a cancer patient and a Māori cancer patient. For the latter there was a sense that a diagnosis of cancer did not just pertain to the individual but also to the whānau [extended family]. There was potential here then for a dissonance between these roles of being a whānau member and being a patient, particularly if they wanted to accommodate a desire to be with whānau to get support from family members yet their whānau lived far away from the cancer treatment centre.

We also noted that for some Māori participants the role of patient did not sit quite so well as it did with non-Māori participants. In the classic discussion of the sick role as outlined by Talcott Parsons (Parsons & Fox, 1952) the patient is responsible for seeking therapeutic help but is then passive, handing over therapeutic responsibility to the health professional. For the non-Māori participants, they did not articulate any tension with this view. They could take on the passive role of patient. For some Māori they articulated a much more active role in their own care and in the obligations they felt inside hospital settings. In in-patient cancer care they might actively work to lift the atmosphere as patients sat in their chairs during chemotherapy—bringing humour to raise the spirits of those around them. In the ward they might make the bed and tidy up on the day of their discharge—to the bewilderment of hospital staff who saw it as their role to undertake such activities. This active role was not like the passive patient, but perhaps more like a guest. A guest has quite a different set of rights and responsibilities than does a patient. Different expectations about roles have the potential to lead to conflict or misunderstanding in mainstream Western medical institutions.

So, from this research we can start to see a whole range of ways in which inequities may appear and misunderstandings could occur, providing insights into sources of confusion and sources of differential treatment, ranging from interactional issues when participants may be attending to different categories, through to raising concerns about the structural issues that disadvantage those who may not have the chance for in-person interaction with members of the multidisciplinary team.

Being Informed by Detailed Considerations of Healthcare Interactions

In other research I was involved in, the research team included academic GPs, research nurses, as well as sociolinguists and sociologists. This combination of expertise meant that the research that was being carried out on interactions between doctors and patients could be immediately transferred to the educational settings of medical schools, as the academic GP taught in that environment. In addition, it is unlikely that the research would have been successful in recruiting participating doctors without having clinicians onboard.

The research started with a focus on understanding decision-making around referrals made by GPs to hospital specialists and understanding how specialists used tools that had been developed to determine whether a patient would have access to elective surgery or not. We then went on to other research issues, like tracking patients from primary care who were referred to hospitals so we could obtain a complete case of an episode of care from initial consultation to being discharged. To find patients who might get a referral, we collected video and audio recordings of hundreds of consultations between health practitioners and patients. This data was archived and over the years has been added to and is overseen by the Applied Research on Communication in Health group, which is based in the Department of Primary Health Care and General Practice at the University of Otago, Wellington. This has become a resource to explore a wide range of issues, including how clinical prioritisation assessments tools are used, how talk about patient use of alternative medicines is responded to, the presence of interpreters in consultations, patient engagement in consultations, and what I will discuss here, how side effects to medications are discussed. I focus on this latter one as it links nicely to the issues raised above about pharmacovigilance.

In this research we again used conversation analysis to try to gain a deeper understanding of what was happening in clinical encounters. Our research team was asked to make a presentation as a seminar series that was to be attended by different clinicians interested in issues of prescription medications, so we decided to look at how side effects were talked about in the consultation: on superficial viewing it looked like it could be interesting, and a closer viewing using conversation analysis indeed showed that it was very interesting. What we found was that when patients raised concerns about a bad reaction to a prescribed medication, GPs would attend to this carefully if the drug was well known as having these kinds of side effects. GPs could then consider changing the dose or trying other medications. This would be the case, for example, with psychoactive drugs. On the other hand, if a drug did not have such a high profile, then patient concerns were usually dismissed or downgraded. We could see this unfold very clearly when we looked at patient presentations and GP responses in detail. I won't show the detail here (see Dew, 2016 for the analysis using conversation analysis conventions) but will provide the gist of the argument.

One feature of the patients' presentations of concerns about negative effects of a drug prescribed by the GP they are talking to is that they would present their concerns very cautiously and hesitantly. Rather than saying something like, 'the rash started as soon as I started taking that drug you prescribed and the drug is the cause" the patient might say "it actually started up around about the same sort of time as you prescribed those pills". The latter is what can be called a tacit linkage proposal (Gill & Maynard, 2006) where causation is not claimed, it is just tacitly suggested. Arguably this is a recognition by the patient that they do not have the right to diagnose in this setting, it is the doctor's right. The hesitancy can be seen in that the patient might change tack in terms of how to say what they want to say. In the case of the patient with a rash that I am referring to here, he starts by saying "it actually started after um (pause) I think you (pause) I came—the first time I saw you". The patient is self-repairing here, starting to say something but then stopping, and trying to say it in a different way. This activity of self-repair indicates that the patient is having some interactional trouble here. We can suggest where the patient might be going with this. In the first instance, he might have been going to say, "it actually started after you gave me that drug", but he did not go there. We can consider why he changed tack. It is likely that he saw this direct statement as a threat to the face of the doctor, and so the patient is working to reconcile two conflicting issues—one to suggest that the drug the doctor prescribed has caused the patient problems, and the other to protect the dignity of the doctor with whom he has an on-going relationship.

In our data we saw many examples along these lines, and almost invariably the GP would look for some other explanation if the drug did not have a well-known side effects profile. In the case of the patient with a rash, he was eventually told that his rash was likely the result of a "stress related thing". In other cases, the patient might simply be told that the drug would not do that with no further explanation. In some cases, the GP would not respond to the concern raised by the patient at all.

This research provided insight into the power dynamics of doctor patient interaction, but also into why adverse reactions to drugs is so dramatically underreported, as I have considered above. If GPs do not recognise a symptom as being possibly caused by a drug, then they are not going to report it to CARM. If it is not reported to CARM then there is missing data on the side effects profile of that drug, and so no reporting from CARM that would make the side effects more widely known. GPs then will not be on the look out for these side effects, as they have not been recorded. This becomes something of a vicious circle. Harold Garfinkel, the founder of ethnomethodology, refers to this sort of scenario as a common situation for us all, and he calls this the documentary method of interpretation. The documentary method of interpretation is where people interpret events based on their understanding of an underlying pattern. The pattern of adverse drug reactions is created by GP underreporting, and GPs interpret what is in front of them based on that underreporting. This finding again reinforces why it is important for pharmacovigilance agencies to find other ways to receive concerns about adverse reactions outside of the clinical consultation, and how sociological research can inform this process.

Concluding Comments

Working in interdisciplinary settings is crucial in healthcare research. Benefits work at multiple levels. For the sociologist, due to the complexities of bodies, the institutions of healthcare and the knowledge-base of medical and clinical disciplines, they can easily be bewildered or be making unwarranted assumptions. Working with people on the ground, such as health professionals, can facilitate a different understanding. Also, for the sociologist the chances of research findings being picked up and used is greatly enhanced. For those working with the sociologist, they can see what the discipline brings to the table, how what might not be easily seen can be revealed more clearly, and how different interpretations of what is going on can enhance reflection of clinical and other types of practice. This also applies in working across cultures. As a Pākehā medical sociologist working in Aotearoa New Zealand, the impacts of colonialism cannot be ignored, and indeed, should as much as possible be addressed. Working with Māori researchers again does the same thing, in that assumptions about how to interpret what one finds can be contested, understandings can be deepened, and this can cut both ways. That is, the approaches used by sociologists can be useful in shedding light on aspects of Māori engagement with healthcare issues, just as Māori led research can provide the Pākehā researcher with insights and access to understandings that they would not possibly achieve by themselves (Dew et al., 2017a).

In his inaugural professorial address, Jim Robb argued that sociology had the difficult task of taking its concern with objective accuracy and balancing it with creative imagination in order to contribute to society's self-improvement (Robb, 1966). Looking at the depth and breadth of sociological work applied to healthcare, I think we can argue that sociologists have worked hard at taking on this difficult task. Sociologists have been concerned with health policy issues, health service organisation and health reform. They have been concerned with disparities in health outcomes, with the role of commercial enterprises in shaping healthcare delivery, and the way in which interactions between people can indicate social structure in action. This great diversity of approaches and topics is to be welcomed and encouraged, as is the engagement of medical sociologists with health service providers, clinicians, advocacy groups, state agencies and others. Through this, sociology can be applied in ways that provide an in-depth understanding of healthcare training and provision, and can shape how they are delivered.

References

Abraham, J., & Shepherd, J. (1999). *The therapeutic nightmare: The battle over the world's most controversial sleeping pill*. Earthscan.

Backstrom, M., Mjorndal, T., Dahlqvist, R., & Nordkvist-Olsson, T. (2000). Attitudes to reporting adverse drug reactions in northern Sweden. *European Journal of Clinical Pharmacology, 56*(9–10), 729–732.

Barker, G. (1999) *Great sex or bad blood? : Expanding the discussion of sexuality after hysterectomy: A thesis submitted to the Victoria University of Wellington in fulfilment of the requirements for the degree of Doctor of Philosophy in Sociology*. Thesis (Ph.D.) – Victoria University of Wellington, 1999.

Blakely, T., Tobias, M., Atkinson, J., Yeh, L. C., & Huang, K. (2007). *Tracking disparity: Trends in ethnic and socioeconomic inequalities in mortality, 1981–2004*. Ministry of Health.

Blank, R. (1994). *New Zealand health policy: A comparative study*. Oxford University Press.

Brickell, C. (2007). Those 'other sociologists': Social analysis before sociology. *New Zealand Sociology, 22*(2), 195–218.

Cohen, B. M. Z. (2016). *Psychiatric hegemony: A Marxist theory of mental illness*. Palgrave Macmillan UK.

Davis, P. (Ed.). (1992). *For health or profit? Medicine, the pharmaceutical industry, and the state in New Zealand*. Oxford University Press.

Davis, P., Lay-Yee, R., Briant, R., Ali, W., Scott, A., & Schug, S. (2002). Adverse events in New Zealand public hopitals I: Occurrence and impact. *New Zealand Medical Journal, 115*(1167), 1–9. http://www.nzma.org.nz/journal/115-1167/271/

Davis, P., Lay-Yee, R., Dyall, L., Briant, R., Sporle, A., Brunt, D., et al. (2006). Quality of hospital care for Māori patients in New Zealand: Retrospective cross-sectional assessment. *The Lancet (British edition), 367*(9526), 1920–1925. https://doi.org/10.1016/S0140-6736(06)68847-8

Dew, K. (2003). *Borderland practices: Regulating alternative therapies in New Zealand*. University of Otago Press.

Dew, K. (2016). Purifying and hybridising categories in healthcare decision-making: The clinic, the home and the multidisciplinary team. *Health Sociology Review, 25*(2), 142–156.

Dew, K. (2021). *Complementary and alternative medicine: Containing and expanding therapeutic possibilities*. Taylor & Francis Group.

Dew, K., Chamberlain, K., Hodgetts, D., Norris, P., Radley, A., & Gabe, J. (2014). Home as a hybrid centre of medication practice. *Sociology of Health & Illness, 36*(1), 28–43.

Dew, K., Cunningham, C., Davies, C., Tavite, H., Stairmand, J., Sarfati, D., et al. (2017a). Māori-centered research and ethnomethodology cancer inequities and research by and for indigenous peoples. *Sage Research Methods Cases*. https://doi.org/10.4135/9781526409218

Dew, K., Gardner, J., Morrato, E., Norris, P., Chamberlain, K., Hodgetts, D., et al. (2017b). Public engagement and the role of the media in post-marketing drug safety: The case of Eltroxin® (levothyroxine) in New Zealand. *Critical Public Health, 1–14*, 388–401. https://doi.org/10.1080/09581596.2017.1329520

Dew, K., Norris, P., Gabe, J., Chamberlain, K., & Hodgetts, D. (2015). Moral discourses and pharmaceuticalised governance in housholds. *Social Science & Medicine, 131*, 272–279.

Dew, K., Stubbe, M., Macdonald, L., & Dowell, A. (2012). Side effects talk in general practice consultations. In B. Bates & R. Ahmed (Eds.), *Medical communication in clinical contexts* (pp. 95–126). Kendall Hunt.

Donovan, S., & Telfar-Barnard, L. (2019). Age of first menstruation in New Zealand : Findings from first ever national-level data and implications for age-appropriate education and support. *New Zealand Medical Journal, 132*(1500), 100–102.

Faasse, K., Cundy, T., & Petrie, K. (2010). Thyroxine: Anatomy of a health scare. *British Medical Journal, 340*, 20–21.

Fenwick, P. (1980). Fertility, sexuality and social control in New Zealand. In P. Bunkle & B. Hughes (Eds.), *Women in New Zealand society* (pp. 77–98). George Allen & Unwin.

Fougere, G. (1974). Medical insurance: The market's quiet counter-revolution. In D. Beaven & B. Easton (Eds.), *The future of New Zealand medicine: A progressive viewpoint* (pp. 86–90). N. M.Peryer.

Gardner, J., & Dew, K. (2011). The Eltroxin controversy: Risk and how actors construct their world. *Health, Risk and Society, 13*(5), 397–411.

Gibbs, A. (2019). An evidence-based training and support course for caregivers of children with foetal alcohol spectrum disorder (FASD) in New Zealand. *Advances In Dual Diagnosis, 12*(1/2), 73–84. https://doi.org/10.1108/ADD-10-2018-0013

Gill, V., & Maynard, D. W. (2006). Explaining illness: Patients' proposals and physician' responses. In J. Heritage & D. W. Maynard (Eds.), *Communication in medical care: Interaction between primary care physicians and patients* (pp. 115–150). Cambridge University Press.

Grace, V. (1997). Reading the silent body: Women, doctors and pelvic pain. In M. de Ras & V. Grace (Eds.), *Bodily boundaries, sexualised genders and medical discourses* (pp. 85–98). Dunmore Press.

Hazell, L., & Shakir, S. A. W. (2006). Under-reporting of adverse drug reactions - a systematic review. *Drug Safety, 29*(5), 385–396. <Go to ISI>://000237955700003.

Hodgetts, D., Chamberlain, K., Gabe, J., Dew, K., Radley, A., Madden, H., et al. (2011). Emplacement and everyday use of medications in domestic dwellings. *Health & Place, 17*(1), 353–360. https://doi.org/10.1016/j.healthplace.2010.11.015. http://www.sciencedirect.com/science/article/B6VH5-51N22G7-1/2/ac3aaa60ddfad669abe72fa68faacb23

Hyde, P. (2000). Science friction: Cervical cancer and the contesting of medical beliefs. *Sociology of Health and Illness, 22*, 217–234.

Jutel, A. (2011). *Putting a name to it: Diagnosis in contemporary society*. The John Hopkins University Press.

Kirkman, A. (2012). Professor James Harding Robb (Jim) - A public sociologist: 28 April 1920–23 June 2011. *New Zealand Sociology, 27*(1), 46–59.

Lopez-Gonzalez, E., Herdeiro, M. T., & Figueiras, A. (2009). Determinants of under-reporting of adverse drug reactions: A systematic review. *Drug Safety, 32*(1), 19–31. <Go to ISI>://000263322300002.

McManus, R. (2013). *Death in a global age*. Palgrave Macmillan.

Mintz, M. (1985). *At any cost: Corporate greed, women, and the Dalkon shield*. Pantheon Books.

Norris, P., Fa'alau, F., Va'ai, C., Churchward, M., & Arroll, B. (2009). Navigating between illness paradigms: Treatment seeking by Samoan people in Samoa and New Zealand. *Qualitative Health Research, 19*(10), 1466–1475. https://doi.org/10.1177/1049732309348364

Opie, A. (2000). *Thinking teams/thinking clients: Knowledge-based teamwork*. Columbia University Press.

Parsons, T., & Fox, R. (1952). Illness, therapy and the modern American family. Journal of Social Issues, 8(31).

Robb, J. H. (1965). *Report on the employment of medical social workers in New Zealand general hospitals*. School of Social Science, Victoria University of Wellington.

Robb, J. H. (1966). *Social science and social welfare: Inaugural address delivered before the Victoria University of Wellington on 14 July, 1966*. Victoria University of Wellington.

Robb, J. H. (1986). Smoking as an anticipatory rite of passage: Some sociological hypotheses on health-related behaviour. *Social Science & Medicine (1982), 23*(6), 621–627. https://doi.org/10.1016/0277-9536(86)90156-5

Robb, J. H. (1996). Some thoughts on beginnings. *New Zealand Sociology, 11*(2), 323–329.

Robb, J. H., & Crothers, C. (1985). New Zealand. In UNESCO (Ed.), *Sociology and social anthropology in Asia and the Pacific* (pp. 460–508). Wiley Eastern Ltd..

Scott, C., Fougere, G., & Marwick, H. (1986). *Choices for health care: Report on the health benefits review*. Health Benefits Review.

Seale, C., Chaplin, R., Lelliot, P., & Quirk, A. (2007). Antipsychotic medication, sedation and mental clouding: An observational study of psychiatric consultations. *Social Science & Medicine, 65*(4), 698–711.

Shaw, R., & Gibson, H. (2022). Kelly needs a new coat: Views on compensating altruistic surrogacy in Aotearoa New Zealand. *Sociological Research Online*, Online first publised August 9, 2022.

ten Have, P. (2004). Ethnomethodology. In C. Seale, G. Gobo, J. Gubrium, & D. Silverman (Eds.), *Qualitative research practice* (pp. 139–153). Sage.

Vallée, M. (2021). Fostering ignorance to maintain public support: New Zealand's 2002-2004 urban aerial pesticide spraying operation over Auckland. *Environmental Sociology, 7*(4), 382–392. https://doi.org/10.1080/23251042.2021.1884341

Wiktorowicz, M., Lexchin, J., & Moscou, K. (2012). Pharmacovigilance in Europe and North America: Divergent approaches. *Social Science & Medicine, 75*, 165–170

Kevin Dew is Professor of Sociology at Victoria University of Wellington. He is a founding member of the Applied Research on Communication in Health (ARCH) group. Current research activities include studies of exceptional cancer survivorship, the sociology of sleep and interactions between health professionals and patients. He is an Associate Editor for Critical Public Health. His books include *Public Health, Personal Health and Pills: Drug Entanglements and Pharmaceuticalised Governance*; *The Cult and Science of Public Health: A Sociological Investigation*; *Complementary and Alternative Medicine: Containing and Expanding Therapeutic Possibilities*.

Fat and (Un)Healthy: A Dramaturgical Analysis of Health, Lifestyle, and Body Size in Healthcare Settings

Aimee B. Simpson

Introduction

In 2016, the New Zealand Ministry of Health released its new health strategy, within which it adopted the World Health Organisation's (WHO) definition of health as the "complete state of physical, mental and social well-being, not merely the absence of disease or infirmity" (Ministry of Health, 2016, p. 4). Despite the framing of this shift as an inclusive and holistic approach, the emphasis on the 'complete state' of health creates innate challenges for marginalised groups. As Harrison (2021, p. 33) explained, "for one to be healthy, they must not only be non-disabled but must also be in an environment that allows for them to feel mentally secure, psychically safe, and socially well". Thus, those who are marginalised are "always already unhealthy because we are always already unsafe" (Harrison, 2021, p. 33).

The broad assumption that a person's weight has a direct link to their overall health and wellbeing is pervasive in Aotearoa New Zealand. Associations between fatness, shorter lifespans, and comorbidities such as diabetes, hypertension and cardiovascular disease are commonly cited by key knowledge producers in calls to action over the public health crisis of 'obesity'. Such conceptualisations make it difficult to have health (Chrisler & Barney, 2017) and to access healthcare as a fat person (Lee & Pausé, 2016). Healthcare is an important site to explore, as stigmatising beliefs about 'obesity' lead to inequitable treatment which can have tangible bodily consequences and diminish the rights of fat people. Indeed, fewer visitations, shorter appointments and discriminatory diagnoses are well documented outcomes of such attitudes (e.g. Lee & Pausé, 2016; Shackelford, 2018).

Applied sociology is well positioned to address such healthcare inequities, particularly that which compiles and analyses marginalised experiences in order to

A. B. Simpson (✉)
Independent Scholar, Auckland, New Zealand

© The Author(s), under exclusive license to Springer Nature Switzerland AG 2023
Z. L. Rocha, K. L. Davidson (eds.), *Applied and Clinical Sociology in Aotearoa New Zealand*, Clinical Sociology: Research and Practice,
https://doi.org/10.1007/978-3-031-36581-2_8

disrupt stigmatising notions (in this case, of fatness) and thus open avenues for designing and implementing more effective and equitable healthcare policy and delivery (Bombak, 2014). This chapter uses a dramaturgical lens to examine how fat people use performance in order to navigate and disrupt stigmatising conceptualisations of 'obesity' and 'health' in healthcare settings. Pointedly, this tension is first expressed in the titling of this chapter as *Fat and (Un)Healthy*. The term 'unhealthy' is deliberately bracketed to mark the way that 'unhealthy' is always lingering in experiences of fatness, in that ill-health is at best seen as a risk or at worst an inevitable part of being fat. Similar to the (No)Vacancy signs that operate outside of motels, which signal at a glance the internal status of the establishment via the illumination of their 'no' switching on and off (but never truly disappearing), (Un)-Healthy speaks to the way that the body is increasingly seen as a public indicator of one's health status wherein the 'unhealthy' part of health never disappears completely from the social experience of fatness. Thus, the complex relationship between fatness and health is something that is both deeply personal and deeply public.

Medical sociologists have, for some time, acknowledged the public-private interplay of health and disease. Peter Conrad (2007) articulated this relationship as the process of medicalisation, wherein aspects of 'normal human life' become annexed and recodified into the realm of medicine: as medical problems and diseases. Thus, broad areas of human experience which at one time were considered to be variations of private, everyday life, are transformed into public conceptualisations of health and disease, and in doing so are both absorbed into medicine's jurisdiction and work to re-signify private understandings of the body, health, and behaviour. In order to unpack the public-private nature of health, this chapter begins by exploring healthism, a concept developed by Robert Crawford (1980) to describe the way that the lifestyle behaviours of the middle class became associated with health. This is a crucial step in understanding how health became a social signifier of moral and social status, and how this presents unique challenges for marginalised groups such as fat people. In positioning health as a social signifier, this chapter finally explores how health is performative, and why convincing performances can be critical in accessing (quality) healthcare. Throughout this chapter, excerpts from interview research conducted in 2017–2018 with 18 self-identifying fat people on the issues of health, body size and identity are drawn upon. These quotes help paint a more fulsome picture of fat people's healthcare experiences and enable the chapter to tease apart some of the more dangerous consequences of having to negotiate one's health in healthcare settings.

Fatness, Lifestyle, and the Concept of Choice

In the late 1970s and the beginning of the 1980s, health started to be framed as a status condition that could be easily achieved through a range of 'lifestyle' adjustments, particularly food choices, smoking cessation and exercise (Crawford, 2006).

Key theorist Robert Crawford (1980) posited that such assertions reflected the values and ideals of the middle class and termed this ideology *healthism*. Specifically, he saw healthism as "the preoccupation with personal health as a primary ... focus for the definition and achievement of well-being; a goal which is to be attained primarily through the modification of life styles" (Crawford, 1980, p. 368). The positioning of health as achievable and optimisable through individual choices emboldens citizens to act like consumers in respect to their health. Not only could they contribute to their health through correct consumption choices, but they could also effectively 'choose' ill-health. As Crawford (2006, p. 409) elucidated "one either changed diet and exercised and thereby avoided heart disease and fatness or not". The assumption that poor health outcomes were the product of equally poor choices, revitalised old moralistic arguments about personhood and physical size. Healthism unleashed what Spitzack (1990) referred to as an 'aesthetic of health' whereby one's appearance informs external judgements about health. Put another way, "standards of appearance replace standards of health and are set as proxy targets" (Jutel & Buetow, 2007, p. 422) for individuals to aspire to. This effectively reduces 'health' into something easily observable by trained and untrained eyes alike: physical size. Unlike other indicators of physical health, it is not easy to visibly mask one's size, and this belief opens the door to acceptable forms of fat stigma, shame, and discrimination that operate under the guise of 'health concerns' (Pausé, 2014).

As Fat Studies scholars have articulated, statements such as 'I'm concerned for your health', 'aren't you worried about your health?', or 'but what about the long-term impacts on your health?' thinly veil underlying feelings of disgust and revulsion over the fat body (LeBesco, 2004; Pausé, 2014). Further, the synonymising of appearance with 'health', as Jutel and Buetow (2007) observed, enables such judgements to colour or even derail clinical encounters. Thus, the "private beliefs of physicians regarding proper appearance" (Jutel & Buetow, 2007, p. 430) bleed into their professional consultations. As Pausé (2014) illustrated, these biases often lead to unequal treatment in healthcare settings, where fat individuals are challenged, overruled, and ignored over the information they share about their health because of their size. Frequently, this type of treatment fosters a distancing from healthcare settings altogether, which can result in acute medical interventions in the future (Forhan et al., 2013). Beyond this, scholarship suggests that the experience of fat stigma alone may produce direct health consequences similar to continued exposure to classism or racism (Chrisler & Barney, 2017).

The equation of 'choice' with health outcomes is a clear symbol of social status. While external factors that can produce ill-health (such as the environment, disease agents and so on) are acknowledged under healthism, they are framed as 'hurdles' for the individual to resist or avoid (Crawford, 1980). However, as Bordo (1993, p. 192 original emphasis) suggested, such behaviours rely upon the "material preconditions that make the *choice* to diet an option". For example, in an interview with Shashank[1] in 2017, there was a perception that exercising throughout the day or

[1] A pseudonym, not his real name.

"keep[ing] your body engaged in fitness" was a core part of an aspirational healthy lifestyle that he saw some 'fit people' engaged in. However, this sat in contrast to Shashank's own means, who, between studying and working, slept on average 4 hours a night during the week. In an effort to have more time to dedicate to his studies, he had started 'meal prepping' on weekends to save himself an hour or two each weekday. Moreover, Shashank did not envision that adopting such a lifestyle would get any easier for him once he transitioned from studying into the workforce full-time. In fact, he anticipated that implementing an ideal healthy lifestyle may even be harder to realise, due to a fixed working schedule during the day, and exhaustion in the evening. In this light, the inability for the working class to engage in such behaviours is *significant*, as the behaviour arguably acts as a proxy for class distinctions (Crawford, 1980; Harjunen, 2017). Such experiences highlight the way that class positions—and indeed other structural features that similarly result in material inequities—can shape outcomes and restrict choice.

Equally significant here is the way that lifestyles are invariably tied to self-identity within modern times (Giddens, 1991). As Giddens (1991, p. 81) astutely pointed out, these "practices fulfil utilitarian needs . . . [and] give material form to a particular narrative of self-identity . . . [lifestyles] are decisions not only about how to act but who to be". In this sense, 'healthy lifestyles' are blueprints for how to live a good life but also how to be a good person. This can therefore be exceptionally important for fat identities in the context of stigmatising dominant ideas about 'obesity', in that the pursuit of a healthy lifestyle can be viewed as a legitimate avenue to redeem an otherwise stigmatised identity, or as a form of respectability politics.

As a concept, 'respectability politics' was initially used to describe the ways that the African American community would police their own members as a civil rights tactic, as it showed that their values and beliefs aligned with hegemonic social standards (Smith, 2014). Those who engaged in respectability politics believed that by showing themselves to be 'respectable' members of society, they and their community may receive better treatment and perhaps advocacy from white Americans (Smith, 2014). However, the issue with engaging in respectability politics is that it does little to change the overarching stereotypes and discriminatory attitudes about marginalised groups (Pausé, 2018). Instead of overturning racist or, in this case, fatphobic beliefs, respectability politics creates space for groups or individuals to be seen as 'one of the good ones'. By positioning the 'good' members as an anomaly, damaging beliefs about marginalised communities are thus reinforced and continued. Indeed, why would they need to be policed if there was not something inherently wrong or awry? As it applies to fatness, respectability politics works to designate acceptable and problematic forms of fatness, by accepting and reinforcing dominant ideas about fatness and fat people, apologising for their fatness, and ultimately expressing that they are trying not to be fat (Pausé, 2018). Thus, engaging in behaviours which publicly display and, in effect, 'prove' one's health status is a significant avenue for fat people to alleviate further stigma and discrimination associated with their body size.

Health as Performance

In arguing that the notion of a 'healthy lifestyle' is a contemporary moral imperative, we can see how 'health' can be understood as a set of behaviours that are enacted for an audience to witness. Critically, such sociological interpretations draw attention to the public-private interplay, and the important role (whether real or perceived) the audience has in determining whether or not social expectations have been met. To draw on the work of Goffman (1956) here, people can be conceived of as theatre actors as we uphold social norms, 'playing' specific social roles while on the public frontstage and only able to slide out of such commitments in the private 'backstage'. In order to be convincing as an actor, the choreography, script, and wardrobe work together to sell the performance as a whole. In applying this sociological framework to healthcare settings, wherein medical professionals are the discerning audience to the patient actor, we can see how these professionals play an active role in accepting or rejecting health performances. In this way, acting, sounding, and looking healthy are all integral to the public signification of an (un)healthy person, and to the successful 'proving' of oneself as such. While this chapter applies such a lens to the case of fatness, we can see how (un)successful performances have led to inequitable treatment and outcomes in other areas, such as the well-documented disparity in physicians' interpretations of heart attack symptoms in women who often present and describe symptoms differently to men (see: Maserejian et al., 2009).

Using the framing of performance to understand health, we can see how behaviour puts the 'act' in 'actor', so movement or 'action' is a critical component of (un)successful performances. There is also the 'script', the specific vocabulary that is used to signal our role and relationship to the wider performance, or the kinds of language that are used in deliberate support or justification of one's role as the healthy citizen. Lastly, the monologue is sold to the public through the costuming of the actor: active wear signals one's commitment to exercise, while the ability to fit into gowns, blood pressure cuffs, and waiting room seats signify one's body size as within acceptable parameters.

Acting Healthy

Focussing on the behavioural aspect of healthy lifestyles, we can see that the kinds of activities that are denoted as 'healthy behaviours' are specifically designated as 'exercise'. One participant, Mira, referenced "swimming, yoga, or [going] to the gym, or hiking every once in a while," suggesting that exercise is something that you 'do' explicitly, at specific locations. The demarcation of 'exercise' as being separate from other, more mundane forms of movement was common among participants. Another participant, Kirsten, talked about the difficultly she had with finding time to exercise between working and studying. When asked about whether or not she saw her active hospitality job as exercise she said no:

> [W]hen I'm working I don't really think "Oh I'm running around" I might've done ten thousand steps but I haven't exercised today, um, yeah and like I walk to bus stop and stuff like that and I don't think of that as exercise.—Kirsten

The example of 'ten thousand steps' is an interesting qualifier used by Kirsten. Here she is suggesting that 'ten thousand steps'—an invention of marketing in and of itself and perhaps a sign of the integration of activity tracking into modern lives—is a threshold for daily activity, while 'exercise' constitutes an additional activity. From this perspective, exercise often operates in conjunction with something that is marketable or consumable in the form of gym memberships, group fitness classes, specific workout gear and so on. This activity is then *always additional*, regardless of how physically demanding the rest of the day is on a person. Undoubtedly this has particularly classed implications, as working class jobs tend to be much more physically demanding (as evidenced by Kirsten's hospitality work above) than more sedentary middle and upper-class occupations.

For example, Lenneis and Pfister (2017) examined the relationship between physical activity and the health outcomes of migrant cleaners in Denmark. These cleaners would frequently hit 20,000 steps a day—double the recommended daily physical activity goal to be a 'healthy' person—but continued to have poor health outcomes. Lenneis and Pfister (2017) posited that the physical activity migrant cleaners engaged in as part of their occupation must not have been providing them with enough of a cardiovascular benefit, and rather what they needed to do was to engage in 'leisure time physical activity' in order to see improvements in their health outcomes. This reasoning renders invisible the role that one's social location and labour conditions play in determining health outcomes, and the emphasis on discrete rather than integrated physical activity reinforces the positioning of 'exercise' as a practice that is performed publicly.

Equally telling are the behaviours which are tracked and monitored through initiatives such as the Green Prescription. The Green Prescription involves the referral from a general practitioner to local community organisations, most often their regional sports trusts, for a range of programmes designed to increase activity levels and improve one's knowledge base through healthy food seminars. They are a popular community initiative, subsidising costs of fitness classes and, depending on the location, reduced fees for gym or swimming pool access. While making facilities such as the gym and swimming pool more financially accessible is a benefit to poorer communities, consider the way in which Maggie described her experience of 'success' on the Green Prescription:

> [T]hey sort of run it concurrently where your doctor keeps an eye on your weight, to make sure you're losing weight, because that's the only success you can have, um... yeah so [laughs] they don't necessarily measure "Hey I could only walk for five minutes yesterday, but today I can walk for *ten* minutes and, next week I hope to walk for fifteen" they don't measure *that*, but they measure how much weight you lose while doing the Green Prescription.—Maggie

As she acknowledges here, fitness was not something that was tracked in her experience, but her weight was. This speaks to the general trend of equating of weight-loss, and thus thinness, with 'health'. In this regard, it is not simply about enriching the lives of communities but ensuring that they meet a certain 'picture of health'. When another participant Lisa, went to the doctors to address her fertility issues resulting from polycystic ovarian syndrome[2] (PCOS), the leading cause of infertility in Aotearoa (Wang et al., 2011), she was told, "the root of the [fertility] problem is obesity". The positioning of 'obesity' as the *cause* of Lisa's infertility signifies weight-loss as necessary to the prospect of having a child, despite the fact that she may still have had to access fertility services even if she were thin, due to her PCOS. This messaging led to a situation where Lisa felt she could no longer talk to people about her infertility, because "they're like, 'Okay so what are you doing to lose weight?' and . . . if I haven't been [losing weight] it's like 'Oh, so then you must not want [to be pregnant].'" By tying her weight so closely into her fertility, the pressure to perform health in this way was expanded from the doctor's office to Lisa's support network of family and friends. This isolated her from her support network and communicated to her friends and family that her fat body was the singular cause of infertility.

As a result of this framing, Lisa's team of doctors had started recommending weight-loss surgery, as a vehicle for accessing publicly funded fertility services which have BMI thresholds that restrict people like Lisa from accessing them. Below, Lisa explained her experiences of being funnelled into weight-loss surgery by her team of doctors:

> I actually talked to the fertility clinic, Fertility [New Zealand], my GP, and I've also seen specialists—endocrinologists, and they've all recommended [weight-loss surgery], so. . . that's kind of a good thing. The only thing is . . . it's quite a lot of money if you go private, and it's quite a *long* waitlist if you go public so it's still a bit of a struggle.—Lisa

Eligibility requirements for surgery require further displays of acting, sounding, and looking healthy. According to Drew (2008), patients must have 'appropriate physiology', which means that patients must meet BMI and/or co-morbid disease requirements. In addition, patients are also expected to display appropriate 'diet history', 'behaviour' and 'attitude', by providing doctors with 'proof' of continuous failed dieting history, and to be compliant with and show enthusiasm for any and all instructions, appointments, and requests. A common stipulation is that individuals must prove to doctors that they are committed to weight loss by achieving an initial percentage weight-loss set by the medical professionals prior to surgery (Simpson, 2015). From a dramaturgical perspective, we can see how various health performances are expected in order for patients to prove their candidacy for medical treatment to medical professionals as, in some instances, surgeries can be cancelled if surgeons are not convinced of individual commitment to weight-loss. For Lisa, the significance of this is that rather than the gateway to children, weight-loss surgery is just the *admission fee* to try fertility services; as it does not guarantee successful

[2]PCOS is a condition where cysts develop on the ovaries and produce elevated levels of male hormones (Norman et al., 2007). The side-effects of this condition are acne, 'masculine hair growth', increased body weight, difficulty losing weight, and infertility (Norman et al., 2007).

pregnancy. Thus, the need for weight-loss surgery in Lisa's case is about being able to *access healthcare*, rather than resolving some inherent fat pathology. This is notwithstanding the additional difficulties Lisa may experience conceiving and carrying a pregnancy full-term as a result of the restrictive nature of the surgery (Iavazzo et al., 2010). In this way, Lisa's experience of health performance is twofold, as she must perform the right behaviours in order to access surgery, and by having surgery she is proving her commitment to—and therefore that she deserves access to—parenthood.

Sounding Healthy

As it applies to health, language facilitates a convincing portrayal that one is healthy, in that we are heard to be essentially 'saying the right things'. In this respect, 'sounding healthy' relates to how specific vocabulary is used to prove one's commitment to 'healthiness' to an audience. Sounding healthy was present in interviews in the way that participants justified 'bad' food choices—or not acting healthy—and deliberately referenced 'good' behaviour in conversation. For example, consider the language that Cheryl used as she described the inner debate she felt when eating potato chips in public:

> [I]t's that idea of... feeling like I'm eating too much in front of other people, and because [...] I didn't eat dinner before I got here [friend's house] and I'm starving and we're drinking [alcohol] and I don't want to drink on an empty stomach so of course I'm going to eat the entire bowl of potato chips you've put in front of me because I haven't eaten in four hours. But nobody knows that, right?—Cheryl

Cheryl felt that eating 'too much' specific foods such as potato chips required justification, and while she never said this out aloud, in relaying the experience in our interview it appeared to be a behaviour that required a qualifier. In this case, eating 'too many' potato chips carried the following justifications: 'I'm starving', 'I didn't eat dinner', 'we're drinking', and 'I haven't eaten in four hours'. The underlying sentiment here is that such lapses in self-control are unusual for Cheryl, that she is aware that the behaviour is 'bad' and that her engagement in the behaviour is only prompted by extenuating circumstances such as alcohol consumption and gnawing hunger, and is thus justifiable or forgivable. This is not to suggest that the moral inscription of potato chips is valid, but instead to highlight how 'sounding healthy' can be used to articulate one's knowledge of and commitment to health performance, by atoning for instances where one is not necessarily 'acting' or 'looking' healthy.

Equally important in 'sounding healthy' is the way that good behaviours are referenced in conversation. This form of sounding healthy is a tactic of respectability politics many fat people employ to position themselves as 'one of the good ones'. Cheryl also reflected that:

> I'm also always quick to drop in conversation that I do do old lady things like Zumba and I do have a really lovely yoga class that I go to once a week, so I do work out three times a

> week y'know? And like I think I'm always quick to throw that into conversation, ... I want it to be clear that that is part of who I am, that if you just looked at me you would think that I sit on the couch all the time, but I don't, like I have interests, like I like going hiking, I like going camping, y'know like I love stand-up paddle boarding and kayaking—I'm terrible at those things but I love them y'know?—Cheryl

One of the most powerful statements in the extract above is "I want it to be clear that this is part of who I am", as it conveys her struggle between harmful internalised beliefs about what it means to be fat (such as 'sitting on the couch all the time') and wanting to be perceived in a manner that is destigmatised. Here we see the importance, and added burden, of 'proving' health for fat people. So ingrained are these degrading stereotypes about fatness into contemporary discourse that 'sounding healthy' is at the forefront of Cheryl's everyday interactions. Thus, the detailing of doing 'Zumba', 'yoga', 'three times a week', 'hiking', 'camping', 'paddle-boarding', and 'kayaking' are all in service of disentangling Cheryl from negative stereotypes about fatness and pre-empting any associated judgments about her. The consistent commitment to 'sounding healthy' in the two extracts from Cheryl, despite speaking to what was ostensibly a fat positive audience, demonstrates how integrated such scripts and performances are in our society, and indeed how few opportunities exist for marginalised groups such as fat people to be their 'backstage' self.

In healthcare settings, the importance of sounding healthy is accentuated as doctors act as gatekeepers to conventional healthcare, and so convincing them of your health can be a fundamental part of accessing treatment, tests, or even advocacy. For example, Kirsten felt that she had to "pretty much explain myself to [doctors]. ... I feel that way each time I go to the doctor ... them sort of being like [sarcastically] "Oh yeah *sure* you eat healthy, *sure ... sure you do, sure you exercise*". Kirsten employed the tactic of sounding healthy in an attempt to offset the significance of her fatness. She explained that she would emphasise that she "eats salads all the time" and that she was "otherwise healthy", yet was met with scepticism and scrutiny, particularly after being weighed. Thus, in 'sounding healthy', Kirsten is illustrating her commitment to other social norms, such as eating healthily and doing exercise, in an effort to reduce the stigma and sanctioning associated with having your fatness confirmed by a scale.

Looking Healthy

The final aspect of this health performance is 'looking healthy', which includes the designating of health-seeking behaviours via active wear, alongside the ability to physically fit into clothes, devices, and the built environment. One's wardrobe signals one's engagement with health and fitness within contemporary societies. Most obviously is the garb that is designated for exercise: 'activewear' or 'workout gear', which includes everything from headbands and sports bras to wicking socks and activity-specific shoes. For example, when I asked Kirsten about her exercise process, she specifically referenced putting on the "good old exercise tights" and "the shoes" as a part of getting ready to exercise. Activewear was not solely restricted to exercise though, but was something that, as Jane suggested, "you walk around in public now in, not something you change out of at the gym". In a performance sense, the increasing presence of activewear outside of workout spaces enables the health actor to become, essentially, a street performer, thereby expanding their performance beyond the confines of the gym-theatre to more public spaces. For instance, to return to the example of Kirsten, she talked about dressing this way specifically to go for a walk through her neighbourhood. In doing this, Kirsten publicly designated this activity as 'exercise', despite walking taking up much of her daily physical activity in the hospitality industry. The wearing of workout gear in public notably indicates that exercise, and thus 'health', is an integral part of your identity which is incredibly significant for fat performers who are invested in portraying themselves as 'one of the good ones'.

The association of body size with health can impede fat people's ability to successfully 'look healthy'. Indeed, the appearance of the fat body is an innate challenge to the aesthetic of health, one which is often emphasised by being weighed and when the body exceeds the bounds of the built environment. This is particularly significant in healthcare settings, where the failure to 'look healthy' can lead to worse care or even a denial of care altogether. As raised in the previous section, Kirsten noticed a distinct shift in her doctor's tone after being told to "step on the scales". The use of scales as part of the examination of the body is a critical example of the way that simple tools are used to establish truths about the body (Foucault, 1995). In this way, participants who initially 'looked healthy', had their fatness confirmed by the scales, and their body thus re-signified as unhealthy. According to Kirsten, any previous positive vital signs such as having good blood pressure and unremarkable bloodwork, were regarded with fresh suspicion in light of her weight. The scale acts similarly for those who do not pass for thin, as they face having the extent of their fatness realised through the scale. In other words, it is not just the appearance of fat which sparks prejudice, but also the separate (but related) pre-existing beliefs about specific weight and BMI ranges. For Kirsten then, the scales were an obstacle in accessing care, in that they were a pivotal force in shifting the focus of her medical appointment towards her fat body.

The denial or deferment of medical treatment on the basis of weight is not uncommon. In Shackelford's (2018) *Fat Census,* 24% of respondents reported being denied or experiencing extreme difficulty in accessing hormone therapy based on their size. Further, in some countries such as the United Kingdom, patients can be denied elective surgeries such as knee and hip replacements on the basis of their weight (Brochu et al., 2014). One participant, Hardy Girl, required regular specialist physiotherapy to treat the lymphoedema[3] she had in her arm which arose following breast cancer treatment. The physiotherapy helped to reduce the size of the limb to make it comfortable and usable. However, in the interview, Hardy Girl

[3]A condition wherein lymph fluid accumulates in one or more limbs due to damaged or removed lymph vessels.

explained, "I was told several months ago by my lymphoedema physiotherapist that she wouldn't treat me unless I lost weight". When asked how this denial of care was assessed, Hardy Girl said it was based on "weighing me and obviously seeing me with few clothes on". So, like Kirsten, Hardy Girl's fatness was confirmed through numbers and subjective visual assessments.

The decision to deny treatment is rooted in the assumption that any weight-loss is/would be a universal health improvement. However, as lymphoedema is an unrelated, chronic condition that can only be managed, it is difficult to understand how weight-loss would have any impact on the condition, other than it providing access to treatment. It is also worth noting that the weight restriction imposed on Hardy Girl was entirely discretionary, as there is no official policy in Aotearoa New Zealand on weight-related thresholds for physiotherapy treatment. Presumably then, Hardy Girl's physiotherapist is unable (or unwilling) to distinguish lymph fluid swelling from fat tissue or track swelling reduction in a fat body. The denial of physiotherapy speaks to the lack of training and knowledge on how to manage medical conditions in fat bodies (Pausé, 2017), and the absence of any kind of reflexivity regarding the role that stigma and discrimination played in shaping these kinds of decisions.

Inevitably this means that professionals are ill-equipped—sometimes quite literally—to respond to the needs of fat patients. As one participant, Jane, described of the experience of her friend:

> [T]he doctor tested her blood pressure and it turned out that her arm was actually, bigger than the uh, circumference of the cuff that they had, which of course was affecting the reading. And the doctor just wouldn't listen to her when she was saying "I think we need a bigger cuff" so... yeah so, it *seemed* like her blood pressure was um, really... concerning. But when they got a bigger one, it was sort of the high side of normal, so there was much less need to go to panic stations.—Jane

The first issue that Jane's anecdote highlights is the lack of appropriately sized equipment to adequately care for fat people in medical settings. This is evident in the limited sizing of blood pressure cuffs available to hand in a doctor's office. In this instance, rather than retrieving a suitable cuff from elsewhere, the physician chose to use one that was too small. As Jane notes, this can have the consequence of producing inaccurate readings and sending doctors to 'panic stations'. As before, the assumption that fat bodies are unhealthy bodies renders concerning blood pressure readings as a sign of fat pathology rather than device malfunction. Similar complaints have been made with respect to the ill-preparedness of medical institutions for fat bodies, such as the restrictive sizing of surgical gowns, the lack of variety in terms of seating options in waiting rooms (Owen, 2012), and the more recent inconsistent usage of appropriate needle gauge when administering COVID-19 vaccines to fat people (Parker et al., 2022). Such restrictions reinforce the notion that fat bodies are unwelcome in medical environments, and actively discourages them from entering those spaces. As Pausé (2017) has advocated, medical professionals need to be educated on how to deal with fat bodies, as having the correct equipment and training is essential to the dispersal of equitable care.

Improving Healthcare for Fat People

The focus on 'obesity' in healthcare settings produces inequitable care and leads to worse health outcomes overall for fat people (Lee & Pausé, 2016; O'Hara & Taylor, 2018). Although this chapter has demonstrated using a dramaturgical lens that fat people have developed a type of healthist respectability politics, which they can perform in healthcare settings in order to combat stigma and discrimination, this is not a viable long-term solution. A fundamental change in the way that healthcare engages with fatness and fat people is needed if we are to create healthcare environments where fat people feel able to 'drop the act' of health performance without sacrificing access to (quality) care.

Sociological insights such as that presented in this chapter highlight the ways that health can be performed, which provide a nuanced perspective that can be drawn upon to think through how healthcare policy and delivery might be transformed to achieve more equitable outcomes in Aotearoa at the micro and macro level. A key consideration within this context is how such transformations might lead to the improvement of the health and healthcare of fat Indigenous peoples. While some inroads have been made towards developing health services that are rooted in Indigenous principles, such as through the *Whānau Ora* initiative[4] and the newly established Māori Health Authority, more needs to be done to ensure that equitable health outcomes are achieved for Indigenous peoples when accessing mainstream services. While a more in depth interrogation of this issue was beyond the scope of this chapter, other scholars have noted that dominant health models problematise these communities as having flawed cultural norms (McCormack & Burrows, 2015), and position non-Western health models as 'alternative' rather than *culturally safe*. This reiterates Harrison's (2021) point that marginalised communities are already unhealthy because they are already unsafe. In this space, key problems to address include: the loss or diminishment of traditional health knowledge and practices of these communities, the homogenising of distinct Indigenous groups and cultures, and how sociology can work to ensure that these nuanced, diverse and *collective* understandings of health can be meaningfully addressed within the current fragmented system (Faleolo, 2003; Meo-Sewabu, 2015; Smith et al., 2019; Thomsen et al., 2018).

At the micro level, by considering health in terms of the way it is socially signified, and thus the burden that is placed upon marginalised groups to signal 'health' in specific ways, we can see how medical personnel and systems play an active role in the kinds of health experiences and outcomes their patients have. Even the WHO, an organisation which is responsible for much of the contemporary concern over the 'obesity epidemic', has acknowledged that 'weight bias'

[4]Whānau Ora, was an initiative launched in 2010 to provide whānau (families) with centralised, wrap-around health and social services through a designated 'navigator', with the explicit intention of addressing the gross "overrepresentation of Māori whānau in poor social and health outcomes" (Smith et al., 2019, p. 506).

contributes to negative health outcomes for fat people, and advocated for a more nuanced and compassionate approach that decentres weight as a diagnostic variable (World Health Organization Regional Office for Europe, 2017). The analyses in this chapter highlights that the implementation of approaches such as Health At Every Size (HAES) into medical encounters could go a long way to improving the healthcare experiences of fat people (Burgard, 2009). The HAES approach emphasises "self-acceptance and healthy day-to-day practices regardless of whether a person's weight changes" (Burgard, 2009, p. 42) in an acknowledgement that factors unrelated to BMI and weight have a direct effect on health outcomes and mortality risk (Matheson et al., 2012). Such change can be immediate at the localised level of medical professionals, by integrating HAES principles into their practices (see Burgard, 2009). In this way, health can be viewed in a more holistic manner, and health goals and priorities can be collaboratively set and understood between the patient and doctor in ways that are body positive, culturally responsive and so on (Burgard, 2009).

To date, the localised uptake in changes to the way we think about and respond to fatness has been, somewhat surprisingly, most readily embraced by dieticians and nutritionists via the implementation of HAES, or other 'anti-diet' models (Bruno, 2017; Gingras, 2006). In part, it is argued that professionals in this field, as a result of working regularly with food and fat people, can more readily see the contradiction that occurs from "prescribing for fat people what we diagnose as eating disordered in thin people" (Bruno, 2017, p. 60). This raises another important issue for sociologists to examine: how medicalised knowledge around eating disorders—a diagnosis which may even specify a BMI requirement such as in anorexia nervosa (American Psychiatric Association, 2013, p. 339)—importantly ignores fat people's experience of them (Bacon & Aphramor, 2011; O'Reilly & Sixsmith, 2012).

However, widespread change cannot occur from the localised level alone, and it is clear that macro sociological analysis and applications are also required. Healthcare encounters such as those documented in this chapter are informed by broader state forces, and thus necessitate fundamental political reform and, relatedly, replacing the dominant ideology on fatness (O'Reilly & Sixsmith, 2012). Indeed, as seen through the experiences of Lisa, although localised change may have improved the interpersonal experience of going to the doctor, she would still be unable to access the fertility services she requires due to the restrictive, weight-based policies in place. An additional strength of macro sociological analysis is its ability to see the general in the specific. In the context of policy reform, this is important as it highlights the interconnected nature of institutions, and how dominant, stigmatising ideologies such as those about 'obesity' can permeate across various policy domains. For example, in 2015, the government of Aotearoa introduced a policy of integrating height and weight assessments into the *B4School Check* programme (Ministry of Health, 2015). This programme assesses the school readiness of four-year-olds in New Zealand on a variety of measures that may impact their learning, such as hearing and vision, so the introduction of height and weight assessments suggests that a child's *body size* is somehow impactful on their ability to learn. From a sociological perspective, we can see how stigmatising medicalised ideologies which problematise the bodies of children have expanded to the education sector—indeed the goal was to have 95% of the 'obese' children identified in this check referred for intervention by 2017 (Ministry of Health, 2015). In this regard, it becomes evident how applications of sociological analysis which lead to shifts in how fatness is approached in healthcare, can have a rippling effect in terms of transforming how fatness is viewed in other spaces, and lead to more equitable outcomes across a variety of domains.

Concluding Remarks

This chapter critically examined the role that healthism, stigma, and respectability politics play in shaping the way that fat people engage in healthy lifestyles. 'Lifestyles' were a critical aspect of how interview participants pursued, performed and, effectively, 'proved' their health status both in and outside of healthcare settings. There was a strong emphasis on the notion of 'lifestyle' in participant narratives of health, and the need/desire to effectively perform health through it. Drawing on the work of Goffman (1956), I conceptualised this experience of lifestyle as a form of performance, and argued that 'acting', 'sounding' and 'looking' healthy was critical to the way that participants experienced their health subjectivities. This highlighted the complex ways that participants engaged in health as a meaningful social practice (Crawford, 2006) while inhabiting bodies that were signified as 'unhealthy'. In this way, the experience of health was enmeshed in the balancing of the tensions and contradictions between dominant understandings of health and their fat bodies.

Participants were often subjected to a weight-based approach to health in medical settings, which resulted in worse care or an outright denial of care. Being seen to be 'saying the right things' as Kirsten did, or 'doing the right things' as Lisa was attempting to, can be crucial steps in being listened to, having your concerns taken seriously, and receiving compassionate care. This raises important questions regarding the kind of healthcare fat people experience, and how such experienced restrictive approaches to health sit in contradiction with official commitments to holistic health, such as that purported by the Ministry of Health (2016).

It is clear from the sociological analysis in this chapter that change to the way that we understand fatness and health(care) is needed. Shifts such as the refocussing on holistic health and meaningful movement, beyond restrictive 'lifestyle' approaches which prioritise and assume that citizens are able-bodied and have the resources to engage with such practices, would be beneficial at the micro and macro level. As a practical step, O'Reilly and Sixsmith (2012, p. 107) have suggested the following strategies to improve the healthcare encounters for fat people: "(1) framing interventions in weight-neutral, Health at Every Size language, (2) implementing anti-weight bias training, and (3) developing research guidelines that mandate variables beyond merely weight are included in research and that evaluations account for possible harm". Moving away from stigmatising approaches to fatness such as via these practical strategies could open up the possibilities of increasing patient engagement with healthcare and thus improving health outcomes and inequities in Aotearoa New Zealand and elsewhere.

References

American Psychiatric Association. (2013). *Diagnostic and statistical manual of mental disorders* (5th ed.). American Psychiatric Association.

Bacon, L., & Aphramor, L. (2011). Weight science: Evaluating the evidence for a paradigm shift. *Nutrition Journal, 10*(9), 1–13. https://doi.org/10.1186/1475-2891-10-9

Bombak, A. E. (2014). The contribution of applied social sciences to obesity stigma-related public health approaches. *Journal of Obesity, 2014*, 1–9. https://doi.org/10.1155/2014/267286

Bordo, S. (1993). *Unbearable weight: Feminism, western culture and the body*. University of California Press.

Brochu, P. M., Pearl, R. L., Puhl, R. M., & Brownell, K. D. (2014). Do media portrayals of obesity influence support for weight-related medical policy? *Health Psychology, 33*(2), 197–200. https://doi.org/10.1037/a0032592

Bruno, B. A. (2017). Health at every size and me. *Fat Studies, 6*(1), 54–66. https://doi.org/10.1080/21604851.2016.1218741

Burgard, D. (2009). What is 'health at every size'? In E. Rothblum & S. Solovay (Eds.), *The fat studies reader* (pp. 41–53). New York University Press.

Chrisler, J. C., & Barney, A. (2017). Sizeism is a health hazard. *Fat Studies, 6*(1), 38–53. https://doi.org/10.1080/21604851.2016.1213066

Conrad, P. (2007). *The medicalisation of society: On the transformation of human conditions into treatable disorders*. The Johns Hopkins University Press.

Crawford, R. (1980). Healthism and the medicalisation of everyday life. *International Journal of Health Services, 10*(3), 365–388.

Crawford, R. (2006). Health as a meaningful social practice. *Health: An Interdisciplinary Journal for the Social Study of Health, Illness and Medicine, 10*(4), 401–420. https://doi.org/10.1177/1363459306067310

Drew, P. (2008). Weight loss surgery patients' negotiations of medicine's institutional logic. *Research in the Sociology of Health Care, 26*, 65–92. https://doi.org/10.1016/S0275-4959(08)26004-7

Faleolo, M. M. (2003). *Talanoa ile i'a: Talking to Pacific Island young people in West Auckland about health* [Master of social work]. Massey University.

Forhan, M., Risdon, C., & Solomon, P. (2013). Contributors to patient engagement in primary health care: Perceptions of patients with obesity. *Primary Health Care Research & Development, 14*(04), 367–372. https://doi.org/10.1017/S1463423612000643

Foucault, M. (1995). *Discipline and punish: The birth of the prison*. Vintage Books.

Giddens, A. (1991). *Modernity and self-identity: Self and society in the late modern age*. Polity Press.

Gingras, J. (2006). Throwing their weight around: Canadians take on health at every size. *Health At Every Size, 19*(4), 195–206.

Goffman, E. (1956). *The presentation of self in everyday life* (Issue 2). University of Edinburgh, Social Sciences Research Centre.

Harjunen, H. (2017). *Neoliberal bodies and the gendered fat body*. Routledge.

Harrison, D. L. (2021). *Belly of the beast: The politics of anti-fatness as anti-blackness*. North Atlantic Books.

Iavazzo, C., Ntziora, F., Rousos, I., & Paschalinopoulos, D. (2010). Complications in pregnancy after bariatric surgery. *Archives of Gynecology and Obstetrics, 282*(2), 225–227. https://doi.org/10.1007/s00404-009-1337-0

Jutel, A., & Buetow, S. (2007). A picture of health? Unmasking the role of appearance in health. *Perspectives in Biology and Medicine, 50*(3), 421–434.

LeBesco, K. (2004). *Revolting bodies?: The struggle to redefine fat identity*. University of Massachusetts Press.

Lee, J. A., & Pausé, C. J. (2016). Stigma in practice: Barriers to health for fat women. *Frontiers in Psychology, 7*(2063), 1–15. https://doi.org/10.3389/fpsyg.2016.02063

Lenneis, V., & Pfister, G. (2017). Too tired for exercise? The work and leisure of female cleaners in Denmark. *Leisure Studies, 36*(4), 530–541. https://doi.org/10.1080/02614367.2016.1216579

Maserejian, N. N., Link, C. L., Lutfey, K. L., Marceau, L. D., & McKinlay, J. B. (2009). Disparities in physicians' interpretations of heart disease symptoms by patient gender: Results of a video vignette factorial experiment. *Journal of Women's Health, 18*(10), 1661–1667. https://doi.org/10.1089/jwh.2008.1007

Matheson, E. M., King, D. E., & Everett, C. J. (2012). Healthy lifestyle habits and mortality in overweight and obese individuals. *The Journal of the American Board of Family Medicine, 25*(1), 9–15. https://doi.org/10.3122/jabfm.2012.01.110164

McCormack, J. V., & Burrows, L. (2015). The burden of brown bodies: Teachings about Pasifika within public health obesity research in Aotearoa/New Zealand. *Cultural Studies <−> Critical Methodologies, 15*(5), 371–378. https://doi.org/10.1177/1532708615611718

Meo-Sewabu, L. D. (2015). 'Tu ga na inima ka luvu na waqa' = (The bail to get water out of the boat is in the boat yet the boat sinks): The cultural constructs of health and wellbeing amongst Marama iTaukei in a Fijian village in Lau and in a transnational Fijian community in Whanganui. *Aotearoa* [Doctoral thesis]. Massey University.

Ministry of Health. (2015). *Childhood obesity: Establishing a health target*. Ministry of Health.

Ministry of Health. (2016). *New Zealand health strategy: Future direction*. New Zealand Ministry of Health.

Norman, R. J., Dewailly, D., Legro, R. S., & Hickey, T. E. (2007). Polycystic ovary syndrome. *The Lancet, 370*(9588), 685–697. https://doi.org/10.1016/S0140-6736(07)61345-2

O'Hara, L., & Taylor, J. (2018). What's wrong with the 'war on obesity?' A narrative review of the weight-centered health paradigm and development of the 3C framework to build critical competency for a paradigm shift. *SAGE Open, 1–28*, 215824401877288. https://doi.org/10.1177/2158244018772888

O'Reilly, C., & Sixsmith, J. (2012). From theory to policy: Reducing harms associated with the weight-centered health paradigm. *Fat Studies, 1*(1), 97–113. https://doi.org/10.1080/21604851.2012.627792

Owen, L. (2012). Living fat in a thin-centric world: Effects of spatial discrimination on fat bodies and selves. *Feminism & Psychology, 22*(3), 290–306. https://doi.org/10.1177/0959353512445360

Parker, G., Pausé, C., Gillon, A., & Gray, L. (2022). Self-identified fat people's understanding of the need for, and use of, long needles when being vaccinated against COVID-19: Findings from a international online exploratory survey. *Critical Public Health, 1–8*, 375–382. https://doi.org/10.1080/09581596.2022.2159789

Pausé, C. (2014). Die another day: The obstacles facing fat people in accessing quality healthcare. *Narrative Inquiry in Bioethics, 4*(2), 135–141. https://doi.org/10.1353/nib.2014.0039

Pausé, C. (2017, September 26). Christchurch firefighters to no longer respond to callouts for morbidly obese patients [Video clip]. *Breakfast*. Retrieved January 29, 2018, from https://www.tvnz.co.nz/one-news/new-zealand/christchurch-firefighters-no-longer-respond-callouts-morbidly-obese-patients

Pausé, C. (2018). *The HAES files: Why I don't care about health*. International Society of Critical Health Psychology. Retrieved January 29, 2018, from https://ischp.info/2018/04/03/the-haes-files-why-i-dont-care-about-health/

Shackelford, A. (2018). *The executive summary of the 2017 fat census*. Free figure revolution Retrieved May 11, 2019, from https://www.freefigure.org/executivesummary

Simpson, A. B. (2015). *Governing obese bodies: Examining bariatric surgery 'post-op' narratives* [Masters Thesis]. University of Auckland.

Smith, M. (2014). Affect and respectability politics. *Theory & Event, 17*(3).

Smith, V., Moore, C., Cumming, J., & Boulton, A. (2019). Whānau Ora: An indigenous policy success story. In J. Luetjens, M. Mintrom, & P. 't Hart (Eds.), *Successful public policy: Lessons from Australia and New Zealand* (pp. 505–529). ANU Press. https://doi.org/10.22459/SPP.2019

Spitzack, C. (1990). *Confessing excess: Women and the politics of body reduction*. State University of New York Press.

Thomsen, S., Tavita, J., & Levi-Teu, Z. (2018). *A Pacific perspective on the living standards framework and wellbeing* (No. 18/09; New Zealand Treasury discussion paper, p. 41). The New Zealand Treasury.

Wang, Y. A., Macaldowie, A., Hayward, I., Chambers, G. M., & Sullivan, E. A. (2011). *Assisted reproductive technology in Australia and New Zealand 2009* (Assisted Reproduction Series, No. 15). Australian Institute of Health and Welfare.

World Health Organization Regional Office for Europe. (2017). *Weight bias and obesity stigma: Considerations for the WHO European region*. World Health Organization. https://apps.who.int/iris/handle/10665/353613

Aimee Simpson examines the ways that discourses of 'obesity' inform understandings and experiences of health(care), bodies, and identities. Her work draws on the sociologies of medicine and health alongside the interdisciplinary field of fat studies. She resides in Auckland, New Zealand, where she recently completed her PhD, and now works as a public servant. Her time is currently occupied with navigating the complexities and wonders of becoming a new parent.

Impulse, Movement, and Collision: Productive Space at the Confluence of Sociology and Psychotherapy

Kathy L. Davidson

Introduction

There is a long-standing debate at the confluence of sociology and psychotherapy and different opinions on whether the two are compatible or incongruent ways of understanding lived experience. This debate is both historic and current and much of what is recorded has taken place outside of Aotearoa New Zealand. In this chapter, I suggest that the two approaches have much to offer one another and that what has sometimes been seen as antithetical is rather an indication of the need to consider the importance of epistemological and ontological underpinnings in whatever conceptual framework is being deployed. In addition, Kegan's (1994) constructivist developmental framework offers a way of thinking about what might be required in order to make such an integrative move. I offer my own experience training as a sociologist first and a psychotherapist second as an avenue to discuss the value a sociological framework has for psychotherapy praxis within Aotearoa New Zealand. I believe the conversation is timely as we as a country continue to grapple with the challenges of what it means to be a bicultural nation within a now multicultural population that is comprised of numerous marginalised voices. Acknowledging psychotherapeutic praxis as socially located draws attention to the various ways that gender, sexuality, ethnicity, able-bodiedness, and socio-economics (just a few of the relevant aspects of the encounter) are inevitably and always at play. Our interconnectedness is also, however, particularly salient right now given the threats presented by climate change and increasing global insecurity. Within such a context

K. L. Davidson (✉)
Independent Practitioner, Masterton, New Zealand

© The Author(s), under exclusive license to Springer Nature Switzerland AG 2023

Z. L. Rocha, K. L. Davidson (eds.), *Applied and Clinical Sociology in Aotearoa New Zealand*, Clinical Sociology: Research and Practice,
https://doi.org/10.1007/978-3-031-36581-2_9

the following Māori whakatauki (proverb) (Metge, 1995) guides the efforts made in this chapter.

> Kua rite te wā, e whakapuru ai tātou i ngā kowhao o te waka
> The time has come when together we must plug the holes in the canoe.[1]

I wish to acknowledge my gratitude for the privilege of having lived in this country for almost 40 years now as tau iwi and to recognise that my presence here is made possible by the manaakitanga (generosity) of mana whenua.

There is much commonality in the topics that interest sociologists and psychotherapists; identity, sexuality, theories of self, social connection, and power, to name just a few. However, sociologists and other social theorists have provided critique of psychotherapeutic theory that is valid and requires consideration (Foucault, 1965; Barrett, 1991; Craib, 1997Chodorow, 1999; Hook, 2002; Hodges, 2011; Brossard & Sallée, 2020; Ratnayake, 2022). Psychotherapy as a body of theory and a practice cannot be removed from the influence of the socio-historic environment within which it began. The various critiques put forward do not render psychotherapy obsolete or even irrelevant but rather suggest that questions of how hegemonic discourse (Gramsci, 1971) shapes the psychotherapeutic encounter must constantly be negotiated. One thing that sociology and psychotherapy have in common is that both arose from Western European origins and have employed approaches that frequently fail to acknowledge the cultural (including ontological and epistemological) biases in their assumptions. In the process, indigenous and other ways of knowing have been oppressed (Metge, 1995; Durie, 2007; Tuhiwai-Smith, 2012) and an overreliance on methodologies more suited to certain types of questions has meant the production of knowledge has incorporated unstated assumptions.

Colonisation of research methodology is one of the ways unconscious biases have been reproduced in the social sciences (Tuhiwai-Smith, 2012). Another element of bias in the production of sociological knowledge has been the dichotomisation of reason and emotion. Somehow, perhaps in the interests of having sociology acknowledged as the scientific discipline it aspired to be, emotion has often been relegated to realms regarded as less important to sociology and instead left to psychological inquiry. Jaggar (1989) sees this division as a reflection of the gendered production of knowledge that has failed to account for experiences of embodiment and emotionality. Others too find emotion as "an experience of involvement ... (as) something that registers in (a person's) physical and dispositional being" to be neglected in sociology's accounts of social life (Barbalet, 2002, pp. 1–2). The sociology of emotions as a body of literature has been addressing issues such as these for some time now (Bericat, 2015), though the assumptions about what emotions 'are' and how we can 'know' about them continue to be core issues. It remains important to hold such issues in mind when reflecting on how emotions are conceptualised in this country. A yet unresearched possibility is that these issues have an influence on what avenues of sociological application have been recognised and sanctioned in Aotearoa New Zealand.

[1] Metge acknowledges the provision of this whakatauiki for her publication came from Rima Eruera of Ngapuhi and Te Rarawa.

Any move towards integration of sociological and psychotherapeutic praxis should be undertaken, however, mindful of the cogent critique that has been launched against some of the problematic aspects of psychotherapy. Much of this argumentation has been directed at specific forms or techniques of psychotherapy, and my experience has been that sociologists in everyday conversations and contexts then take these techniques to be representative of all of psychotherapy. This is misleading. There are distinct and critical differences in the different schools of psychological and psychotherapeutic thought with relationships to ontological, epistemological, and methodological issues. Some evaluations of psychotherapy are best understood quite specifically as critique of a particular school of thought; for instance, Moussaieff-Masson's (1988) analysis of what is problematic in the psychoanalytic tradition. Humanistic and transpersonal psychologies operate from different suppositions and psychotherapists working in these traditions share sociologists' concern about the problematisation of everyday life experience.

A common complaint about psychological approaches (including psychiatry) is that they construct narratives which pathologize and medicalise everyday experiences. Ratnayake (2022) argues that while much of this critique has focussed on psychiatry, psychotherapy is equally guilty. However, the claim Ratanayake then makes is supported by demonstrating how cognitive behavioural therapy (CBT) pathologizes and medicalises experiences such as heartbreak, misfortune and bereavement. CBT is an approach to therapy that meets the needs of some people who access mental health services, but more importantly operates from a particular set of beliefs that reflect a worldview that is not shared by all psychotherapeutic approaches. CBT's amenability to quantitative evaluation has led to its wide acceptability and even preferability for the likes of insurance companies, where such evaluation is considered simple and unproblematic. Many psychotherapists are similarly concerned with the pathologizing and medicalising of everyday experience and find CBT limited. While critique of psychotherapy's preponderance to pathologizing and the implications of power dynamics is important, and not a fault that is limited to CBT, the collapsing of all psychotherapeutic approaches to one psychotherapeutic approach is problematic. Likewise, discarding the 'baby with the bath water' is not helpful. I have found the approach of psychosynthesis psychotherapy as taught in Aotearoa New Zealand addresses both these issues in ways that allow me to do psychotherapeutic work with sociological integrity. The post-modernist, linguistically attentive, psychospiritual model operates from a very different set of beliefs about the nature of human existence and how we might better 'know' ourselves than other psychotherapies, for instance, CBT.

In addition to the theoretical issues produced at the intersection of sociology and psychotherapy, there is also a more pragmatic problem that faces anyone wanting to become a clinical sociologist or sociotherapist here. While there is no official registration process for applied or clinical sociologists in Aotearoa New Zealand, the possibility of constructing a professional identity as a sociotherapist is remote. I have long been enlivened by the possibility sociology offers to understanding biography as something more than an individual's story and equally been disappointed that there was so little room for carving out the kind of work life (as a researcher/practitioner) that I desired within my chosen field.

Practicing psychotherapy has brought to light (and life) some of the most pertinent and perplexing sociological concepts and issues. For instance, intellectual understanding of embodiment and reflexivity alone is insufficient when faced with the task of engaging with another person in the therapy room and no amount of academic learning can prepare a person entirely for the experience. Not only has psychotherapy brought alive such concepts for me but I see the aims of psychotherapy as inherently sociological and emancipatory; and sometimes more hopeful than sociology would have it. If the study of sociology "enlarges our sympathies and imagination" by helping us to take "a step back from our own personal interpretations of the world (to) look at the social influences which shape our lives" (Giddens, 1989, pp. 1–5) in a liberating manner, then I see the psychotherapeutic endeavour as inherently sociological. While changing the way society conceptualises things like sexual identity, or ethnicity, might be a long and sometimes fruitless-seeming task, the experience of changing perceptions within the psychotherapeutic encounter can be liberating and more immediately achievable in a way that is hopeful. Therapeutic encounter has the potential to bring the confluence of agency and structure into sharp relief as people grapple with 'reality' as they have been taught to see it and consider other possibilities of meaning making in their present lives. Within the dynamic interplay, individuals can begin to see the powerful social forces at play in their lives. From here, there is at least the possibility of an enhanced capacity to engage in social change whether that be through how they engage in their interpersonal relationships, or through the way they make decisions in the workplace, or—for some—through participation in social activism and politics. At the very least, this is the possibility and the hope that I hold in my therapeutic work.

The efforts I describe above could be supported by additional measures. Vissing (2022) documents the important role of addressing micro, meso and macro levels in battling extremism in school students in the United States. While micro applied sociology remains poorly understood and developed in Aotearoa New Zealand, such opportunities are more elusive. My acknowledgment here is that in 'ideal' world, attention to all levels of engagement is needed for social change to be most effective. I currently work within the social limitations inscribed upon my practice at the same time as I continue to challenge the productivity of binary notions around agency/structure, personal/political, and individual/social.

My suspicion is that many sociologists can remember an early experience of having social theory alter the way they viewed the world in a way that was transformative. Perhaps it was Emile Durkheim's (1951) analysis of the relevance of social conditions to the 'individual' act of suicide, or Karl Marx's (cited in Tucker, 1978) contention that the material conditions of lives shape thoughts about that life. Or the promise that C. Wright Mills' (1959) offered through the connection of private troubles with public issues via the sociological imagination. Or perhaps it was the more recent work of Dorothy E. Smith (2005) regarding the way that knowledge production is imbued with viewpoints steeped in situated meaning making and power dynamics. Whatever the source, sociology is replete with opportunities for new understandings; understandings which can be challenging both professionally and personally. Perhaps it is this aspect of the sociological enterprise that leads to strong attachment to professional identity and the border skirmishes common between sociology and other disciplines. Becoming a sociologist does not only involve the attainment of proficiency in a knowledge area but is for many a transformative experience; a training in how to see the world in a way that is different and complex—in a way that becomes a marker of identity.

Training to become a psychotherapist is also an inculcation into how to see the people who inhabit this world in a different and complex way. It is a training in the examination of what it is that structures a person's meaning making process and their world view, including their view of themselves. And, like training to be a sociologist, it is for many practitioners a transformative experience. In each case, the learning draws on concepts and the development of a shared disciplinary language that portrays a way of seeing in particular ways. Like any culture, it is helpful to learn to speak the language in order to really understand the perspective and although it is common to combine sociology and psychology in an undergraduate degree, it is less common—in New Zealand, at least—to train at an advanced level in both cultures. I reflect here on the challenges and the value of attaining a level of proficiency in both ways of viewing ourselves and the world. In the current climate we find ourselves in, it is timely to also consider the way that sociological identity is recognised institutionally. New applications of the sociological imagination can support a shift in how we understand the contribution that sociology makes to psychotherapy as well as how psychotherapy can contribute to more vibrant sociological praxis.

I continue to look for greater integration of sociological and psychological perspectives as I search for a way to be both sociologist and psychotherapist in the work that I do. This is a task that is particularly difficult and to date I have been unable to find any guidance on how this might be achieved for someone located in this country, although there has more recently been some discussion of the inherent challenges of being, for instance, both social scientist and psychoanalyst (Chodorow, 2014). What I provide here is therefore exploratory in nature, my thoughts still in a process of development; seeds for a broader conversation regarding the value of bringing together sociological and psychotherapeutic perspectives in Aotearoa New Zealand.

In considering how to tell the following story, several issues arose. First, does my own biographical trajectory have any relevance for others? If it does, and if it is worth telling, how might I tell it? (Wall, 2008). What ethical dilemmas might be produced if I allow my own personal experience to become public? (Dashper, 2015). Such questions are commonly asked by those who write from a personal position or who employ autoethnographic methodology (Ellis & Bochner, 2000 in Denzin & Lincoln, 2000). In answer to the first question, "personal narratives such as autobiographies, biographies, and life stories are likely to present fuller pictures, ones in which the meanings of events and relationships are more likely to be told than inferred" (Lasslett, 1999, p. 391). The value of telling such stories has already been well-established by those who have wrangled with the dilemmas involved in qualitative research generally (Denzin & Lincoln, 2000). Though I would not claim what is produced here is autoethnography in its pure sense, it is in the spirit of such an approach that I produce this account. It seems the best method for telling this story.

The last question regarding the ethics of using my own experience as data is hardest to answer. However, turning to authors of autoethnography, I find inspiration to take the risk that I do (Wall, 2008; Dashper, 2015).

My experience of becoming a psychotherapist following completion of a PhD in sociology is an experience shaped by location in many ways: geographic, cultural, and temporal as well as being located through my ethnicity, my gender and my sexuality. The experience of becoming a psychotherapist was made possible through the generosity of so many others. Hence, I incorporate elements of my own whakapapa and the whakapapa of the institution that provided my psychotherapy training in recognition that what is written here is made possible as a result of both. Having earlier rejected psychology and psychotherapy as approaches that I could align myself with, primarily because of sociological critique of the two, I found myself needing to reconsider when faced with an impulse to create a career that allowed me to actively incorporate theory with practice.

A Case in Point

What follows here is a personal story of my attempt to integrate two perspectives which have provided me with a map for understanding myself and the world we live in. As noted above, sociology and psychotherapy are not always easy bedfellows, but they have shaped the trajectory of much of my life. As a city-born Canadian immigrant to this country, I have felt caught between different cultures for most of my adult life as I live on a farm near a small rural town in Aotearoa New Zealand. My academic and professional interests have also straddled two different (cultural) disciplines and my undergraduate education was a bachelor's degree majoring in sociology and psychology. However, it was the broader and more critical perspective of sociology that won me over when it came to postgraduate study. Reading Foucault's *Madness and Civilisation: A History of Insanity in the Age of Reason* (1965) at the same time as *Abnormal Psychology* (1998) contributed to my dissatisfaction with purely psychological accounts of human experience. The possibility of postgraduate study in the sociology of emotions cinched my enrolment in the discipline. With a scholarship for PhD study in hand, I began an exploration of the complexity of emotional labour within the New Zealand parliamentary workplace (Stuart, 2008). An investigation of the sociological literature on emotion left me also dissatisfied with the dichotomisation of reason and emotion that continued to permeate and the location of my research was chosen out of a desire to 'study up' and to disturb the more usual (gendered and class-based) assumptions regarding emotion work (Hochschild, 2012).

Gender and socioeconomics have shaped my academic interests and my working life. As the first person from my family of origin to complete high school, let alone university study, the academic world was an entirely unknown entity. While it is (thankfully) no longer entirely remarkable to be a 'first in family' university graduate, this lack of cultural capital (Bourdieu, 1973) may have contributed to some naivety on my part later in my career. In addition to the lack of understanding or guidance in negotiating 'the system', there was also the challenge of carrying out my entire undergraduate and postgraduate education while raising children and living on a farm. There were many barriers to education to overcome. This information is relevant as the background to the account I produce here. Suffice it to say, my academic 'career' did not follow the usual pathway and its novelty made completion and gainful employment that much more challenging. In addition, the financial support our family farm provided me with made the path I have followed possible.

On completion of my PhD studies, I entered fixed-term contract work for two universities. After 5 years that involved teaching at least one new course every semester that I was employed, I made a bid for a permanent position in a New Zealand university. That bid included a proposal to create a postgraduate diploma in clinical sociology.[2] The first time I came across the concept of clinical sociology was just after my postgraduate studies were complete. At no time during my undergraduate or postgraduate education had I realised that there were others, albeit in countries far afield, that were applying sociology at the micro level in direct therapeutic encounters. My reasons for wanting to create this kind of programme remain important. I was concerned at the time with anecdotal accounts of people with undergraduate sociology degrees in jobs at the local supermarket or others with postgraduate qualifications involved in policy work which they described as uninspiring. I hoped to create a new avenue for those who were drawn to the sociological study of emotional life and who might want to apply their education and training to a form of praxis.

The job bid was unsuccessful, and I was devastated. Other more experienced colleagues later suggested that including in my application the proposal for a programme in an applied sociology such as clinical sociology was unwise. There wasn't an appetite, in their opinion, for the application of sociology in such a micro-focused manner. Had I consulted others prior to the application, I would not have likely done anything differently. By then I had decided that the sociological study of emotions addressed only some of the problems I was concerned with and was seriously limited. What I believed was required was a more feminist-inspired, experientially based approach, one which acknowledged the embodied experience not only of emotion but of learning. And so it was that at this point I relinquished the dream of being a sociologist within the academic world and turned to training to be a psychotherapist. Sadly, at the time I did not see a way to be both while I continued to live in this country. Letting go of the dream of creating Aotearoa's first clinical sociology programme brought with it a moment of deep despair. I felt no option but to also relinquish my professional identity as a sociologist, tied up as that was with employment in the university system. I continue to hold the conviction that this

[2]The Commission on the Accreditation of Programs in Applied and Clinical Sociology (CAPACS) is an American body with an interest in sociological practice and provides a means for such programs—national and international—to be evaluated and monitored. CAPACS was formerly known as The Commission on Applied and Clinical Sociology but was renamed in 2010 to better reflect the activities of the organisation.

choice should not have been necessary; that there ought to be room within the sociological identity to be both. I see clinical sociology at the micro level, or sociotherapy as I would now prefer to call it, as one form of the more general category of applied sociology.

Enter Psychosynthesis

At the time I discovered that clinical sociology was a possibility in North America, I also found it was possible to apply for registration via the USA if I lived in a country where such registration was not possible (provided I had the qualifications to meet their requirements). In addition to a postgraduate degree in sociology I required some form of qualification that demonstrated an ability to work one to one with people. Previously, while still involved in fixed-term contract work, I had discovered the Institute of Psychosynthesis N.Z. in Auckland and begun block-course study there in the hopes of meeting the American requirements. I intended to use the training in psychosynthesis to gain registration.

While it is the work of Sigmund Freud that is most closely associated with psychotherapy because of his early development of the psychoanalytic perspective, it is the work of the lesser-known Italian psychiatrist Roberto Assagioli that underpins the institute where I studied and consequently the thinking within this chapter. Psychosynthesis is a psychospiritual psychotherapy emphasising personal growth and viewing the experience of self as an ongoing process of both being and becoming. It differs from some other Western psychotherapeutic approaches in important respects: the basic working assumption is of an already whole and intimately interconnected 'self' yet a self that experiences separateness. In his development of psychosynthesis, Assagioli is said to have integrated Western 'depth' psychology with Eastern 'height' psychospiritual traditions (https://www.psychosynthesis.co.nz/introduction/). His theorising is holistic in nature in that it does not valorise any one aspect of human experience at the expense of another. Sensing, feeling, imagining, thinking, desiring, intuiting, are equally important psychological functions. As functions, however, they do require direction. What provides direction is the concept of will, which I elaborate shortly.

From early in his career and until his death in 1974, Assagioli preferred to maintain a separation between his own biography and the approach he developed. He desired that psychosynthesis stand on its own as a scientific approach and likely realised that the breadth of his interest in human experience beyond three-dimensional time and space might prove a distraction. Psychosynthesis is an approach that acknowledges the contribution that unconscious and early life experiences make to understandings of self and adds in the presupposition of human longing for a sense of connection to something greater than material life or an individual self.

In the interests of acknowledging the socio-historic origins of this approach, Assagioli's life is briefly summarised here. Born in 1888 in Venice to Italian Jewish parents, Assagioli's father died soon after when Assagioli was just 2 years old. His mother remarried a Dr. Emanuele Assagioli. Roberto's early life contained both the unfortunate loss of his father and the good fortune of becoming part of a family that enjoyed significant privilege. Assagioli appears to have had an active and inquiring mind from a young age and was afforded the luxury of a stimulating educational life that led to him choosing to study medicine at university. He quickly found himself a home in the field of psychiatry with its integration of physical and behavioural sciences (Guggisberg Nocelli, 2017).

Assagioli was influenced by the work of Freud and is known to have communicated with him through letters, though the two never met. Indeed, Assagioli declares that his own framework is precluded upon Freud's psychoanalysis, a necessary but not sufficient condition of psychosynthesis (Assagioli, 1965, 2000). Although fellow psychoanalyst Carl Jung wrote to Freud of his hopes that Assagioli might prove a prospective adherent of psychoanalysis, Assagioli's impulse was to prove far more independent than Jung's comment implies (Guggisberg Nocelli, 2017). For Assagioli, Freud's approach, though significant in the recognition of unconscious process, neglected what he saw as the most important aspect of psychological work: to facilitate human potential and growth by attending to the whole of the human being and to the on-going process of synthesis. Freud did also believe in the desirability of synthesis in the human personality, but he saw it as something that would spontaneously develop out of sufficient analysis (ibid.). Assagioli, on the other hand, sought a way of working that directly encouraged synthesis by addressing all levels of human experience. In recent times, the value of mindfulness and body-based practices such as yoga to emotional health and well-being has been noted (Carsley et al., 2018; Varambally & Gangadhar, 2012; Duraiswamy et al., 2007). Assagioli discovered the benefits of meditation and yoga for himself back in the early 1900s, though he did not explicitly advocate for either in the development of his theory. For Assagioli, psychosynthesis took participants to the 'doorway' of religious or spiritual experience but did not direct a person in how they ought to move through that doorway. Assagioli was imprisoned for a short time in 1940 by the Italian fascist regime and he credited the experience as an opportunity to deepen his own spiritual practices.

A significant difference between Assagioli and his predecessors Freud and Jung is Assagioli's development of the concept of will. He contended that what was most notable about human beings at the turn of the century was that although people could act upon their environment, they did not show the same capacity to engage with their inner worlds. He thought that modernisation brought with it much that was good but also much that was problematic.

> To some extent everyone is able to resist the attractions of the world and the pace of modern life, eliminate many unnecessary complications, re-establish closer contact with nature, and practice the art of relaxing and resting at intervals. But past a certain point, one encounters great difficulties. Duties of every kind, family ties, professional obligations keep us bound to the wheel of modern life and often compel us to conform to its hurried pace (Assagioli, 2010, p. 4).

The answer to being unreflectively driven by the demands of modern life was a "direct existential experience" of will (ibid., p. 5). While a full discussion of the concept of will is not possible here, suffice it to say that Assagioli is not referring to will in the way we might know it. He identifies four aspects of will—strong will, skilful will, good will and joyous will—some of which map onto more common notions of will and others which do not. It is through direct engagement with will that we find greater purpose, meaning and value in life.

An important aspect of psychosynthesis is that it includes but is not limited to recognition of "transpersonal experiences as … life-changing or meaning-giving events" (Evans, 2012). For the most part, transpersonal is an umbrella term that covers a myriad of religious and spiritual expressions and experiences. It is a concept associated with the humanistic school of psychology and key theorists include Albert Maslow (1943) and Stanislav Grof (2008).[3] In my view, the production of a PhD in sociology can be a 'transpersonal' experience, though perhaps not necessarily so. The PhD process involves the researcher engaging with concepts and theories that connect to things much larger than self, to a literature that spans centuries and is enlivened by the recorded thoughts and findings of theorists and researchers who have gone before. It is often a life-changing and meaning-giving event. It is not uncommon for a researcher to experience a 'dark night of the soul' once deep in the research process. I had such an experience at one point as a I wrestled with notions of self, identity, and epistemological issues related to the subject of emotion. As awareness developed of the consequences of issues that had until then been in shadow, there came a moment when the entire thesis, and indeed my knowing of myself, fell apart and the decompression that resulted felt like annihilation; at that moment, just months before I thought I would be submitting, the thesis was reduced to ashes in the face of fiery challenges to what I thought I knew. It was, of course, at this point that production of my own thesis really began.

A Local Approach

The framework that underpins my thoughts and informs my experience of integrating the sociological and the psychological is born from the work of Assagioli and the London Institute of Psychosynthesis, for it was at the London Institute that New Zealanders Helen Palmer and Peter Hubbard trained and taught before establishing the Institute of Psychosynthesis N.Z. in Auckland in 1986. Palmer and Hubbard have developed psychosynthesis in their own way, informed by their learning and by the issues relevant in this place. For over 30 years their Auckland institute trained counsellors and psychotherapists and people interested in their own psychological and spiritual development; the work continues now through their own

[3]Transpersonal psychology as part of the humanistic school of psychology differs from some other psychologies with its inclusion of consciousness as an important aspect of human experience.

Psychosynthesis Research and Education organisation as well as the new and independently established Psychosynthesis South Pacific Trust.

The work Hubbard and Palmer undertook at the Auckland institute was shaped from the beginning by the local landscape. In applying to write her master's thesis through the London Institute and its affiliated Middlesex University in 2009, Palmer wrote:

> We were raised in a society where the official governmental policy for race relations in New Zealand was one of assimilation and integration, based on the dominant ideology that 'we are all New Zealanders'. Such ideology ignored alternative world views and differing cultural aspirations, preferences and practices, particularly of Māori as the indigenous minority. It also failed to acknowledge the sad history of colonization and post-colonial power imbalances entrenched by land dispossession, suppression of language and identity, and institutionalized policies based on Western values at the expense of Polynesian traditions (unpublished communication with the London Institute of Psychosynthesis).[4]

The Treaty of Waitangi Act was passed in 1975, at about the same time as Palmer and Hubbard headed (separately) overseas. When they returned together in 1986, they found a changed country, one where awareness of the Treaty as a living, foundational, national document was growing. Tensions between Māori and Pakeha (and a desire to be in respectful relationship) is but one of the ways the Institute's trajectory has been informed by its location in the South Pacific. The theoretical development of psychosynthesis that has taken place in this country differs from the work of psychosynthesis theorists and practitioners in other parts of the world, namely Europe, Scandinavia and the United States of America. Palmer declares psychosynthesis as conceptualised here is a psychospiritual psychology, devoid of the implicit (and potentially problematic) association of psychosynthesis with the perennial philosophy[5] (Palmer, 2012). The version of psychosynthesis developed in Aotearoa also departs from iterations in other parts of the world with an aversion to reification through linguistic deployments such as *the* will and through introduction of the term personal centre of identity (PCI). "We noticed ... people would think of 'The I' as a place to get to, an identity to be achieved, a step towards Self-realisation" so they introduced the new term in order to "identify the developmental and experiential functioning and capacity of the personal self" (Palmer, 2012, p. 50). PCI functioning became part of case formulation for psychosynthesis psychotherapy trainees. Training as first a counsellor and then a psychotherapist (or a guide, as is the term often used by psychosynthesis trainers and practitioners) at the Institute, I found the directors avoided some of the pitfalls I had earlier struggled with when faced with more conventional and modernist-influenced approaches to psychotherapy. Self was not a destination, but a process that was continuous; an experience of both being and

---

[4]I wish to acknowledge the help of Helen Palmer with this information.

[5]In this way, psychosynthesis as developed and taught in Aotearoa by Palmer and Hubbard seeks distance from Assagioli's vague but arguably problematic association with the perennial philosophy. The perennial philosophy is the idea that all religious and spiritual systems have a core or essential similarity in spite of the different ways this is expressed. For more on the connections between psychosynthesis and the perennial philosophy see Kenneth Sorensen.

becoming. Neither was self reductively individualised but understood through relationship and manifested through will.

In addition, the influence of postmodernism and the insistence on a psychospiritual frame for psychotherapeutic work (Palmer, 2012) make for a more sensitive (and sociological) holding than might be expected given critiques of psychology and psychotherapy. Rather than ignoring social stratification, the training relationally embraced my sociologically trained perspective. Palmer draws on British epidemiologists and academic researchers Kate Pickett and Richard Wilkinson to suggest why it is so important that dichotomy not prevail, and this is relevant when it comes to thinking about the prospects of sociotherapy and clinical sociology. "How people become sensitive to inequality 'cannot be understood in terms either of social structure or of individual psychology alone. Individual psychology and societal inequality relate to each other like lock and key'" (Wilkinson & Picket, 2010, cited in Palmer, 2012, p. 45). The application of sociological inquiry in the micro-setting of the therapy room is entwined with other sociological endeavours that seek to contribute to emancipatory potential at all levels of society.

Sociology and Psychotherapy: At the Confluence

Key concepts that permeated the New Zealand psychosynthesis training programme, with relevance to possibilities for the development of sociotherapy within Aotearoa, are the capacity of holding 'a point of tension' between ideas that might seem at first glance oppositional (such as we find at the confluence of structure and agency, or sociology and psychotherapy) and the notion of 'disidentification'. Disidentification is a core practice in psychosynthesis and involves recognition of the difference between ideas and thoughts about self or of the topic at hand. It is a difficult practice to express linguistically, and its understanding is best aided through an experiential process. Holding a 'point of tension' allows for on-going engagement without the necessity for resolution of the tension through premature conclusion.

Another important aspect of Assagioli's approach is that although he speaks of development, he does not see this process as linear or continuous. Rather he speaks of finding one's own voice and subsequent 'synthesis' through a process of exploring one's personality without being caught in the content of that experience (Palmer, 2012). In this, I find psychosynthesis to be both sociological and psychological. Without abandoning the notion of inner knowing, but by identifying the way that knowing may be constrained by personality and social conditions, it is possible to discover new ways of being in the world; new ways of experiencing self and others. The process of 'disidentification' aids in an understanding of self as something more than the product of earlier life experiences or the trauma responses that may be a part of that experience. This process requires first 'identification' of those aspects of experience that have shaped our thoughts about ourselves and those experiences. It is identification in service of disidentification and this allows for a much broader understanding and perspective than might otherwise be possible. I believe a similar process occurs in sociology as we identify the value in a particular theoretical approach at the same time as we might elaborate its limitations.

Ascribing to the notion of 'both and' rather than 'either or' creates opportunity for working within areas where contradiction is current. Also helpful is Robert Kegan's (1982, 1994) constructivist developmental framework for understanding what he calls 'orders of the mind'. His model demonstrates that thinking that can hold a point of tension moves us away from reductivity and towards complexity. According to Kegan's model, the development of mind is continuous, flexible, lifelong, and intrinsically shaped by the relationship between what we can hold as subject and object, aligning his framework with the ideals of psychosynthesis psychotherapy.

At the point at which I realised I would need to create my own path to a career incorporating my sociological interests and my desire for an applied practice, I thought I had no option but to 'let go' of one aspect of my professional identity in order to find personally meaningful work. I experienced the loss of a 'consolidated' sense of self (Kegan, 1982, p. 232) and that initiated a deep sense of grief. I did not undertake 6 years of postgraduate study in order to arrive at the place I found myself in. I undertook another 5 year training and, with registration as psychotherapist, began to describe myself and what I did in a new way. However, I continue to experience tensions between the two professional identities and how I understand myself and the work that I do. I believe this is evidence of a stage of transition from one order of mind to another, in Kegan's terms. It is also a reflection of the unavailability of a formally recognised professional identity as a sociotherapist or even, less specifically, clinical sociologist in New Zealand.

Kegan suggests that as human beings we experience distress when there is a mismatch in the complexity of our world and the order of mind we are operating from. At such times we might feel "in over our heads" (the name of Kegan's 1994 book). It is then that a shift in the lens through which we view our selves and the world is necessary. The shift from interpersonal to institutional self, or put another way, from the self-authoring (fourth order) to the self transforming (fifth order) order of mind enables "a perspective on (the self-regulating) system, a dawning recognition of how it works and a questioning of its costs" (Kegan, 1982, pp. 225). Kegan's model emphasises the important growth that takes place in the transition space between the different orders of mind. It is within the transition space from the self-authoring (fourth order) to the self-transforming order (fifth order) of mind that I find myself as I continue to develop my understanding of myself as both sociologically informed psychotherapist and psychotherapeutically informed sociologist.

No longer bracketing off that which is 'sociological' from that which is 'psychological' in the perspective I bring to my *kanohi ki te kanohi* (face to face) work, I am recognising that the theories I operate from are intrinsic to who I am in the therapy room. Is it important—or even possible—to say when I am being a sociologist versus when I am being a psychotherapist in my work? A colleague recently asked what it is that I thought I did differently in the therapy room as a sociologist. It is a good question, yet one that is no more easily answered than is the question of what difference culture or ethnicity makes to the encounter. Both perspectives or cultures are embedded within me, informing what I notice and say, and at times causing dissonance when there are unarticulated clashes of ontological and epistemological positions.

Within the confines of the therapy room (my therapy room, the one whose location I have chosen, the room that I have furnished in a particular way) those lessons acquired during my training as a sociologist take on new relevance. My own able-bodiedness, my heteronormativity, Scandinavian and Canadian heritage, my economic and educational privilege, are all a part of the therapeutic encounter. Even when clients from marginalised social positions say otherwise and attempt to reassure me that they want to do their personal exploration with me, these social identifiers influence what happens between us. I cannot bracket off who I am, and neither can my clients. I enter the exchange and must face the possibility that I may make a mistake—indeed, if I want to be effective, it is important that I am willing to do just this. In this regard, sociology alone has been insufficient for equipping me with the intrapsychic tools I need in order to navigate the complex issues that face me in a micro-level setting such as the therapeutic encounter. Yet my training as a sociologist is what has predisposed my attention to include awareness of the various ways social locatedness is central in the intersubjective space of my work. Being exposed to the sociological critique of power in the therapeutic relationship prior to beginning psychotherapeutic training has led to an emphasis on transparency in the work that I do. I view myself and anyone I sit with as companions on a journey poet David Whyte[6] (2009, 2015) describes as one that is "impossible to accomplish alone".

Conclusion

Sociology's contribution to understandings of human life is important given the range of locations across which it has application. While areas of sociological research may overlap with psychological research areas, the attention sociology pays to the structural forces at play even in the seemingly internal experience of emotion is part of what makes its explanations powerful. Psychotherapy is a vehicle through which we can understand how it is that the social lives within us; how it is that even the best intentions do not dissolve the ways in which social structures can encage our thoughts and selves. For those who seek to address the myriad of issues facing Aotearoa New Zealand today, sociology avoids an excess of introversion while I have found the psychospiritual approach of psychosynthesis helpful in circumventing an excess of extroversion and what Assagioli calls an illusion of no will (or a sense of being without agency). As sociologists we study society and the patterns that structure society at all levels because these levels are entwined. Age,

[6]Whyte is a poet living in the Pacific Northwest, of Irish and Welsh descent, with a particular interest in the transformative possibilities of work.

gender, ethnicity, economic, sexuality, regionality, religiosity, and spirituality—are all organising principles actively at play in the therapeutic space.

One thing missing from my sociology education was an embodied experience of meaning-making patterns. Reflexivity aside, sociology did not teach me to understand the deep limbic pull that could happen when sitting with another human being experiencing emotional pain. Not only does sociology have so much to offer psychology generally and psychotherapy particularly, but it is my contention that psychotherapy also has much to offer sociology in terms of understanding the deep and often unconscious structures of our meaning-making.

Sometimes I think that my dual training has equipped me to understand the two very different worlds and cultures of sociologists and psychotherapists in a manner that is enriching. At other times I feel the result of this dual training is an absence of ever feeling fully understood by either set of colleagues. That can produce a sense of isolation and may play into the desire to encourage others in the same endeavour in order that the conversations may deepen, and to create more coherence and integration in a world where those things are glimpsed only fleetingly. Further research could be done on what would encourage sociologists outside academia to build a more vibrant sense of shared professional identity. Questions could also be asked regarding what would help build a stronger collegial community so that applied sociologists as well as those who would identify as sociotherapists might not be left to individualise that which is better understood collectively.

For others who come to the end of a postgraduate education in sociology and continue to yearn for something more, the path into sociotherapy is not an easy one but it is a fruitful and meaningful one. I have offered this personal account because I continue to care deeply about sociology in Aotearoa New Zealand and I would like to see more avenues of application for those who have studied the discipline here. The ideas offered here are offered in the spirit of what Peter Hubbard calls "quarter thoughts and half thoughts"; as stimulation to further discussion and elaboration. I write this because I do not believe that sociology or psychotherapy alone are sufficient to address the state of our nation or our world, but they have made for a powerful combination in my pursuit of finding purpose, meaning and value in the work that I do and in the life that I lead.

References

Assagioli, R. (1965). *Psychosynthesis: A manual of principles and techniques*. Hobbs, Dorman.

Assagioli, R. (2000). *Psychosynthesis: A collection of basic writing* (2nd ed.). The Synthesis Centre.

Assagioli, R. (2010). *The act of will*. The Synthesis Centre Press.

Barbalet, J. (Ed.). (2002). *Emotions and sociology*. Blackwell Publishing.

Barrett, M. (1991). Psychoanalysis and feminism – A British sociologist's view. *Signs, 17*(2), 455–466.

Bericat, E. (2015). The sociology of emotions: Four decades of progress. *Current Sociology, 64*(3), 491–513. https://doi.org/10.1177/0011392115588355

Bourdieu, P. (1973). Cultural reproduction and social reproduction. In R. Brown (Ed.) *Knowledge, education and cultural change*. Routledge.
Brossard, B., & Sallée, N. (2020). Sociology and psychology: What intersections? *European Journal of Social Theory, 23*(1), 3–14.
Carsley, D., Khoury, B., & Heath, N. L. (2018). Effectiveness of mindfulness interventions for mental health in schools: A comprehensive meta-analysis. *Mindfulness, 9*, 693–707. Accessed 12 January 2023, from https://doi.org/10.1007/s12671-017-0839-2
Chodorow, N. (1999). *The reproduction of mothering: Psychoanalysis and the sociology of gender*. University of California Press.
Chodorow, N. (2014). Why is it easy to be a psychoanalyst and a feminist, but not a psychoanalyst and a social scientist? Reflections of a psychoanalytic hybrid. In L. Chancer & J. Andrews (Eds.), *The unhappy divorce of sociology and psychoanalysis: Studies in the psychosocial*. Palgrave Macmillan. https://doi.org/10.1057/9781137304582_6
Craib, I. (1997). Social constructionism as a social psychosis. *Sociology, 31*(1), 1–15.
Dashper, K. (2015). Revise, resubmit and reveal? An autoethnographer's story of facing the challenges of revealing the self through publication. *Current Sociology, 63*(4), 511–527.
Denzin, N., & Lincoln, Y. (2000). *Handbook of qualitative research*. Sage.
Duraiswamy, G., Thirhalli, J., Nagendra, H. R., & Gangadhar, B. N. (2007). Yoga therapy as an add-on treatment in the management of patients with schizophrenia – A randomized controlled trial. *Acta Psychiatrica Scandinavica, 116*(3), 226–232.
Durie, M. (2007). Counselling Māori: Marae encounters as a basis for understanding and building relationships. *New Zealand Journal of Counselling, 27*(1), 1–8.
Durkheim, E. (1951). *Suicide: A study in sociology* (J. Spaulding & G. Simpson, Trans.). The Free Press.
Ellis, C., & Bochner, A. (2000). Autoethnography, personal narrative, reflexivity: Researcher as subject. In N. In Denzin & Y. Lincoln (Eds.), *Handbook of qualitative research* (2nd ed.). Sage Publications.
Evans, J. (2012). *Forward in H. Palmer, Psychosynthesis in the South Pacific: Ontological and epistemological considerations in the context of Aotearoa New Zealand*. London Institute of Psychosynthesis.
Foucault, M. (1965). *Madness and civilization: A history of insanity in the age of reason*. Random House.
Giddens, A. (1989). *Sociology*. Polity Press.
Gramsci, A. (1971). *Selections from the prison notebooks* (Q. Hoare & G. Nowell Smith, Trans., Eds.). International Publishers.
Grof, S. (2008). Brief history of transpersonal psychology. *International Journal of Transpersonal Studies, 27*(1), 46–54.
Guggisberg Nocelli, P. (2017). *The way of psychosynthesis: A complete guide to origins, concepts, and the fundamental experiences with a biography of Roberto Assagioli*. Synthesis Insights.
Hochschild, A. R. (2012). *The managed heart: The commercialization of human feeling*. University of California Press.
Hodges, I. (2011). Queering psychoanalysis: Power, self and identity in psychoanalytic therapy with sexual minority clients. *Psychology and Sexuality, 2*(1), 29–44.
Hook, D. (2002). Psychotherapy, discourse and the production of psychopathology. In D. Hook & G. Eagle (Eds.), *Psychopathology and social prejudice*. University of Cape Town Press.
https://www.psychosynthesis.co.nz/introduction. Retrieved December 4, 2022.
Jaggar, A. M. (1989). Love and knowledge: Emotion in feminist epistemology. *Inquiry, 32*(2), 151–176.
Kegan, R. (1982). *The evolving self: Problem and process in human development*. Harvard University Press.
Kegan, R. (1994). *In over our heads: The mental demands of modern life*. Harvard University Press.
Lasslett, B. (1999). Personal narratives as sociology. *Contemporary Sociology, 28*, 4.

Maslow, A. H. (1943). A theory of human motivation. *Psychological Review, 50*(4), 370–396. https://doi.org/10.1037/h0054346
Masson, J. M. (1988). *Against therapy: Emotional tyranny and the myth of psychological healing.* Common Courage Press.
Metge, J. (1995). *New growth from old: The whanau in the modern world.* Victoria University Press.
Mills, C. W. (1959). *The sociological imagination* (Vol. 46, p. 355). Oxford University Press.
Palmer, H. (2012). *Psychosynthesis in the South Pacific: Ontological and epistemological considerations in the context of Aotearoa New Zealand.* London Institute of Psychosynthesis.
Ratnayake, S. (2022). 'I will never love anyone like that again': Cognitive behavioural therapy and the pathologisation and medicalisation of ordinary experiences. *Medical Humanities, 48*(7), e7.
Smith, D. E. (2005). *Institutional ethnography: A sociology for people.* Altamira Press.
Stuart, K. (2008). *Emotional labour and occupational identity: Passionate rationality in the New Zealand parliamentary workplace.* (PhD thesis, Massey University, Palmerston North).
Tucker, R. C. (1978). *The Marx-Engels reader* (2nd ed.). W.W. Norton & Co.
Tuhiwai Smith, L. (2012). *Decolonizing methodologies: Research and indigenous peoples.* Zed Books.
Varambally, S., & Gangadhar, B. N. (2012). Yoga: A spiritual practice with therapeutic value in psychiatry. *Asian Journal of Psychiatry, 5*(2), 186–189.
Vissing, Y. (2022). Extremism vs. human rights: How ideology is built, nurtured, and transforms societies. In J. Zajda & Y. Vissing (Eds.), *Discourses of globalisation, ideology, and human rights* (Globalisation, comparative education and policy research) (Vol. 28).
Wall, S. (2008). Easier said than done: Writing an autoethnography. *International Journal of Qualitative. Methods, 7*(1), 38–53. https://doi.org/10.1177/160940690800700103
Whyte, D. (2009). *The three marriages: Reimagining work, self and relationship.* Riverhead Books.
Whyte, D. (2015). *Consolations: The solace, nourishment and underlying meaning of everyday words.* Many Rivers Press.
Wilkinson, R., & Pickett, K. (2010). *The spirit level.* Penguin.

Kathy L. Davidson is a sociologist and registered psychotherapist currently working in private practice in Wellington and the Wairarapa. She has a PhD from Massey University, an honours degree in sociology, and a BA with a double major in psychology and sociology also from Massey University. She holds diplomas in Psychosynthesis Counselling and Psychotherapy from the Institute of Psychosynthesis NZ. Kathy's diverse research interests include emotional labour and occupational identity, disaster management, and mental health. She has coordinated a bicultural participatory action research project into the mental health and well-being of youth/rangatahi.

Glossary of Māori Words

Aotearoa	New Zealand
Aroha	Love, caring, compassion, empathy
Aroha ki te tangata	Respect for people
Haka	Ceremonial dance
Hapū	Sub-tribe
Hui	Meeting, gathering
Iwi	Tribe
Kaiako	Teacher
Kaikaranga	The woman (or women) who has the role of making the ceremonial call to visitors onto a marae
Kaikōrero	Speaker, narrator
Kaitiakitanga	Guardianship, protection
Kai	Food
Kanohi ki te kanohi	Face to face, in person
Karanga	To call, summon
Kapa Haka	A group which performs traditional dance and song
Kaumātua	Respected elder or elders
Kaupapa Māori	A philosophical doctrine, incorporating the knowledge, skills, attitudes and values of Māori society.
Koha	Gift, present, offering, donation
Kōhanga reo	Māori language nests (whānau led early childcare)
Kōrero	To tell, say, speak, read, talk, address
Kuia	Female elder
Kura	School
Mana	Prestige, authority, control, power, influence, status, spiritual power, charisma
Manaakitanga	The process of showing respect, generosity and care for others.

© The Author(s), under exclusive license to Springer Nature Switzerland AG 2023

Z. L. Rocha, K. L. Davidson (eds.), *Applied and Clinical Sociology in Aotearoa New Zealand*, Clinical Sociology: Research and Practice,
https://doi.org/10.1007/978-3-031-36581-2

Mana whenua	Power associated with possession and occupation of tribal land
Marae	A communal or sacred place that serves religious and social purposes
Mātāpono	Principle
Mātauranga Māori	The body of knowledge originating from Māori ancestors, including the Māori world view and cultural practices
Ngā Tamatoa	An activist group to promote Māori rights, fight racial discrimination, and confront injustices
Pākehā	New Zealander of European descent
Pōwhiri	Welcome ceremony
Tāne	Man
Tangata Moana	Pacific peoples
Tangata Tiriti	People of the Treaty, New Zealanders of non- Māori origin
Tangata whenua	People of the Land, Indigenous people
Tangi	Funeral, rites for the dead
Taonga	A treasure, something prized
Tau iwi	Non-Māori people of New Zealand
Te ao Māori	The Māori world
Te reo Māori	The Māori language
Tikanga	A customary system of values and practices that have developed over time and are deeply embedded in the social context
Tino rangatiratanga	Self-determination, sovereignty
Tūpuna	Ancestors
Tūrangawaewae	Place where one has the right to stand
Wāhine	Women
Wahine	Woman
Waiata	Song
Whaea	Mother, Aunt
Whakamā	(Collective or individual) shame, embarrassment
Whakamana	Endorsement, confirmation
Whakapapa	Lineage, descent
Whakataukī	Proverb, significant saying
Whakawhanaungatanga	Establishing relationships, relating well to others
Whānau	Family
Whanaungatanga	A relationship through shared experiences and working together which provides people with a sense of belonging
Whare	House, residence
Wharekura	School, place of learning

SPRINGER NATURE

GPSR Compliance

The European Union's (EU) General Product Safety Regulation (GPSR) is a set of rules that requires consumer products to be safe and our obligations to ensure this.

If you have any concerns about our products, you can contact us on ProductSafety@springernature.com

In case Publisher is established outside the EU, the EU authorized representative is:

Springer Nature Customer Service Center GmbH
Europaplatz 3
69115 Heidelberg, Germany

The manufacturer's authorised representative in the EU is Springer Nature Customer Service Centre GmbH, Europaplatz 3, 69115 Heidelberg, Germany. If you have any concerns regarding our products, please contact ProductSafety@springernature.com

Printed and bound by CPI Group (UK) Ltd, Croydon, CR0 4YY
28/09/2026
02224070-0002